From Darkness To Light

AN AUTOBIOGRAPHY OF REDEMPTION

SUPRIYA K. DEAS

BALBOA.PRESS
A DIVISION OF HAY HOUSE

Balboa Press books may be ordered through booksellers or by contacting:

Balboa Press
A Division of Hay House
1663 Liberty Drive
Bloomington, IN 47403
www.balboapress.com
844-682-1282

Print information available on the last page.

ISBN: 978-1-9822-5986-0 (sc)
ISBN: 978-1-9822-5988-4 (hc)
ISBN: 978-1-9822-5987-7 (e)

Library of Congress Control Number: 2020923676

Balboa Press rev. date: 12/29/2020

I dedicate this book to all the lost and broken people who live without hope, and to those who help them along the way.

I dedicate it to the children who are neglected and hurt in the crossfire of addiction, and to those who love them and help them to be safe.

I also dedicate this book to my parents, Jack and Mary, to Hippie, and to my children, Joshua, Terra, and Isaac. My love for you and the pain of losing you caused me to change and become a better person.

And last but certainly not least, I dedicate this book to Baba Hari Dass, my spiritual Master. By following your guidance and being influenced by your impeccable example as a human being, I was finally able to understand that every saint has a past, and every sinner has a future.

CONTENTS

ACKNOWLEDGEMENTS

I offer my humble thanks to my yoga Master, Baba Hari Dass, for giving me the chapter titles when I was stuck and for encouraging me to write my story to help others.

I would also like to extend special thanks to my dear friends, Christine Hinch and Sam Maniatis of Total Home Training, Roy (Mahesh) Naud, Brajesh Friedberg, and Prem Mohan for believing in me and financially sponsoring my book.

I wish to express my deep affection and appreciation for my cherished friends, Anuradha Star Hannah, Maheshwar (Sylvain) Robillard, Cynthia Moore, Bunny Shannon, Gwen Nickerson, Laurie Burns, and Leslie Lord Humphrey for being my cheerleaders when my self-confidence waned; for my brothers and my children for their unconditional love; to Dona Cadman for her kindness; and for all the unnamed people on my journey who instilled in me the trust and faith needed to raise myself up out of the darkness and into the light. You know who you are.

FOREWORD

by Leslie Lord-Humphrey

I never met Sissy; but I'm certain that I would have recognized her by the stay-away smile and the vacancy behind her eyes, as once they were my own. I did, however, meet Supriya, now many years ago, through a sequence of coincidences, God-incidences, which are indicative of her life.

Supriya's autobiography chronicles the journey from being one of nine children born into the ravages of multi-generational alcoholism, and further fractured by the death of her mother at the young age of two. Sissy was a father's daughter, which is far different from being "daddy's little girl". The former is an assignment fraught with the role reversals of the daughter attempting to distract from the family pain, to take care of her father's emptiness, and the latter being a term of endearment. Additionally, she assumed the role of mother to her younger siblings, a weight far too heavy for a child such as herself to carry.

Sissy was drawn to unavailable men who reflected her father and to friends containing the same woundedness as her own. Incrementally taking on the shame of her father's alcoholism, and in search of relief, she was ensnared by the siren's call of drugs and alcohol herself. The first chapter's title, "Growing in the Dark", aptly charts this course. Fear grows in the dark. Shame grows in the dark. Secrets grow in the dark. Dis-ease grows in the dark.

Aborting her first child at 18, Sissy later gives birth to three children, whose lives are also tainted by parental addiction. Years later, following her indwelling light and guided by the real-life angels who always seem to surround her, Sissy becomes Supriya under the tutelage of her guru, Baba Hari Dass.

The sufferings she endured, and through which she eventually flourished, are hers to tell. I invite you to follow Supriya's words through a nearly unbelievable transformation from darkness into light.

PROLOGUE

I always felt close to Jesus, having had a mother with the same name as his. Mary was the middle child and eldest daughter among six brothers and two sisters. She loved to clown around, doing cartwheels and handstands to please her audience. After graduating from college, Mary's tender love of children and keen sense of humor drew her to teach elementary students in a one-room schoolhouse of Butte, Nebraska. At the age of twenty-four, she left her parents' home and moved to San Francisco, California to live with her sister, Marge. As her parents waved goodbye, they couldn't have known it would be the last time they would see their daughter alive.

My father, John Edward, (nicknamed Jackie) was born third of six children and raised in Richmond, California during the Great Depression of the 1920's. By day, his father worked as a laborer for the Standard Oil Company. At night, he was prone to drunkenness, which caused constant friction between him and his devout Catholic wife. Jackie detested the incessant bickering between his parents and often lay powerless in the darkness of his room, knowing his mother's face would be bruised and swollen in the morning.

Sundays occasionally brought with them a melancholic mood for young Jackie. When he didn't come in for breakfast, his mother would find him sitting alone on the back porch, crying for no apparent reason. One day he overheard his father cursing the black family that was moving in next door.

"I'll be damned if I'm gonna sell out to those niggers like the rest of the God damned whites in this neighborhood!" he yelled, before storming out to nurse his resentments on the jug of cheap red wine he kept hidden in the tool shed behind the house.

Every morning before school, Jackie and his older brother Jimmy shared the responsibility of milking the family goat. Since Monday was Jackie's day, he grabbed the milk pail off its hook and bolted down the back steps into an unusually silent backyard. Butterflies, red, yellow, and periwinkle blue, did not flutter here and there, but sat with wings folded like hands in silent prayer. A murder of crows huddled on low bending tree limbs, as though painted on a canvas of foreboding and gloom. Their beady black eyes sparkled with knowing and their brackish morning squawks sounded muffled with dread.

Young Jackie stopped abruptly as he neared the fence. Tears blurred his vision as he stared down at the flies swarming his dead goat's face. One of her eyes dangled weirdly from its gaping socket, and off in a nearby patch of weeds was his baseball bat, still bloodied with the rage of his father's drunken frenzy the night before.

Dropping the empty milk pail, Jackie ran to find his mother who was stirring bubbling porridge on the woodstove. Before he could speak, Inez glanced furtively at her husband and then back at the boy.

"Get washed up for breakfast, son," she whispered, showing no emotion at all.

The sensitive boy understood his mother's warning and went quietly to the back porch to wash his hands. After school he ran straight to the backyard, but the dead goat and his baseball bat were gone, never to be mentioned again.

As soon as they were old enough, Jackie and his best friend, Al, spent their weekends caddying at the local golf course. On his way home from work one evening, Jackie found a girlie magazine laying in the gutter. Pulled by the curiosity of youth, he peered at the voluptuous nudes smiling at him from their glossy pages. Too innocent to understand their seductive glances, Jackie ran home and naively handed the magazine to his mother who was busy cooking the evening meal. Inez let out an anguished gasp.

"This is where women like these belong!" she scolded, hooking the iron lifter into one of the heavy, round fire lids.

As the scourging flames leapt from their fiery depths, the boy watched them devour the nude women he had so innocently placed in his mother's hands. Without another word, she replaced the lid on her woodstove and went back to cooking supper.

Social life at school both intrigued and dismayed my father, who was unlike his older, more charismatic brother, Jimmy. At the age of seventeen, he enlisted in the United States Air Force and then went to Germany to fight for his country in World War II. As his feelings of separation and loneliness intensified, Jackie did as his father before him and reached for the bottle he had so despised in his youth.

My parents met and married the year my Dad got out of the service. After their honeymoon, they moved to South San Francisco to a housing unit provided by the government for soldiers returning from the war. Donny and Bobby were born a year apart and two years later, my mother gave birth for the third and last time.

When I was small my family mostly called me Sister or Sissy, except when I got into trouble, and then it was clearly Kathleen. About the time of my second birthday, we moved to a newly developing tract of homes in Antioch where warm evenings brought neighbors out to work in their yards. Lawns were seeded, saplings planted, and young children pressed their hand and footprints into the freshly poured sidewalks. At one end of our street bulldozers cleared the way for a new elementary school and at the other, a haunted house dared all kids to enter, especially after dark.

The stage of my childhood seemed to be set for a lifetime of happiness, but an unexpected turn of events suddenly altered my fate. It was not until many years later that I would learn there were two truths behind the tragedy that was to shape my life, but only one could be explained by my father. We were alone in his apartment one morning, when I broached the forbidden subject of my mother's premature death. The seventy-year-old man's voice trembled with emotion as he began his long-withheld tale.

"I came home from work at about five o'clock one evening," he said, his gaze reflecting on the far distant past. "As usual, your mother anticipated my arrival and greeted me at the front door. Her soft, wavy hair was curled and combed, but her radiant smile was missing, which let me know right away that something was wrong."

Sliding his chair back, Dad got up to boil a cup of water in the small aluminum pot he kept at the back of his stove. He stirred two rounded teaspoons of sugar into his cup of instant coffee and then sat back down to continue his story.

"Your mother sounded weak," he recalled, tinkling his spoon round and round in his cup. "She reported being ill all day with an unbearable headache. Although headaches were not uncommon for Mary, she seemed in more pain than ever before. When she went into the bedroom to lie down, I became alarmed and called the doctor.

"The physician's arrival was prompt. After a brief examination, he told me to give your mother a couple of aspirins and then hurried out the door. When Mary reached out for the water, her hand went limp and the glass fell to the floor."

My father's voice choked with emotion.

"Mary's speech was slow and there were words missing at odd intervals from her sentences," he said, wiping his eyes with the cotton handkerchief that he pulled from his pants pocket. "When she lost control of her bladder, I put you and your brothers beside her in the back of the station wagon and rushed to the nearest hospital."

Dad paused a moment to blow on the hot liquid in his cup before taking a sip.

"On April 27th, just one month before your second birthday, your mother was pronounced dead on arrival from a cerebral hemorrhage."

From the depths of his grief, my father realized he had three small children to raise and the demands of an accounting firm to answer to. His loneliness and despair fuelled his already progressive tendency for alcoholism, and his life quickly spiralled out of control. Sensing his distress, his co-worker, Dorrie, took a special interest in his life and just eight months after my mother's funeral, the two of them were joined in a marriage that would last only three short years.

The rest is my story.

There seems to be a lonely calling deep within our hearts beginning in early childhood. Although each person's calling is different, its essence is the same search for our divine Selves. In my attempt to tell the truth, I took great care not to exaggerate or minimize my experience but have changed or omitted some of the names to protect the innocent and forgive the guilty.

CHAPTER ONE

Growing in the Dark

My teacher, Mrs. Plum, went all out for Valentine's Day. She covered the walls of the kindergarten with our innocent decorations and taped large red envelopes to every desk. Heart-shaped cookies that said I love you were piled high on a platter at the back of the room, and her fizzy sweet punch stained our lips pink. Children ran happily about the room delivering their valentines, but I saw only Steven West. He smiled at me when he dropped his card in my envelope and I smiled right back.

Steven was a quiet boy, unlike the boisterous Charlie Baxter who turned his eyelids inside out trying to make me laugh. By the time I got home I forgot all about the cookies and sweet punch, but the smile of the timid blond boy remained vivid in my mind. I pinned his valentine on my wall and felt warm inside my heart.

As soon as school let out for the summer my family took a trip to Butte, Nebraska, to visit my real mother's parents. The combination of the car's motion and my parents' cigarette smoke made me feel sick. Several times I had to ask Dad to pull over so I could throw up, but for some reason, when I got out in the fresh air all my queasiness disappeared.

The drive across the country was long and tiresome. When my brothers and I got fidgety, Dad sang to us in his deep, melodious voice: "Row, row, row your boat, gently down the stream. Merrily, merrily, merrily, merrily, life is but a dream." He taught us to sing together in rounds and for a while, all our boredom slipped away. As soon as the car got quiet again,

I wondered about the stream we were to row down and what Dad meant by life being just a dream.

On the first day of our visit, Grandpa took us on a walking tour of his small town. Before heading to the park, we stopped at his friend's farm to visit a large white horse. Grandpa wanted to take my picture, so he hoisted me up on the kind animal's back. I immediately recognized the powerful being as an old friend and spoke to him without moving my lips.

The park was magnificent with its green grass and flowers of every color blooming along the walkways. Wearing shoes made me feel like I couldn't breathe, and I yearned to touch the vibrant, soft grass with my bare feet. My grandfather proudly introduced us as Mary's children to the people we passed. One of the women bent down and patted my head. Her touch caused feelings of deep sadness to course through my body. Looking deeply into my eyes the woman exclaimed, "Why, this little girl looks exactly like her mother!"

Besides overseeing the post office in Butte, my grandfather also had the responsibility of taking care of any prisoners waiting for trial. On the way home we followed him down the stairs in a red brick building he called the courthouse. There was a large cage in the far corner of the room where a dark-skinned man sat hunched over on a cot. When Grandpa unlocked the steel barred doors, the man got up to accept his lunch and a cup of hot coffee.

"Here you go sir. Just the way you like it!" Grandpa said, joking and laughing as though they were good friends.

After introducing us as his daughter's family, my grandfather locked the door and bade the prisoner good-bye. On the way home I was confused.

"Why does such a nice man have to be locked up in a cage?" I wanted to know.

Grandpa's voice was kind. "The man did something wrong, but he is still a human being and deserves good treatment."

When we returned home from our walk, Grandma seemed to be expecting us. The aroma of freshly baked apple pie wafted out from behind her when she opened the door to welcome us inside. While untying her apron, she led us down a hallway lined with photographs. She bent down and picked me up.

"That is your mother," she said, tenderly gazing at the picture of a young woman with soft green eyes.

The same deep sadness that had permeated my body when the village woman patted my head now betrayed the elderly woman's smile as she absent-mindedly stroked my back. I didn't remember my mother, but understood that these people had loved her very, very much.

Lorena was the youngest of my grandparents' nine children. She rarely spoke, but sat alone, staring placidly at the world around her. At the supper table, Grandpa cut up Lorena's food while Grandma draped a large bib around her daughter's neck. After Grandpa asked the blessing, Grandma put a fork in the twenty-five-year-old woman's hand, trying to encourage her to feed herself.

That afternoon I was anxious to play with the new miniature tea set my grandparents gave me for coming to see them. With my doll tucked beneath my arm, I went outside to sit beneath the large shade tree on the front lawn. While pouring my doll an imaginary cup of tea, Lorena came out and squatted down beside me. Picking up one of my little cups she held it out for me to fill. When I looked deeply into most people's faces, I could know their thoughts, but Aunt Lorena was different; her face was blank and so was her mind.

"It's not polite to stare, Sister," my father's words suddenly echoed through my mind. Diverting my gaze, I dutifully pretended to fill Lorena's cup.

"Time to eat, girls!" Grandma called, waving cheerfully from the front porch. "Come on in and get washed up for supper!"

Lorena shadowed my every step as I peeked in closets and looked behind doors on my way to the bathroom. After exploring the space beneath my grandparents' bed, I opened the basement door at the end of the hall. The plunging stairwell gave me an idea.

"Wait here, Lorena," I said, and ran to find my suitcase.

When I got back, my aunt was still standing right where I left her. Soberly hovering over my shoulder, she watched without a blink as I squatted on the top step of the plunging staircase to bounce my coiled Slinky into the darkness below.

That night Dad said I should be a good girl and sleep with my aunt Lorena. Ignoring my protests, he carried me down the steps to the musty smelling basement where the blank woman waited in her pyjamas. Spiders peered at me from their webs as we descended the stairs, and I wondered if they would crawl across my face as soon as I went to sleep.

After the long trip home my brothers and I were glad to be back with our friends. Skating back and forth on the cement sidewalks, my girlfriends and I called out nursery rhymes and waved our arms like butterfly wings. Our laughter rang out as we rolled down the neighbors' sloping lawns and on my way home, I picked flowers for my new mother from any garden I chose.

My brothers and I loved Dorrie. She was good to us and it was easy to call her our mother. On the weekends I liked to follow her around, listening to her talk while she did the housework. Fascinated by her long red fingernails, I watched as they slipped easily across the piano keys and clicked on the kitchen table whenever she played solitaire in the afternoon sun.

That summer Donny and Bobby played baseball with the Antioch Little League. Donny's team was the *Spaghetts* and Bobby's, the *Comets*. Whenever they had a game, my parents and I would go to the park to cheer them on. While Mom and Dad talked with the other parents in the bleachers, I sat in the sandbox eating cotton candy. The sky was vast and blue, and the sun felt warm on my skin.

Dad liked to work outside on the weekends. While he pushed the mower back and forth across the front lawn, I would sit beneath the flowering walnut tree, seeking shelter from the sun. The prickly green grass made my legs itch, but nothing could get me to leave my father's side, except the sound of the ice cream truck that arrived every afternoon, right after lunch. Without a care in the world I rolled my silver dime through my fingers, listening for the familiar jingle. When it finally turned onto our street, kids of all ages came running to catch it before it disappeared around the corner by Debbie Stokes' house on Bigelow Drive.

Mom's friend, Zola Karr, was our babysitter during the week while our parents were at work. Arriving early in the morning, she stayed until Mom and Dad got home from work at five o'clock. The elderly woman's ankles swelled over the tops of her thick-heeled black shoes making her hobble when she walked. She wore silky flowered dresses, long pearl necklaces, and always smelled of sweet perfume.

One day Zola asked us kids to call her Grandma which suited us just fine. Whenever she sat me in her lap to clean my ears, I would caress the soft pouch of skin that hung beneath her chin. It was from Grandma Karr that I learned some of the most important secrets of womanhood like knotting our nylon stockings just above the knee and powdering our noses with a puff from a little round compact with a mirror. When my brothers and I misbehaved, Zola would pinch her eyebrows together and pucker her lips up to her nose making a clucking sound with her tongue. She laughed right out loud one morning when she caught me walking round and round in the living room trying to pucker my lips up to my nose.

As soon as I turned six, Dorrie enrolled me in tap and ballet lessons at Doreen's Dance Studio. On the night of my first recital, I felt beautiful in my red lipstick, gold sequined halter-top, and purple hula skirt. Like a proud mother, our teacher nodded and patted our heads as we pranced one by one onto the stage to take our places. When the familiar music began

5

to play, the heavy black curtains whisked open and the blinding lights flooded my vision. The other little girls began to smile and dance around, but I stood perfectly still, looking for my father. Sensing my plight, Dad stood up and waved.

"Over here, Sissy!" he called from the dark sea of faces. "I'm over here!"

Content to know my father was near I entered the dance, but it was too late, I had already lost my routine. Each time I tried to get back in step with the other girls they twirled in the opposite direction. Due to my intense excitement hot urine flooded down my legs, but somehow, I knew the show must go on. As the miniature ballerinas slipped and slid in the puddles of my despair, I just held up my chin and kept on dancing.

Several times over the years my father tried to teach me to stop wetting my pants, but the harder he tried, the worse I failed. At first, he calmly explained why I should not do it. When that didn't work, his face turned red and his voice became stern. Finally, he got so mad that he pulled my pants down to give me a spanking. Terrified of his anger, I lost control of my bladder and we both learned a very important lesson: Dad should not put me across his lap to spank me, and I should hide my wet clothes to prevent him from getting mad.

There were starting to be many nights when my father did not come home after work. Pacing back and forth with her lips pressed together, Mom made supper without saying a word. My brothers and I became quiet in her distraction, but her worried thoughts kept her from noticing.

I felt a strong sense of protection for my father whenever he drank, as though he were my own child. If he did not come home before I went to bed, I would lay awake in the darkness, waiting to hear his voice. One night I awoke to a crashing sound coming from the living room.

"Whose lipstick is this on your collar?" Mom angrily demanded.

Worried for my father's safety, I huddled close behind my bedroom door until I fell asleep. The next morning, I followed Mom around like usual, but I could sense something was wrong. Instead of washing the laundry and dusting the furniture, she packed her belongings into a large wooden chest.

"This is mine and this is mine," she said, as though I understood.

Suddenly her voice became quiet and she sat down on the bed. Big tears formed in her eyes and then spilled down her cheeks. I climbed up beside her and put my hand on her shoulder.

"I left my three-year-old son, Roger, in Minnesota," Dorrie confided through heart-wrenching sobs.

My mind reeled back to the long summer trip we took to see my real mother's parents in Nebraska. Dorrie had taken the car and gone off by herself to a place called Minnesota. When she came back, she hardly spoke. On the way home she didn't laugh or sing with us like before, but stared out the window, absorbed in a world all her own.

That night while making supper, more tears rolled down Dorrie's face.

"Why are you crying?" I asked.

"It's the onions," she whispered, wiping her cheeks with the sleeve of her shirt.

Ever since my real mother died there was an empty place in my heart that nothing else could fill. No pictures of her were displayed in our house and we were not allowed to talk about her whenever Dad was around. I thought about Dorrie's son and wondered how any mother could be alive and not stay with her own child.

The following week Dad and Dorrie came home early. They were sitting in the living room when my brothers and I came in from school. The curtains were drawn, and Zola Karr had already gone home. Dad directed us to sit down.

"We have something important we need to discuss with you kids," he said in his serious voice. "Dorrie and I are getting a divorce and you kids must decide who you want to live with; her or me."

Sitting just as close to Bobby as I could get in our favorite place beneath the piano I whispered, "What is a divorce?" but my brother simply shrugged and stared straight ahead.

Bobby had always been the quiet one, but there were three things about him I knew for certain: he loved Dorrie like his own mother, he hated Dad's drunken kisses, and he only played dolls with me so I would not be lonely. Although I was certain that life without my brothers would be painfully empty, I had no decision to make. I would be staying with our father.

Donny suddenly remembered our first mother's death and began to cry. I thought about Dorrie's anger over the lipstick, and the wooden chest she packed saying, "This is mine, and this is mine." The heavy feeling in my heart and her onion tears finally made sense; our second mother was leaving.

Shortly after Dorrie left, Grandma Karr stopped coming to babysit. Now that the house was empty when we came home from school my brothers and I would climb up on the kitchen counters to forage through the cupboards, looking for food. At first, I continued to practice my dance routine, but with no one home to clap for me, all my enthusiasm disappeared. We rarely changed our school clothes or did homework anymore. Since no adults were home to make supper, we ate bologna and mustard sandwiches, potato chips, and drank a pitcher of Kool-Aide with lots of extra sugar before running back outside to play with our friends.

Whenever I was afraid at night, I would climb into bed between my two brothers. Lying together in the darkness of their room we discussed our worst fear that Dad would get killed while driving drunk, leaving us alone in the world without any parents to call our own.

Sometimes I stayed in my own room trying to figure out the answers to my many serious questions. If there was a God, then why did our mom have to die and leave us so alone? I wanted to know what die meant, and why our father drank so much alcohol. At Sunday school the nuns said God created everything, but if that was so, then who created God? To stop the endless trail of thoughts from circling round and round inside my mind, I learned to beat my head against my pillow until I fell asleep.

For some reason people treated me as though I was a fragile and helpless child. Although I knew it was not true, affection with pity was better than no affection at all, so I acted according to their belief. The women Dad brought home from the bowling alley often stayed the night. In the morning I liked to climb up on the toilet seat to watch them put on their lipstick.

"Are you gonna be my new mommy?" I'd ask, but each one just patted my head and hurried out the door.

California's warm summer evenings brought the neighborhood kids outside to play hide and seek beneath the streetlights until well after dark. While one of the children closed their eyes to count, the rest of us scurried off, looking for a place to hide. One night, wanting to avoid the whispering of the other children, I went off to hide by myself in the shadow of a large tree. One by one I heard my friends being caught, so I held my breath whenever the seeker came close to me. After a long period of silence, I realized I was all alone. The moon shone full and bright above my head, and I was certain that this was the last time I would ever play the game of hide and seek.

Kaye Quinn was a beautiful Italian woman who lived right across the street. She loved to paint things turquoise and work in her flower garden in the afternoon. When I came home from school she would look up and wave like she was glad to see me. One day I got an idea. I put on my shrinking tap shoes and white sailor costume from Doreen's dance recital and went over for a visit. Kaye was delighted. Pulling the dirty gloves from her hands she opened the front door.

"Won't you join me for a little snack?" she laughed.

She pressed her finger to her lips and then motioned toward the couch.

"I have to check on the baby," she whispered. "Go on in and sit down. I'll be right back."

A bearded sage sat peacefully on Kaye's coffee table. His porcelain head was bald on top with long silver hair trailing over the shoulders of his pure white robe. With great reverence, I slipped off my shoes and sat on the floor in front of him just as close as I could get.

"Don't be afraid or worry about a thing," he cautioned without moving his lips.

Beyond all activity of life, there was another world just behind my eyes. It was a secret place, a silent garden, where people moved slowly, and kindness was the way. I never told anyone about the sage's advice or my secret world because I was certain the adults would not believe me, and most children already knew.

When Kaye came back from checking on the baby, I followed her into the kitchen. After sprinkling our two plates with potato chips, she cut my sandwich into triangles and arranged them in a special design. I giggled as the bubbles from the 7-Up popped up on my nose and the cheery way she served me kept me coming back for more.

One day Kaye offered me a dime to babysit her two-year-old son, Kevin, while she went outside to hang up the laundry. Since the baby was asleep, I got right to work scraping the turquoise paint off my friend's door handle to reveal its original gold. When Kaye came back and saw what I had done she asked me to sit beside her on the couch. At first, I thought she was going to scold me, but her voice softened, and she began to whisper.

"Kevin is sick with leukemia and the doctors say he will die soon," she confided.

I knew that word die. It meant Kevin would be leaving and no one would talk about him anymore. Although I secretly wished Kaye could be my mother, I knew that leaving my father was just not going to happen. After saying goodbye, I went home and drew a wavy blue line on my bedroom wall with a crayon. I knew it was the ocean but when Dad came home, he thought it was just idle scribbling and made me wash it off. I had no words to tell him I was lonely, and it made me feel better to have the ocean nearby.

Donny and Bobby were becoming accustomed to running the streets, even after dark.

"Wait for me!" I called one evening, chasing after them as fast as I could go.

"Go home!" they yelled as they ran up ahead to be with their friends.

Since all kids know that monsters hide in the bushes at night, I walked down the middle of the street. The nuns had taught me to sing whenever I was afraid, so I decided to give it a try.

"This little light of mine, I'm gonna let it shine. This little light of mine, I'm gonna let it shine. Let it shine, let it shine, let it shine."

At the top of our driveway I stopped and stared at the house. According to my brothers' reports after returning from the Saturday afternoon matinee, there was a good chance that the mummy was hiding inside our house. If I went in alone, the monster was certain to make me suffer a horrible death like the poor people Donny and Bobby had seen in the movie. Although I longed to run over and knock on Kaye's door, I had been taught the good manners of not bothering people after five o'clock.

Hungry and tired, I grudgingly went in and sat on the living room couch. Sinking back into the cushions, I watched as the last bit of sunlight disappeared into the backyard. Large, foreboding shadows flickered and grew into shapes as the room expanded and contracted in the growing darkness. Terrified, I stood up on the couch to see if Kaye's light was still on, but each time I turned my head, the bandaged corpse advanced a little closer. A bright light shone from its forehead, and I could see a deteriorating body beneath dirty strips of peeling gauze. My mind, now riveted with fear, made my head jerk uncontrollably, back and forth, back and forth, between Kaye's house and the mummy until finally, I got mad!

Getting up off the couch I flicked on the hall light and then entered every room, turning on the lights as I went along. Determined to conquer this demon of darkness, I forged ahead, checking behind doors, under beds, and in closets. Gaining power with every step, I passed through the kitchen heading for the garage; the place where children never go alone, especially after dark. Although my fear was paramount, my resolve to face the bully was not to be thwarted. Opening the door just wide enough to slide my small hand along the wall, I groped for the light switch. The smell of gasoline made me think of my father's car.

"Remember Sissy, there is nothing to fear but fear itself," Dad always advised when I was afraid at night.

I looked up at the giant cobwebs drooping from the rafters. Ghosts lurking behind boxes of old clothes and family photographs silently threatened to come out of the shadows and scare me to death. A shiver rushed up my spine.

"There is nobody here but my own self!" I declared, and ignoring my hunger, I went to bed and fell asleep.

The next day I told my father I had been alone and afraid the night before. His face turned hard like stone. Instead of realizing the error was his, he took off his belt and called my brothers into the room. His sensitive voice was now stern and cold.

"Donald did you and Robert leave your sister alone last night?"

"We were just up the street playing," Donny defended, afraid of the whipping he was about to receive.

"Go to your room!" Dad yelled, and then looked over at Bobby. "Both of you!"

My brothers' cries pierced the silence as I cowered behind my bedroom door. Covering my ears so I could not hear their screams I felt ashamed that I had been the cause of their suffering.

That summer Dad decided to stop drinking. He got out his wheelbarrow and began digging a hole in our backyard. Content to have my father home I stayed nearby, watching as he worked. Large drops of sweat poured down his face as he leaned forward to rest on his shovel.

"Just think, Sissy," he exclaimed. "One day this will be a swimming pool!"

The warm dirt felt good on my bare feet as I ran here and there, playing in the sun. One afternoon, I tripped on a rake that was lying in the path. One of its thick iron prongs drove right in between my toes. When Dad saw my blood oozing out of the gaping hole, he immediately dropped what he was doing and ran over to make sure I was alright. Seeing the worried look on his face I began to cry.

"Jesus, Sister, we had better get you to the doctor," he said with concern. "You will probably need a tetanus shot so you don't get lockjaw."

I figured lockjaw must be serious since Dad no longer believed in doctors after they let our real mother die. Whenever my brothers or I needed stitches he just pulled our skin together and held it in place with two Band-Aids.

"I learned this in the war," he explained. "It's called the butterfly method."

On the way to the hospital I looked down at the blood-soaked cloth wrapped around my foot.

"They must have needed a lot of butterfly methods to help people during the war," I said, but Dad was off in his faraway place and couldn't hear me.

I adored my father with his tall stature and wide, genuine smile. When he wasn't drinking, he called me his crown jewel and always came home right after work. Some nights I felt lonely even when he was home. Unable to sleep, I would go into the living room where he was sitting on the couch, reading the newspaper.

"What's the matter, Sissy?" he asked one night with his kind voice.

"I can't sleep," I complained, rubbing my eyes.

"Come on up," he said, patting his leg.

I lay my head in his lap and he caressed my face with one hand while holding the newspaper with the other. I quickly drifted off to sleep knowing he would be home and safe throughout the night.

One evening it was so hot that I was restless. As usual, I went out to find my father.

"Come on Sis," he said. "Let's go for a swim!"

I thought it was a great idea and ran down the hall to get my bathing suit.

"Never mind, Sissy," he called. "The body is nothing to be ashamed of. Let's go in the nude."

At first, I felt nauseous at the sight of his genitals, but when he grabbed my hand and ran toward the pool, I forgot all about it.

"Be really quiet," he whispered, as we slipped into the water. "We don't want to wake the neighbors!"

Off in the distance there was a rumble, and then a bright light flooded the starlit sky.

"Quick Sis!" Dad laughed. "Don't let the engineer see you! Dive under the water!"

It was great fun splashing and ducking in the cool water with my father so late in the night.

That year for Christmas the presents were loaded under our tree. Silver tinsel and delicate glass bulbs shimmered on branches strung with colored lights. Day by day our anticipation grew until finally, it was Christmas morning. At the first sign of daylight my brothers and I tore into the living room to see if Santa had come. I was delighted to see my new roller skates and a wooden cradle for my dolls but when I saw the faraway look in my father's eyes, the new toys lost their charm.

He's leaving, I thought.

Pacing back and forth, Dad jingled the keys in his pocket. Feeling sad for his plight I went over to stand by his side. The tender hand that had caressed my cheek just nights before now changed to an absent-minded pat on the top of my head.

"Take care of your brother and sister, Donald," he commanded. "I'll be back in a little while."

When our father returned that afternoon, he took me in his arms and began to cry. His warm tears tasted salty as they spilled down his cheeks and into my mouth. Squeezing my small body close to his he cried, "You're going to leave your ole papa one day!"

His breath smelled sour and his bristly whiskers hurt the soft skin on my face. I longed to go outside and play with my friends, but I would not struggle to get free from his grasp. Instead I felt sorry for him and promised I would stay forever.

Every time we got desperate for food Donny went across the street to ask Kaye for help. None of us spoke about the whippings from our father because we were ashamed of being bad and believed we deserved them.

Whenever I was not in school, I tended my dolls the way I knew children should be cared for. I dressed them, took them for walks, fed them their meals, and every night before going to bed, I tucked them safely into their new cradle. When Dorrie caught wind of our father's neglect she phoned social services and then let our relatives know what she had done. My brothers and I were outside playing in the yard when Uncle Jim's Cadillac pulled up to the curb. Aunt Jane got out and hurried into the house with all three of us kids running close behind.

"You won't be coming back for a long time," she said, stuffing our clothes into large bags. "Take only your favorite toys and go get in the car with Uncle Jim."

I quickly gathered up my dolls.

"Does Dad know we're leaving?" I asked, but Aunt Jane didn't have time to explain.

As soon as I got to the car, I remembered my goldfish and dashed back inside the house. On the way to the car I saw Kaye out in her yard, tending her flowers. Handing the fishbowl to Bobby I started to run across the street to say goodbye, but Aunt Jane took hold of my arm and hustled me into the car. As Uncle Jim pulled out from the curb, I stood on the backseat between my brothers, waving until Kaye disappeared out of sight.

The next day Aunt Jane enrolled us at the Franklin Elementary School in Alameda. As the weeks dragged by, I tried to be part of my relative's family, but a thick blanket of fog had covered my heart. I missed my dad and could not understand why he didn't come to get us. Refusing to attach to the new kids and teachers, I stayed aloof at school with the firm resolve that no matter what happened, I would be going home to be with my father.

Over the next couple of months, I shared the upstairs bedroom with my seventeen-year-old cousin, Charlene. Trying to be friendly, she bought me a coloring book and taught me to stay inside the lines by using little circles. When I came in from school one afternoon Charlene was sitting on her bed with a strange look on her face.

"What's wrong?" I asked, sitting down beside her.

"I have to go to the doctor in a few minutes," she responded shyly. "Mom says I need to have my breasts examined."

Before turning out the lights that night my cousin came over and sat on the edge of my bed.

"When I was twelve my real mom contracted a serious illness and died," she said. "Since my father didn't want me, your aunt and uncle adopted me as their own daughter."

Charlene reached over and touched my shoulder.

"I know how it feels to be taken away from your only living parent," she said, and then went back to her bed and began to read.

I pulled the covers up to my chin. For as long as I could remember Aunt Jane and Uncle Jim had three children: Jimmy, Gary, and Charlene. It felt good to know someone understood what I was going through, but as soon as my cousin turned out the light, I covered my face with the pillow, and cried myself to sleep.

It was late one evening when my father finally came for a visit. He spoke with my aunt and uncle in the kitchen and then carried me into the garage so we could be alone to talk. When he sat me on the washing machine, I was so happy to see him that I clung to his waist with all my might.

"Please Dad, take me home with you!" I begged.

As soon as our private talk was over, he carried me back upstairs and set me down in the hallway.

"Wait here, Sissy," he said. "I need to talk with your aunt and uncle alone in the kitchen for a while."

When my father came out of the kitchen, he picked me up and squeezed me real tight. I happily put my arms around his neck thinking he was taking me home but instead, he gave me a hug and kissed me goodbye. As he walked out the door that night, I noticed a strange droop in his shoulders that I had not seen before. Certain that I alone knew his heart, I missed the man who could love people with just his eyes.

A few weeks later Dad came to take my brothers and me home. Since nothing had changed, things got worse instead of better. Every day found me soaked in my own urine. School, birthday parties, and even the aisle of my First Holy Communion were all saturated with the same yellow trail that had spilled across the stage of Doreen's tap and ballet recital. I was terrified that my father would punish me with a spanking or shame me by sending me to school in cloth diapers with large pins I could not undo. To prevent his upset, I did everything in my power to hide my shameful problem.

Dad's mother was a religious woman who prayed on her knees every afternoon in the downstairs bedroom where Nanny died. That summer she and my grandfather came to take us three kids to their house for a two-week vacation. The first afternoon of our visit my brothers ran outside to play, but I stood outside Grandma's slightly open door, watching her speak to the God I longed to know.

On Sundays after church Grandma and I walked to the convent, bringing the nuns gifts of homemade bread and raspberry jam. Her eyes sparkled with delight as she stopped in the middle of the sidewalk to introduce me to her friends. For some unknown reason, my shameful problem of wetting my pants completely disappeared whenever I was with my grandmother.

I considered my third-grade teacher my favorite because he looked out for the welfare of all children. After the last bell rang one afternoon Mr. Stevenson called me up to his desk.

"*The Nun's Story* is playing at the theatre tonight," he said with an easy smile. "If you would like to go with me, be ready at six o'clock."

I ran all the way home to tell Kaye who got so excited that she painted my fingernails pink and pinned my hair up in a bun on top of my head. At the show Mr. Stevenson bought sodas and popcorn and then led the way into the darkened theatre. As we took our seats, a blue stream of light flowed above our heads, illuminating the screen at the front of the room. Tears sprang to my eyes as I watched nuns like my grandmother's caring for the lonely, screaming people locked behind doors that separated them from the rest of the world.

The house was dark and empty when Mr. Stevenson dropped me off, but I was no longer afraid. I just waved goodbye and went to my room to get ready for bed. Lying awake in the darkness, I told God that I wanted to be like the nuns in the movie and help people find peace, even when everything around them seemed hopeless and cruel.

Now that I was eight, I was finally old enough to walk to church by myself. Ashamed of my clothes when people turned to stare, I would sit in the back pew trying not to be noticed. Since the priest spoke in a language I could not understand, the sun told me the story of Jesus through the colored glass windows lining the walls of the church. Although I didn't know how I would do it, I was certain that when I grew up, I too would make colored windows that told the story of love.

That summer Dad started seeing a woman named Sue and came home even less than before. One morning I went to his room to find that his bed had not been slept in at all the night before. When I started to cry Donny came to comfort me and Bobby tried to make me laugh, but nothing could take the place of my own father.

Since I had been to Sue's once before I was certain I could find my way back again. Knowing Donny would never let me go by myself, I slipped out the back door without telling him. Holding the picture of Sue's pink house clearly in my mind, I walked downtown looking for the gray front steps that were framed with two white pillars.

A small dog barked as I approached the door. Two little girls pulled back the curtains to see who was there. Six-year-old Susan recognized me as Jack's daughter and shyly let me in. Without saying a word, she led me down the hall and pointed to a closed door.

"He's in there," she said, and then went back to the living room to play with her younger sister, Liz.

Feeling hesitant, I pushed the door open. Putrid smells of stale breath and cigarette smoke rushed out to greet me. I felt sick to my stomach seeing Dad lying naked in bed next to Sue in the dimly lit room. He tried to speak when he saw me, but his words came out stupid, so I closed the door and went back to the living room to find Susan and Liz.

Sue's teenage sons, Sparky and Mike, were in the kitchen cooking breakfast. I tried to keep my mind focused on playing with the little girls, but all I could think of was their food, so I said goodbye and walked back home to be with my brothers.

After that Sue started coming to our house every weekend. She cooked, cleaned, and made sure that my brothers and I had plenty of food in the refrigerator. One day she caught me staring at her swollen belly.

"There is a baby in there," she said, possessively cupping her abdomen with her hands.

I didn't know how a baby got inside her stomach or how it was going to get out, but I felt relieved when she promised we would not be alone or hungry anymore.

Over the next few months Dad left his accounting firm and bought a cocktail lounge in Sunnyvale.

"We will be moving soon," he announced one night at the supper table.

I finished my meal and went to my room. My heart felt sad. Moving meant I would have to say goodbye to my friends, and leaving Kaye was like abandoning my own mother. Understanding my upset, Dad came in and sat on my bed. Stroking my hair, he tried to console me while I packed my dolls into boxes.

"If we had never moved to Antioch from San Francisco, you would not have met Kaye in the first place," he said. "There will be plenty of new friends at our next home. Just you wait and see."

When we got to the new house, I looked around for the new friends Dad spoke about, but no one was there. The large moving van pulled in shortly after our arrival. As soon as the truck was unloaded, I rummaged through my boxes looking for my dolls, but they were gone! Like any real mother I was heartbroken. I had poured so much love into those dolls that they had become real. How could I tell that to my new mother? I heard the harsh way she spoke to her own children, and I was afraid of her sarcasm. Masking my hurt, I quietly arranged my clothes in the appointed drawers and settled into the room I would be sharing with my new sisters.

After my brother John was born, Dad and Sue went away to get married. The following year Sue gave birth to my youngest brother Greg, making me like my original mother; the middle child and eldest daughter among six brothers and two sisters. At first Dad came home every night right after work. It was fun seeing him laugh and play with the babies before they went to bed.

Our relatives rarely came to visit because they did not accept Sue as our father's wife. By the way Sue spoke she did not care for them much either. My brothers and I were not happy with the situation, but the food was good, and the house was no longer dark or empty when we came home after school.

One weekend my parents decided to take the whole family to the beach. While the other children ran off to play, I stared at the ocean, recognizing it as the wavy blue line I had drawn on my bedroom wall. Without a word to anyone I took one of the large black inner tubes and paddled out near the rocky cliffs. My body turned numb with cold and then warm all over as I rocked gently in the arms of the great Mother. Disappearing into my silent place deep inside, I could hear the ocean's roar as though off in the distance. Out of the corner of my eye, I suddenly noticed my father waving his arms. Through cupped hands he was hollering from the distant shore.

"Come back, Sissy! Come back!"

Longing to stay with the ocean I pretended not to see him at first, but when I realized he was worried, I turned my little boat around and paddled back to shore.

My new school was in Alviso, a small town mainly inhabited by poor Mexicans. I thought the black stuff the girls wore on their eyelids made them look beautiful, so I let them put a little on mine. When I got home, Sue was irate.

"Get that crap off your eyes before your father gets home," she scolded. "You look like a harlot!"

Halfway through the fourth grade a handsome brown boy joined my class. As soon as our eyes met, we fell instantly in love. During recess he spoke to me with a kind and loving voice and let me wear his jacket while we walked around the schoolyard. When the teachers weren't looking, he would put his arm around my shoulders and together, we would walk out beyond the playground, where the grass grew tall and green. I felt safe in the comfort of his arms and when his soft lips touched mine, all my troubles slipped away.

"Rocky, Rocky, Rocky," I wrote in my diary and wherever I went, I thought only of him.

Paula Reinhart became envious of our happiness and decided she was going to be Rocky's girlfriend. On her way to the pencil sharpener one morning she dropped a note on my desk with a scowl.

"Stay away from Rocky or I will beat you up!" it threatened.

Paula was a year older and much bigger than the other kids in our class. When I didn't follow her demands she passed me another note.

"I told you to stay away from Rocky. Now we are going to fight. Meet me out by the baseball diamond right after school!"

I didn't know anything about hitting people or why anyone would want to do such a thing over love. When the last bell rang, I slipped past the teacher and walked out to the field, ready to face my foe. Unsure what to do when it came time to fight, I tried to envision myself punching someone in the face like the men in the cowboy movies. For some reason, the picture would not come and fortunately, neither did Paula.

Just before school let out for the summer, Sue found a letter I wrote to Rocky in one of my dresser drawers. At the supper table that evening she read my youthful longings aloud as the rest of the family passed around the mashed potatoes and gravy. Horrified to have my intimate words to my boyfriend flung irreverently before the whole family I sat perfectly still, waiting for Sue to finish. Sensing my embarrassment, Susan and Liz giggled and my brothers teased, but none of their reactions mattered like the look on my father's face.

"God damned dirty Mexicans," he said, and forbade me to see or talk to Rocky ever again.

The way Dad talked it sounded like it was the color of the boy's skin that upset him, but I sensed even more, he had a hard time realizing that his little girl was growing up. Now that my privacy had been violated, I felt hurt and confused. Not wanting to make a scene, I picked at my dinner and then excused myself and went to my room. A few minutes later Sue came and stood at my bedroom door.

"If you are not careful the boys will stick their hard thing up inside of you and it will hurt a lot!" she warned, her eyes cold as steel. "You may not understand right now, but trust me, what I did tonight was for your own good."

As she walked away, I missed the advice of the porcelain sage in Kaye's living room and the path behind my eyes was now obscure.

Just before leaving Antioch, Donny ran away from home looking for Dorrie. When he knocked on her door her answer was unexpected.

"You belong to your father. You have to go back," she told him.

Trying to fit in with the other children my brothers and I started calling Sue Mom, but our hearts were not really in it. Discussing our hurt bound the three of us even more firmly together. The new rules were being imposed on us too fast and Donny was the first to rebel. Having been our father, brother, and boss for so many years he did not appreciate his power being taken away without his permission. Not knowing how else to express his anger, he began climbing out of his window at night to smoke and drink with his friends.

Dad didn't believe in God but taught the whole family to say the Catholic blessing before we ate our meals. Sue had been raised a Protestant and did not approve of the Catholic Religion.

"Why pray to saints or confess your sins to a priest?" she demanded with distaste. "Go straight to God!"

One morning I heard Liz screaming in the living room. When I ran to see what was wrong, I saw Sue whipping her daughter's legs with a belt. Many times, I had asked God for a mother, but now I was confused.

"Please God," I prayed. "If this is a mother then I don't want one!"

A few days later I walked in on Sue spanking her favorite daughter, Susan, with the same belt she used on Liz. Desperately wanting to be loved like Sue's real daughter, I decided that I too would like to be hit just like Susan and Liz.

That summer it was time for my brothers' Confirmation in Catholic Church. Father Sullivan directed the boys to meet in the appointed room to receive their final instructions before going into mass. While waiting for Donny and Bobby in the front hall, I was happy to see Rocky standing nearby with a group of his friends. Without reserve I went right over to say hello, but Rocky was no longer kind like he had been at school, offering his coat and talking in a soft voice. When I tried to explain that my parents wouldn't let me answer his phone calls he said, "Oh well," and laughed with the other boys.

"I'm dying," I whispered, as I turned and walked away.

One night my parents threw a party. Wanting to introduce his children to his guests, Dad called us all out to the living room. As soon as the introductions were over, we were sent back to our rooms to play until bedtime. At nine o'clock Susan and Liz climbed up on their bunks while I pulled out my trundle bed and turned off the light. Shortly after my parents moved the party out to the backyard, the three of us drifted off to sleep.

It was late when I awoke to one of my father's friends sitting on the edge of my bed. The obnoxious laughter from the backyard had ceased and the house was dead quiet. I could smell the stink of alcohol on the man's breath as he leaned in close and caressed my cheek with the back of his hand. He whispered something in my ear, but his speech was slurred, and I couldn't understand what he wanted. The door suddenly flew open and the hall light flooded into the room.

"Get out!" my new mother whispered with a vengeance.

Her dark eyes flashed with anger as she pointed toward the hall. The man struggled to get up and then staggered out the door.

"If you tell your father it will only upset him," Sue warned before closing the door.

The last time I had confided in my father he beat my brothers with his belt. Not wanting to cause any more strife, I did as Sue asked and kept the incident to myself.

Although Sue rarely drank alcohol, she spent most of her time at the bar with our father. The younger kids resented being raised by their siblings and started running the streets the way Donny, Bobby and I had in our early years. After school I tried to help them with their homework, settle their fights, and cook their meals, but I was only young myself, and their aggressive behavior was beyond my control.

Sue did not believe in stylish clothes or makeup, so I felt uncomfortable in the social setting on campus. After two weeks of wandering the halls alone, I found my best friend, Joan, sitting right in front of me in history class. One day she slipped a bag of potato chips into my lap during a movie. She wanted to know if I could open it without getting caught by the handsome Mr. Baxter, who we both had a crush on. Passing the bag back and forth, we held the salty morsels on our tongues until they dissolved without a sound.

Joan's father let her dye her hair blonde and wear as much makeup as she pleased. He also let her smoke cigarettes and gave her spending money every morning before school. My friend wore endless combinations of expensive new clothes and for her sixteenth birthday, her dad bought her a car.

I thought Joan had the perfect life until I went to her house to spend the night. Teen magazines, crumpled candy wrappers, and plates of moldy food pierced with cigarette butts littered her bedside table. The expensive clothes I had admired at school were strewn about her bedroom floor, and a variety of perfume bottles, mascara, and open tubes of makeup cluttered her bathroom shelves.

Hungry for adventure, we painted each other's faces with colorful paisley designs and then walked up to the local department store. We were proud of our ability to ignore the stares of passing shoppers and before going home, we panhandled like the hippies were doing in San Francisco. When we got back to Joan's we washed our faces and then lounged on the couch with our feet propped up on the coffee table. Feeling as important as the adults looked, we stayed up late into the night smoking cigarettes and discussing the important issues of life.

"My mom died, and my brother Bob is in the Marines," Joan began. "I don't get along with my dad's new girlfriend, so he hardly ever comes home."

"Me too!" I exclaimed, surprised by the likeness of our stories. "My mom died when I was a little girl and my dad drinks a lot, so he hardly ever comes home either. My stepmother can be really cruel sometimes. I've been secretly marking the days off my calendar, just waiting until I'm old enough to move out on my own."

In 1965 Dad sold our home in Sunnyvale and bought another one in San Jose. The new house was nice, but I had spent so much time with Joan that I felt lost without her at the new high school. Making friends was difficult and inviting anyone into our home was out of the question. Sue's suspicious mind and self-righteous ways frightened me. Twice I got up the courage to ask her if I could stay after school to get involved with the student body and both times the answer was the same.

"I need you at home to take care of the kids," she snapped. "Your father is drinking. If he calls, I'll have to go downtown to drive him home."

Bitterness began to choke my heart and self-pity dominated my every thought. One day after school I noticed a book on the coffee table in our living room titled *Edgar Cayce, the Sleeping Prophet.* With great interest I read about the uneducated man from Kentucky who, when just a little boy, had seen a bright light in the shape of a woman while playing in the woods behind his home. The radiant woman asked Edgar if there was anything he wanted.

"Why, yes ma'am, I would like to help people," the boy answered without hesitation.

Over the years, Cayce's love for God continued to deepen. One afternoon he unexpectedly went into a sleep-like trance with his wife Gertrude sitting nearby. From his altered state Edgar saw what caused people's sickness and began speaking about their cure. When Gertrude heard the strange guidance coming from her unconscious husband, she ran for a pen and paper to begin a series of notes that would one day help many people. The more I read about the holy man, the more I realized that I too could *see* and help people heal. When Sue came home, I asked her about the book.

"I don't believe in such foolishness!" she said, dismissing it with a shrug.

The subject was closed. Afraid of her criticism, I hid my ability to *see* and after a while, I forgot all about my desire to help people heal.

After school one day I went to the hospital with Joan to visit her friend, Gary String. While making her way through traffic she explained that five months before, Gary had found a black spot on his baby toe. Since it would not go away his mother took him to the doctor to have it tested. When the report came back, the doctor told Gary he had cancer and gave him six months to live.

All the way to the hospital I looked forward to seeing the tall, handsome boy from our high school. When we got to his room, I could hardly contain my shock. Gary's young body was emaciated, and his pallid skin stretched taut across his now bony frame. The teenaged boy seemed happy to see us. He sat up in his bed and joked a few minutes before taking four neatly rolled marijuana cigarettes out of his bedside table.

"The chemo makes me feel nauseous, so the doctor prescribes marijuana. Smoking pot makes me feel hungry!" he laughed.

Dropping two joints in each of our hands, Gary lay back in his bed and pulled up the sheet. "I'm tired," he said, and flashing one of his charming grins, he cheerfully bade us goodbye.

On the way home Joan did not have much to say. Gripping the thinly rolled joints in my fisted hand I thought about my father's lectures on the harmful effects of marijuana.

"Call me later," Joan's voice broke the silence as she pulled up to the curb in front of my house.

"I will," I said, and got out of the car.

Still trusting my father's words, I waited for my friend to drive away and then threw the joints into the bushes before going inside the house. The next afternoon the telephone was ringing when I came in from school. It was Joan crying. She had found her mother's death certificate while snooping through her father's private papers. The document claimed that her mother had died from self-inflicted asphyxiation in a mental institution.

Joan was afraid that she would end up crazy like her mother. Since the papers were found in the off-limits of her father's bedroom, she couldn't talk to her dad about her discovery. I could not imagine anyone holding a plastic bag over their face until they died, but never said anything to my friend.

The underlying racial prejudice between students was beginning to surface at school. A riot broke out one afternoon between the Mexicans and Anglophones in the corridor outside my classroom. When my Spanish teacher heard the commotion, he ran outside to help the other teachers stop the fighting. Crowding up to the window with the rest of the students, I saw Manny Rodriquez take off his wide, spiked leather belt and beat Mr. Stanton across the back.

I was horrified! Mr. Stanton had always been kind to me, silently whispering "I love you" with his lips when the other students weren't looking. Remembering how my father had called Rocky a damn Mexican, I realized the other parents must be saying the same cruel words to their children. Turning away from the window I quietly went back to my desk.

That summer Dad accepted a challenge from his partner at the bar.

"I bet you a hundred dollars you can't stop drinking for one year," Glen wagered.

It worked. Dad stopped drinking. Now that he was sober, he tried to make up for lost time by working seven days a week. When he came home in the evening, he was restless and distant, and his fondness for children had completely disappeared. The only time his face lit up anymore was when he watched the National Geographic travel logs on TV every Tuesday and Thursday evening at precisely seven o'clock. Although I had no idea what a real life was, I was quite certain my father never had one. Sensing his loneliness, I would sit on the floor beside him and massage his feet.

"Look Sissy," he would say, pointing at the black-skinned primitives dancing naked on the television. "Isn't that fascinating?"

He tried to get me to watch, but all I was interested in was his feet. For some reason when I touched them, I could see pictures of my father in those far-away places, but none of us kids, Sue, or the station wagon ever appeared in the visions.

It was hard to see that Sue had problems of her own because she covered her symptoms of cigarette smoking, sarcasm, and faultfinding with her ability to talk about the Bible. Now that Dad was sober, he came home every night right after work. Trying to avoid the marital bickering of his childhood, he isolated himself with a thick shield of silence. Sue often closed her bedroom curtains, took pills for her migraine headaches, and told me to watch the kids while she tried to get some sleep.

Late one night I got out of bed and walked out to the living room. Dad and Sue were sitting together on the couch watching TV. Although all the lamps were on, the room was extremely dark. My eyes were open and I was fully aware, but everything looked different, like being awake in a dream. Without thought of reproach by my parents, I walked over and switched off the lamps and the television.

"You need to turn on your lights!" I commanded, and casually went back to bed.

"You were sleepwalking last night," Sue informed me when I came into the kitchen for breakfast the next morning.

Since I had no words to explain what had really happened, I just smiled and kept the truth to myself.

Don liked to lift weights after school so he would go out to the garage where it was cool and quiet. Wanting to be near him I often went out to watch. It was so hot one afternoon that he took off his t-shirt. Up near his shoulder I noticed that his name had been freshly tattooed in blue ink. He became nervous when he realized I had seen it.

"Swear you won't tell Mom and Dad!" he said.

"Don't worry," I said calmly. "I won't tell."

Not wanting to cause any more grief in our family I promised to keep his secret. When I went back inside the house, I decided that one day I too would get a tattoo of my name on my arm, just like my brother Don's.

Right after his 18th birthday, Don received a formal letter from the United States government saying he had been drafted into the Army. The day before his induction, my brother and some of his friends got together for a going away party. We were just finishing supper that evening when the telephone rang. It was someone from the hospital wanting to speak with Dad. As usual I watched my father with a careful eye. His six-foot-three frame contracted, and his face broke out in a sweat as he listened to what the caller had to say. When Dad hung up the phone, I knew he wanted to cry.

"Donald has been in a serious car accident," he stoically announced. "His friend, Roddy, was driving too fast and rolled his car three times before landing in the Alviso slough."

When Dad got to the hospital, he was told that the two young men were drunk at the time of the accident. After freeing himself from the wreckage, Roddy somehow made his way over to the passenger side of the car. Unable to swim, he struggled in the dark water to pull Don's six-foot frame through the window of the sinking vehicle. The driver of a passing car heard Roddy calling for help and went to the nearest house to call an ambulance. According to Sue, the doctor's voice was quiet and grim when he spoke to my father.

"Your son's body was so cold by the time he got to the hospital that he went into shock. Due to his shivering the x-rays didn't come out clear, but your son can't move his legs and I suspect he has a broken neck."

Over the next few weeks, I watched my father suffer. Worried that his son would never walk again, Dad went to the hospital every evening right after supper. One night, Sue's migraine headache was so bad she could not go with him.

"Come on, Sis," Dad said, slipping on his jacket. "Let's go visit your brother."

When we got to my brother's room a strange energy pulled me to the foot of his bed.

"Look Dad," I said. "Don's big toe is moving!"

With disbelief, my father rushed to my side.

"My God, look at that!" Dad said, as Don grinned and wiggled his toe back and forth.

When I saw my father's radiant face, I was certain that God was going to let my brother walk again.

32

Our neighbor, Mary Patton, was the director of nursing at the Beverly Manor Convalescent Home in Santa Clara. She heard a rumor one day that the nurses' aides were going on strike and called to ask me if I would like a summer job.

"My daughter Cyndy is also going to work," she said, and encouraged me to give it a try. Our age and lack of experience didn't seem to matter.

As soon as my parents gave their permission I sat down and added up my future paychecks, dreaming of the new clothes I would buy for school. After a couple of weeks, the phone finally rang. It was Mary.

After apologizing for the short notice, she said, "The nurses' aides went on strike this morning at six o'clock. If you can be ready in twenty minutes, I will meet you in the driveway in front of my house."

Feeling professional in my new white uniform and soft-soled nursing shoes I ran across the street to meet Mary. She had just come out of the house as I approached her driveway. Her pillbox nursing cap and starched white uniform reflected the many years of disciplined training she had received in nursing school. Mary gave a nod of approval as I got into the car beside Cyndy. After backing carefully out of her driveway she drove to the end of the cul-de-sac and turned left. The clicking blinker magnified her serious mood.

"I will be dropping you girls off at another facility," she said, merging into traffic on Saratoga Avenue. "Just go inside and wait by the front door. Someone will come by to pick you up in a laundry truck."

When the driver arrived, he helped me, Cyndy, and a few others into the back of his van and then drove to Beverly Manor. At the head of the long, unpaved driveway the laundry truck crossed the picket line. The angry strikers were not fooled.

"Scab!" they yelled, while hitting the van with heavy wooden signs.

"Stay low," the driver warned as he drove up the road to the front of the nursing home.

He pulled up to the curb and then came around to the back of the van and unlocked the doors. A sloping sidewalk lined with brilliantly colored marigolds led to the sliding glass doors. Directly inside was a large sitting room scattered with comfortable looking chairs. Soft elevator music drifted out from unseen speakers and oversized oil paintings adorned the pastel walls.

I was relieved to see Mary waiting for us at the front desk. After introducing us to the staff, she asked us to follow her down a long corridor to what she called the senile section of the nursing home. As soon as we turned the corner, the soft table lamps and plush carpets disappeared. Fluorescent ceiling lights glared off white tiled floors and silver framed clocks ticked from yellowing walls. The strong stench of urine wafted out into the hall as elderly patients with vacant stares watched pathetically from their unkempt beds.

This has got to be one of life's cruelest endings, I thought as I passed by their rooms.

At the nursing station, Mary left us under the direct supervision of Mrs. Dawson, an ancient-looking charge nurse. Her voice was harsh, and her chin bristled with stiff gray whiskers.

Why, she is more of a drill sergeant than a comforter! I inwardly exclaimed, as Mary returned to her office on the other side of the building.

After a few weeks of training I was asked to work a couple of night shifts. While the sleepy looking charge nurse read her book in the lunchroom, the early morning hours found me poring through the patients' files. I wanted to know how these people, once vibrant and alive, had ended up in such a miserable condition.

Rosie Galloway's frantic screaming spells caused her intense blue eyes to bulge from their sockets. Her grossly distended stomach came from her refusal to have a bowel movement for sometimes weeks at a time. Wandering up and down the corridor with a rigid back and clenched fists, she muttered over and over under her breath the same conversation between two people.

"Get up on the bed!" the grisly male voice demanded.

"No! No! I don't want to!" squealed a high-pitched cry.

"I said get up on the bed!" the deep voice insisted.

"No! No! No!" the hysterical woman screamed, digging her fists into her face until several nurses came running to calm her down.

As I delved into Rosie's chart, I found out that she had been in mental institutions for more than fifty years before ending up at Beverly Manor. The terror ingrained in her mind was due to the rape she had experienced as a sixteen-year-old girl. When I flipped to the back page, I noticed a warning scribbled at the bottom of the original paper in faded blue ink.

"Rosie's father is a well-known member of the Mafia," it said. "The rape was most likely an act of revenge."

According to the file, seventy-year-old Rosie had never had a visitor.

While making the rounds with Mrs. Dawson I noticed a large gouge in Mrs. Heppe's skull. Her file revealed that the hideous scar was the result of a lobotomy. The detailed report explained that before the operation, thirty-four-year old Janet Heppe had been prone to violent outbursts. Now fifty, Mrs. Heppe laughed even when she broke her leg trying to climb over the bars of Jim Cooke's bed in the middle of the night.

Jim Cooke was a thirty-one-year-old paraplegic. While trying to get his son's cat down from the top branches of a tall tree he fell and broke his neck. Part of my duties was to put an external catheter on him so he could urinate into the bag hanging on the side of his bed. Although I was old enough to know about sex, my mind was still pure, and I felt no embarrassment when I took care of the paralyzed man.

Mr. Cooke kept a pint of whiskey in his bedside table and Playboy centerfolds taped inside his closet door. One day he told me that his wife was cheating on him and would probably leave him soon. I thought about my Dad's drinking and Dorrie's anger over the lipstick on his collar. Not knowing what I could say or do to make things better, I just listened to Mr. Cooke talk while I did my work.

The nurses kept a special high-backed chair out in the hall for Mrs. Fenucchi. As soon as she sat down, they would give her a cotton diaper to fold over and over in her lap, speaking a language no one understood. One afternoon I tried speaking Spanish to Mrs. Fenucchi. Her elderly face lit up as she responded in her native tongue, but the words sounded different from the ones I knew. When the old woman realized my limited vocabulary, the light drained from her face and she slumped back in her chair. Picking up the diaper, she began folding it in her lap, mumbling words I wished I could understand.

Celia Davidson weighed eighty-five pounds soaking wet. Her scabby, wrinkled skin hung from its skinny frame like long underwear two sizes too big. Restrained in a braked wheelchair, the ninety-year-old woman inched her way down the hall yelling in a loud southern drawl.

"I've gotta git to work! I've gotta git to work! I've GOTTA GIT TO WORK!!!"

The driving force behind these frail bodies fascinated me, and I had a strong desire to find the cause of their suffering.

Our days were filled with emptying bedpans, changing beds and diapers, and bathing and feeding the patients. The diapers were often soiled with feces and needed rinsing before going to the laundry. One morning Nurse Dawson sent me to do the terrible job.

Alone in the utility room I tried to avoid the awful stench by turning my head to one side. Pinching my nose with the fingers of my left hand, I carefully dipped the offensive material into a large toilet with the thumb and forefinger of my right hand. Wondering what was taking so long, Nurse Dawson came looking for me. Standing unseen in the open doorway, she watched for a moment and then let out an impatient snort. Grabbing my arms from behind, the strong old nurse plunged my hands and the diaper up and down in the messy hopper as the fetid brown water mixed with my repulsion.

"Hands will wash miss!" she scolded, as she washed hers and left.

The strike lasted longer than everyone predicted. Desperate for resolution, one of the workers threw a stink bomb inside the nursing home forcing us to evacuate the patients from their rooms. The following week a brick was thrown through the window of the regional director's home. When I heard that the brick as well as the broken glass had fallen into the crib of his newborn child, I was appalled at what people would do for the sake of more money.

One morning I sat up in bed with a start. I dreamed that Mrs. Fenucchi was gone, and her mattress was stripped of its linens. As soon as I got to work, I went straight to her room only to find that the curtain had been drawn shut around her bed. Taking a deep breath, I opened the thin drape and stepped inside the enclosure. Mrs. Fenucchi's once rosy complexion now had a pale waxy sheen and her bright eyes were shut forevermore. Lost in thought, I didn't hear Mrs. Dawson enter the room. Throwing the curtain open she startled me out of my reverie.

"Take out her teeth and wash the body!" she demanded, and then hurried out the door to finish her rounds.

My heart pounded as I went to the sink to get a bowl of warm water. I had never touched a dead body ever since my grandmother's funeral. I was thirteen when we got the call from the convalescent home saying my grandmother had died. The doctor informed the family that diabetes was the cause, but I was certain it was the loneliness that took her away.

At the funeral service, Aunt Phyllis encouraged me to go up and kiss my grandmother goodbye. When I got to the coffin I looked down at the waxen figure before me. The pleasant fragrances of homemade bread and blackberry jam were now replaced by a scent I could not identify. Bending over the casket, I pressed my lips into her sunken powdered cheek. The skin was clammy and cold. I recoiled in disgust.

This dead body is not my grandmother! I inwardly protested and hurried back to my seat.

Setting the water down by the bed I took Mrs. Fenucchi's teeth out of her mouth and fondly washed the stiffening corpse. When I was finished, I pulled the sheet up over her face, grateful that my old friend had come in the night to tell me goodbye.

That summer Aunt Phyllis and Uncle Lee called my parents to invite me to go with them and their two daughters to Clear Lake. Although elated with the prospects of going on a two-week vacation, I knew I had to be careful as life could be a cunning and dangerous enemy, not to be trusted. I had begun to realize that whatever I wanted the most could be used as a punishment and whatever I got attached to left me suffering when taken away. Trying to be the perfect child, I cooked, cleaned, and took care of the children until I was safely out the door.

The ride into the mountains was exhilarating. Unlike the stale, dirty air of the city, this air was fresh and alive. When we got to the cabin my cousin Carol, who was one year older than I, took me out back and unlocked the door of a Silverstream trailer.

"This will be our home for the duration of our stay," she explained as we made up the beds.

The next morning after breakfast Uncle Lee hitched up the boat to the back of the car and took us to the lake to go water skiing. Gliding in and out of the waves Carol and I gave the thumbs-up signal to go faster and faster until Aunt Phyllis finally stood up and waved her arms.

"Drop off!" she yelled. "It's time for lunch!"

Letting go of the ropes, my cousin and I sank into the water and took off our skis. As soon as we climbed into the boat Uncle Lee flicked off the engine. The hot afternoon sun flashed off the glassy water as the boat creaked and bobbed on the wake of the occasional skier. The combination of suntan lotion, gas fumes, and my aunt's cigarette smoke made me feel sick to my stomach, so I leaned over the boat's edge to get some fresh air. The rolling waves lapped against the side of the boat and I quickly became mesmerized by the feathery strands of algae swirling beneath the water's surface. Uncle Lee suddenly fired up the engine.

"Put on your skis girls!" he called. "I'll take you for one more spin around the lake and then we're heading back to shore!"

While my aunt and uncle cleaned out the boat, Carol and I went for a quick walk along the beach. There, sitting in the shade of a large oak tree, was a handsome dark boy looking my way. It felt as though a strong magnet was pulling me to him right through all the people on the popular shore. Seeing our attraction, Carol took my arm.

"C'mon," she whispered. "He is a boy from my high school. I don't know him very well, but I can at least introduce you!"

There was something familiar about the boy I could not place. He looked deeply into my eyes as though he knew me, and my blushing cheeks exposed my shyness. When we turned to leave, he smiled and waved. I never looked back but could feel his eyes watching me all the way to the boat.

The next evening Carol and I were excited as we got dressed. Aunt Phyllis had given us permission to walk into town to play miniature golf.

"I want to go!" begged eleven-year-old Donna, but Carol refused, knowing it would ruin our chances of meeting boys.

My aunt's friend Marion was a lot of fun. When Carol asked if we could drink a beer before leaving, she bubbled up with laughter.

"Go on Phyllis," she coaxed my aunt with a twinkle in her eyes. "Let the girls have a can of beer before they go! They're old enough, and besides, it's Saturday night!"

"Yeah baby," Uncle Lee said, as he patted Aunt Phyllis's leg. "Try to remember what it was like when you were young!"

"Okay, go ahead, but only one!" my aunt said, passing us each a can of beer.

Carol sipped hers while chatting with her parents, but I gulped the fizzy liquid right down. Marion was delighted.

"Woo hoo, look at her go!" she laughed, cheering me on like I was her hero.

The beer was so cold it seared my throat like liquid fire, but the attention from my aunt's friend was well worth the pain.

"Be home by midnight!" Aunt Phyllis called as the screen door banged shut behind us.

I felt like I had died and gone to heaven.

"Do you know where the miniature golf place is?" I asked naively.

"Miniature golf?" Carol laughed. "You don't really think that is where we are going do you? Come on! We're going to have some fun!"

Carol seemed to know exactly where she was going, and I quickly followed her lead. The alcohol had begun to sedate my senses and I happily surrendered to the elixir's soothing effect. The thrill of freedom made the small town come to life. Loud music blasted from wildly painted cars filled with teenage boys honking and waving at the giggling girls with ponytails who ignored them from the sidewalk. Multi-colored neon signs blinked and flashed while the aroma of buttered popcorn, hot dogs, and greasy french fries permeated the night air from a variety of outdoor concession stands.

The boy I met at the beach that afternoon was standing in front of a take-out stand with a group of his friends. I was delighted when he raised his arm and waved us over. Jimmy's dark eyes flashed, and his charming smile made everything appear to be part of him. The bitter resentments I had kept pent up inside seemed to dissolve just by being in his presence. When he teased and flirted, I did not play coy but let him take me in his arms and hold me close. I felt loose inside my skin and when he kissed me, I became immersed in an ocean of dark, blue silk.

At the end of the night I was afraid to tell the handsome boy where we lived because of the color of his skin. My sleep became fitful and I was sure it was him beckoning to me from the cars passing our trailer late in the night. The following week I was tortured by desire, wondering if Jimmy thought of me the way I did him. While water-skiing, eating, and visiting my relatives' friends, my mind went constantly to him and the warm feelings of release I had experienced in his touch. At the end of the two weeks it was time to go back to San Jose. As we drove out of the mountains it felt as though my heart was breaking into a thousand and eight pieces.

"Promise me you will give Jimmy my phone number the next time you see him!" I whispered in my cousin's ear.

Once school started my work at the nursing home diminished to weekends. I saw none of the boys in my classes but held Jimmy's image firmly in my mind. At lunchtime I had no interest in food but spent all my time drawing Jimmy's name on the covers of my books. When the last bell rang at the end of the day, I ran all the way home to wait for his call. I continued to look after the kids when my parents were not home, but my attitude had changed from resentment to distraction. When Jimmy finally called, he described the many sexual acts he would like to perform with me. Although repulsed by his words I was at the same time, strangely attracted.

41

One afternoon Jimmy called to say he was coming to see me. I began to panic. My father tended to over-react toward any boy coming near his daughter, especially one with dark skin. Torn between loyalty and passion I told Jimmy where I would be babysitting that night. I knew that if my father found out I would lose his trust, but the power of my lust was now growing in monstrous proportions.

Jimmy lived in Richmond, about an hour's drive from my home. The kids were asleep when he arrived, so I shyly let him in. The drone of the handsome boy's voice was intoxicating. He tenderly pulled me into his arms and I easily gave into his embrace. As Jimmy pressed his pelvis deep into mine, I felt something hot and hard rise in his jeans just beneath his belly. My heart began to pound with excitement as a warm, sticky fluid seeped out between my legs.

Jimmy led me into the living room where his passionate kisses passed eagerly down to my neck. His arms slipped from my shoulders allowing his skillful hands to probe parts of my body not yet touched. When he tried to persuade me to go into the bedroom to make love, I felt like one awakened from a dream. No longer feeling safe the way I had with my cousin Carol nearby, I told Jimmy he had to go.

The year of my father's sobriety was up, and he had won the bet. With the hundred dollars securely in his hands, my sole refuge went back to the bar to drink with his friends. Now that Don was getting around on crutches, he was able to leave the rehabilitation center and move in with Roddy's parents, Pola and Frank Mendoza.

At school I didn't belong to any one group in particular. The kids were now changing from surfers to hippies and there were rumors of pot being smoked on campus. During lunch one day I heard a group of students gathered in the food court talking about a music festival that was coming to Woodstock, New York that summer. I listened as my peers boasted with indifference that they were going no matter what their parents said. I admired their courage to hitchhike across the country to attend a music festival, but I could not imagine leaving the children alone or disobeying my parents in such a blatant manner.

While getting ready for work one afternoon I peeked out my bedroom window. The clear blue sky had darkened with clouds and the wind began to howl. Raindrops bounced off the cement patio and gushing sheets of water poured off the roof. Before leaving for the bar Sue had promised to be home in time to drive me to work. I had been coughing all day and my face felt feverish, but it was too late to call in sick. It was already three o'clock and I had to go.

"Take care of the kids!" I called to Susan before heading out into the rain.

Angry and frustrated by my parents' neglect I thought, *maybe if I get sick Mom and Dad will see the error of their ways!*

Pushing through the torrential rain I opened and closed my coat, encouraging the icy wind to weaken my body. By the time I got to work I was soaking wet and burning with fever.

"What are you doing here honey?" the charge nurse asked when she heard me coughing. "You should be home in bed!"

After calling another girl to take my shift she insisted on driving me home. Shivering with chills, I gratefully climbed into bed. My temperature continued to rise during the night and my lungs gurgled with phlegm. When I would not get up for school the next morning Sue got worried and took me to see Dr. Lane.

"She has walking pneumonia," he reported, lifting the stethoscope from my chest.

WALKING pneumonia? I thought. *How did he know? If he tells my parents, it will ruin my plan!*

"You are a very lucky young lady," the doctor admitted as he wrote me a prescription for antibiotics. "Keep her in bed for the next two months," he advised my stepmom. "If she gets any worse, she will have to go to the hospital."

At first Sue served me special meals on a tray and Dad came home every night right after work. Sitting on the edge of my bed, he would touch my face and speak with his gentle voice like he had when I was small.

One morning Bob came home saying he had a surprise for the whole family. He had just gotten his pilot's license and wanted to take us for a plane ride. Since it was Saturday, the kids were home from school. One by one they came to my room to say goodbye and then dashed out the door. Hearing the last car door slam shut, I reflected on what I had done. My brother was important to me and I wanted to acknowledge his accomplishment with the others. Lying alone in the empty house I decided there had to be a better way to get parents to care for their children than by making myself sick.

Every night after supper I sat near my father watching the atrocities of the Vietnam War flash across the television screen. Young men all over the country were being drafted, creating an air of vacancy in the homes they had left behind.

By 1969 the six o'clock news was flooded with reports about the degeneration of society's standards by America's youth who were calling themselves hippies. San Francisco's Haight Ashbury grew in popularity as the media produced streams of people taking pictures and gawking at the flower children through the open windows of their cars. Peace rallies, sit-ins, and draft dodging were a sign of the times as adolescent girls burned their bras and young men grew their hair long. Frightened parents tried every trick in the book to bring their children home, but it was too late; a wave of rebellion was moving fast across the country, mirroring a desperate cry for peace.

Adorned with a feather boa and rose-colored glasses, Janis Joplin drank Southern Comfort and wailed the blues in crowded auditoriums. While the Beatles insisted that love is all there is, the Rolling Stones opened the doors of promiscuity on the stage of our easily influenced minds.

Just as my high school peers predicted there was a three-day music festival in Woodstock, New York that summer. Over 400,000 peace-loving fans gathered as the Who, Santana, Janis Joplin, Jefferson Airplane, Crosby, Stills, Nash & Young, and several other well-known bands played on the open stage while torrential rains transformed Mr. Yasgur's lush farmland into an overcrowded stretch of mud. Seventy-year-old Richie Havens opened the legendary concert by crying out his spontaneous song, "Freedom", to the massive crowd who had parked their cars and walked to the concert site Friday afternoon. As the weary and very dirty fans headed back to their vehicles on Monday morning, Jimi Hendrix could be heard off in the distance electrifying the National Anthem.

Marijuana euphoria was giving the nation's young people a temporary feeling of peace, and LSD created flower children in its psychedelic wake. Feeling out of control, red-faced parents tried to convince their teenaged sons and daughters to stay away from the orgy-indulging bunch of young Americans who refused to stand up and fight for their country.

Now that I was back in school things at home fell back into their old routine. Dad stayed out drinking late into the night and Sue's frequent headaches increased. After threatening divorce many times, my stepmom finally called a lawyer. When I came home from school one afternoon, she was sitting alone in the living room reading a book.

"Your father came to get his things this morning," Sue said without looking up.

I remained silent as the confused thoughts raged through my mind.

I am a part of him! How can he just leave without telling me where he is going?

The following week my brother Bob enlisted in the Air Force and Joan called to say she was dropping out of school. Feeling as though there was nowhere to turn, my world began to collapse.

"Mom can't make you stay now that Dad is gone," Don advised when he dropped by to visit one afternoon. "If you want to come live with me at the Mendoza's get your clothes and be ready to leave in fifteen minutes."

I felt like a deserter saying goodbye to the kids. Sue did not say much when I told her I was leaving. As I kissed her goodbye I wondered if maybe her world was falling apart too. That night at the supper table Mr. Mendoza tried to include me in his family.

"Have a little chilito Catalina," he urged in his sensitive way. "It will make you strong!"

When the hot pungent tomato sauce hit my tongue, my throat seized shut and my face burned bright red. Gulping down a glass of water, I ran to the sink for more. Everyone began to laugh, and I realized I had just been initiated into the Mendoza family.

Every day after school Pola Mendoza met me at the door to kiss my face and whisper words in Spanish that I knew meant she loved me. Staying close by her side I would follow her into the kitchen, which was my favorite place to be. As she stirred the beans and rolled her tortillas perfectly round, I watched to learn what she knew.

Frank Mendoza drove the school bus for the elementary kids in Santa Clara County. When any of us got into trouble, he would raise his eyebrows with sincere concern. He loved his family and always kept his voice soft, even when he was angry. One morning I convinced his youngest daughter Melinda to pierce my ears.

"Here Sissy," she said, handing me a cube of ice wrapped in a wet washcloth. "Hold this on your earlobes until they are numb."

Melinda soaked a needle and red thread in alcohol and then proceeded with the operation. Although painful, the piercing felt like a rite of passage that would prepare me to experience the world as an adult.

Don was getting tired of driving me to school, so he bought me a second-hand car with his earnings from the gas station. At first, I went every day, but my mind was so distracted that I could not focus on my studies. After a few weeks I had every intention of going directly to class, but my little white Ford Falcon with the red interior just could not seem to get past the turn off to Joan's new apartment.

There was a constant party going on at Joan's and I had fun with her friends. Steve Shiver had an innocent air about him as he played his guitar and moved his hips like Elvis Presley, making us all laugh. We called Greg Hanson the Stork because of his long, skinny legs, and Joey Elder was the enthusiastic one, always full of great ideas. Although none of us were romantically involved, we stuck together as good friends do. We played bingo at the community hall on Saturday afternoons and listened to music until late in the night, telling each other everything that was on our minds.

Finding it hard to pay the rent, Joan found a roommate to share the expense of the apartment. Tina was older than the rest of us and never joined in with our group. While Joan was at work one day Tina came in with her new friend Diane. Diane was different than the girls Joan and I knew from school. She wore low, revealing blouses and such tight jeans that she had to lie down on the bed to zip them up. I sensed trouble in her presence right away, but it didn't seem right for me to judge Tina's friends.

Over the next few weeks Diane started coming to the apartment even when Tina was not there. Since Joan and I were not strong enough to oppose Diane's forceful opinions, we put up with the tough guys she brought with her. Before long we started to experiment with their drugs and we didn't even notice that Steve Shiver, the Stork, and Joey Elder had stopped coming around.

Bags of garbage began piling up in the kitchen and the apartment now smelled of stale beer and cigarette butts. Joan's bedroom floor was once again strewn with clothes, and dirty dishes with food and cigarette butts cluttered the top of her bureau.

Diane painted her eyelids with a thick black line making her look like a modern-day Cleopatra. With her dyed black hair ratted up high on her head, she emulated the tough Mexican girls from east side San Jose. Drunk and stoned most of the time, Diane had sex with any guy that wanted it.

Strutting around when she came out of the back room, she acted like she was wonderful.

What a fool she is! I thought. *The guys are laughing at her behind her back calling her Diane the Snake, and the girls are calling her a whore!*

Diane liked to call Doug Harrison her boyfriend. She got jealous whenever he spoke about a girl named Suzy who would read him the Bible and encourage him to be a good person. Listening to Diane's threats about what she would do to Suzy if she ever found her near Doug made me think of Paula Reinhart wanting to beat me up over my love for Rocky. Like Paula, I was certain Diane would not be the one to show up if it ever came time to fight. One morning Doug sounded anxious.

"Hey Sissy, how about letting me borrow your car for a couple hours?"

I shook my head no.

"I will take you wherever you need to go, but I don't loan my car to anyone," I replied.

"Come on," he pleaded as though we were good friends. "Don't be like that. I just have to move a few things from my old apartment. I will be back in less than an hour."

The more I refused the more Doug persisted until finally, going against my better judgment, I threw him my keys.

"All right Doug but swear you won't drink or use drugs while driving my car."

"Don't worry so much!" he called on his way out the door. "You'll see. I'll be right back!"

One hour passed and then two more. Pacing back and forth I wrung my hands, worrying about my car. About seven o'clock that evening I got a telephone call. It was the police inquiring about a white Ford Falcon registered to my brother's name.

"This is Officer Sorenson," the man's voice was serious. "About two o'clock this afternoon a Mr. Doug Harrison smashed into three parked cars. He was apparently intoxicated and lost control of the car. He's not hurt, but the cars he hit are pretty smashed up."

Terrified of their reaction I did not call my father or brother but got stoned with my friends and decided I could never go home again.

Now whenever Joan was at work, I spent most of my time with Diane. She made life seem exciting, saying we were going here and going there, but we never made it further than the nearest Burger King. One day I tried to get her to stop using such foul language.

"Guys don't respect girls who talk like that," I said, hoping to make her life a little better.

"You think you're so pure!" Diane retorted. "If you don't like the way things are around here then why don't you leave?"

I felt hurt by her words. I loved my friend Joan and remembered the days when Steve Shiver, the Stork, and Joey Elder were our friends. Now that I had ruined my relationships with my family and missed so much school, I didn't know how to go back. Worried about my delinquent behavior, the principal called my father. When Dad finally got in touch with me, he was irate.

"Your brother is being sued for the damaged cars," he said, and then, "Why haven't you been going to school, Sister?"

Still afraid of his anger I tried to lie about where I had been, but the tension in my voice gave me away. How could I tell him I was afraid of the future? The students I admired were making plans for university, but I didn't know where to begin. My father had so many problems of his own that I couldn't ask him for money, and I was too proud to ask my teachers for help.

"Get yourself back to school Sis," he said. "One day, you are going to need that diploma and you will be glad that you graduated."

As we hung up the phone, I was relieved that he cared, but at the same time, confused. My father offered no solutions to my problems, or proof that he was dealing with his. I needed his love and support to recognize and develop my abilities. Without that, I was lost.

That afternoon I voiced my concerns about going back to school in front of Diane. To my distress she decided to go with me the following morning. Thoughts of being seen with her on campus made me cringe, but I could not think of how to tell her without hurting her feelings. By the time we got to my classroom it was empty. A passing student stopped and pointed to the gym.

"The seniors are having graduation practice until noon," she said, and then disappeared into the bathroom.

With Diane the Snake close by my side I endured the disapproving looks from my peers as I went shame-faced up to my teacher. Without time for reproach he gave me a cap and gown and told me to get in line. I saw no point in the diploma or the graduation ceremony but showed up every day with a strong desire to please my father.

When the big day finally came, Aunt Jane and Uncle Jim arrived early. While presenting them to my friends and teachers, my eyes scanned the crowd, looking for my dad. Just as the ceremony was about to begin, I saw him weaving his way through the people. The sway of his body and the sombre expression on his face explained why he was late; my father was drunk.

Shame and anger burned inside my chest as my father hung his limp arm around my shoulder. His stupid talk and the familiar stink of his breath fuelled the fire of my rage. Sensing my discomfort Aunt Jane talked fast, trying to cover the situation. Uncle Jim said something about his brother under his breath and then lowered his eyes.

I was relieved when the principal finally called all the graduating students up to the stage. After the last speech was over, we cheered and threw our hats up in the air just like in the movies. Feeling different and alone I gathered with my peers who were now huddling in groups, laughing, and talking about the grad parties they would attend later that night. When they asked what I was doing I kept my plans vague.

After the ceremony was finished Aunt Jane and Uncle Jim offered me a ride back to the Mendoza's. When they pulled into the yard, I thanked them for coming and got out of the car. Pretending to be happy, I smiled and waved until they were gone and then went inside the house. Pola greeted me at the door.

"Congratulations Sissy," she said in her quiet demure manner.

"Yes, congratulations Catalina!" Frank added. "How will you celebrate your success tonight?"

Offering the same vague answer I had given the others, I changed my clothes and then went off to get stoned and drunk with Diane and her friends at Joan's apartment. On the surface I was glad the whole affair was over, but underneath I knew I had missed out on some of the most important years of my life.

Over the next few weeks, I began to dye my hair black and lay on the bed to zip up my pants like Diane who now proudly signed "The Snake" beside her name. The warm California nights made it easy to hang out in the streets with my friends. Our camaraderie reminded me of my childhood years of surviving with my brothers by sharing what little we had. With no plans for the future, I now smoked a lot of pot, cussed worse than Diane, and could chug down a can of beer faster than most of the guys.

That summer a friend of Doug's began coming to the apartment. A thick red scar slashed the left side of his forehead and his mischievous grin seemed to be hiding a secret. It never occurred to me that the name Robert Burns might be a warning.

When Joan's brother was released from the service, he came to stay at the apartment for two weeks. Bob was a decent guy who wore clean clothes and knew how to express himself without using foul language. One morning after the others left the apartment, he went into Joan's bedroom to meditate. I was attracted by his goodness and wanted to know more about the meditation he was doing, but it was too late; I had already become Robert's girlfriend.

Before leaving, Bob gave me a book called *The Prophet* by Kahlil Gibran. Inside was a simple poem he had written on a small piece of paper.

"You are only seventeen and you thrive on the action scene, but Sissy, I'm down on my knees, begging you please, don't throw your life away."

I put the poem in a safe place and wondered why he sounded so worried.

One afternoon Diane said if I got pregnant the welfare office would give me a monthly check. I was shocked by her advice.

"I want a baby to love not to provide a Welfare check!" I retorted with contempt.

One night while reading *The Prophet* I came across the poem, "On Children." From as far back as I could remember it had seemed as though my father suffered from his strong attachment to me. Wanting to ease his suffering I took out Joan's manual typewriter and typed out one of the verses of the poem. In an attempt to keep it anonymous, I disguised the handwriting on the envelope and mailed it from another town.

Joan was getting tired of supporting the group of young people hanging out at her apartment. Suspecting that I too had become part of her burden,

I gathered up my belongings and went to live with Robert at his mother's house in Cupertino. As he pulled out in traffic his ominous grin alerted my awareness that something was wrong. Shifting my attention, I looked over at the people in the passing cars. They appeared to know where they were going, but I was lost, wandering through life without an aim.

"How did you get that scar on your forehead?" I asked, trying to subdue the fear now surfacing in my mind.

"A car accident," he replied.

His inappropriate grin reminded me of a smiling theatre mask.

As Robert pulled up in front of his mother's house my breath sucked inward of its own accord. The lawn was severely neglected, and a thick patch of weeds choked the flowers in the bed near the porch. A trash barrel was tipped over on its side. Wedged underneath was a dirty tennis shoe.

Robert's thick-soled boots sounded heavy on the cement. His wavy, black hair reached just below the collar of his buckskin jacket. Its long, leather fringes swayed to the rhythm of his indifferent saunter as he led the way up to the house. Reaching his hand through the broken screen, my new boyfriend opened the front door.

I followed Robert inside and sat down on a sofa that was covered with a clean white sheet. The smell of beans cooking in the kitchen made me think of Mr. and Mrs. Mendoza's simple home in Santa Clara. They had worked hard to furnish it and keep it clean and their yards flourished in their care. I looked at the scratched hardwood floors. Cheaply framed pictures of saints had been cut from magazines and hung in no certain order on the faded blue walls. The back of a wooden chair was laden with clothes; its crossbar was broken, and the seat splotched with yellow paint. Hearing voices in the living room, Mrs. Burns came out of her bedroom.

"This is Sissy, Mama," Robert said, a little too casually.

With lowered eyes, the humble Mexican woman crossed the room to greet me. I stood up and offered my hand.

What are you doing with this crazy boy? her timid gaze seemed to ask, as she lowered her eyes and placed her limp hand in mine.

Margaret Burns was a religious woman who lit candles in the window whenever her son did not come home at night. Widowed early in life, she worked under the table babysitting the neighbor's children and cleaning people's houses to supplement her welfare check. Every couple of weeks Margaret's cousin, Ramiro, stopped by to take her to see Mrs. Walters in East San Jose. For just two dollars a reading, the psychic woman would spread her cards to tell Margaret her son's future. One evening while Robert was out, Margaret came home with some interesting news.

"I went to see Mrs. Walters today. She told me she saw a girl who will get pregnant soon, but no baby could be seen in the cards."

It wasn't long before Robert's devious smile began to show its true colors. Every evening after supper he would grease back his hair and put on his leather jacket saying he had to go downtown. Feeling courageous one night I spoke up.

"I'm going with you," I said, carrying my dinner plate to the sink.

"No," he snapped with a mean glint in his eye. "I don't want you downtown. Stay here with my mother until I get back."

Steeped in boredom and intimidated by fear I sat beside Margaret, watching the lights flash across the television screen. I missed my friend Joan and all the fun we had in the early days at the apartment. As usual, it was late when Robert came home. His speech was slurred and everything I said provoked his violence, leaving my arms bruised from his rough treatment. The following night, I called Joan to come get me as soon as Robert's car pulled out of the driveway.

"What's wrong?" she asked, hearing the tension in my voice.

Peering around the partition that separated the living room from the kitchen, I tried to make sure Margaret could not hear my plan.

"I have to get out of here right away," I whispered. "Can you come get me?"

"Of course! Where?"

"Just pull up to the curb in front of the house next door. But please, come right away! I don't know when Robert will be back."

A sense of urgency pressed me to haphazardly stuff my clothes into a garbage bag. After dropping it out the bedroom window, I walked nonchalantly into the kitchen to clean up the dishes. When I was done, I told Margaret I was going outside to empty the trash and then slipped out the back door to wait for Joan.

Fear shrouded my awareness as I watched through the pouring rain for my friend's car to pull up to the curb. When two headlights appeared, I waited until I was sure it was Joan and then ran out and threw my bag of clothes on the backseat of her car. As we drove up the street, I was aware that I was running away from something bigger than myself and it was not Robert Burns. My inability to be firm with my convictions kept me weak, and my refusal to tell the truth perpetuated my fear.

Later that night I awoke to someone pounding on Joan's apartment door. Not wanting to cause trouble for Joan with the landlords, I put on my robe and undid the latch. It was Robert. He was intoxicated and insisted we talk.

"You can come in, but you have to be quiet," I whispered, trying my best to keep the peace.

Robert was aware that two months had passed since my last menstrual cycle. Knowing my desire for children was a weak point in my mind, he used it with turned on charm.

"Please stay with me Sissy," he said, ending our lengthy discussion. "If you will just come back things will be better for you, me, and the baby. I promise."

The dark sky was just beginning to fade into daylight as we pulled into Margaret's driveway. The winking candles in her living room window gave me the strange feeling that I was a puppet dangling from the strings of an ill-humoured marionette. As Robert climbed in beside me in the single bed of his childhood, I pressed my face against the wall, deeply lonely for the truth.

Over the next few weeks Robert's behaviour went from bad to worse. In an attempt to control me, he now demanded I stay in the bedroom whenever he left the house. Since I refused to do as he asked, the bruises on my arms spread to other parts of my body. My pregnancy was now advancing into the third month and I felt pressured to make a decision right away.

Robert is already half crazy, I thought. *If I have this baby and don't stay with him, he will haunt me for the rest of my life. If I have an abortion and he finds out, I might be beaten or even killed.*

Night after night I sat on the sofa beside Margaret, worrying about my future. Outwardly I appeared to be gazing at the flashing screen, but inwardly my prayers for freedom intensified. One morning, Robert got up early.

"Where are you going?" I asked, as he put on his jacket.

"I have some business to take care of in town," he said, and the tattered screen door banged shut behind him.

When he returned a few hours later he had a formal looking document in his hand.

"I have decided to enlist in the Marines," he announced.

The thick, wormlike scar on his forehead glowed bright red as he deposited the paper on the table before me.

"The military will be good for our future now that we have a baby on the way!" he grinned.

Realizing my prayers had been answered, I contained the surge of gratitude flushing up in my mind.

"Yes Robert," I agreed, controlling the inward and outward flow of my breath. "If you join the service it will be very good for our future."

On the day of his induction, I drove Robert to the airport. As I pulled into the parking lot to drop him off, Mrs. Walter's prediction flashed through my mind.

"A girl will get pregnant soon, but no baby can be seen in the cards."

I suddenly knew what I had to do. I watched until Robert's plane disappeared out of sight and then drove back to Margaret's to call my friend Joan.

CHAPTER TWO

Unreality Seems Real

Wanting to rest and re-evaluate our lives, Joan and I decided to move in with her father. She made all the arrangements for my abortion and the following Monday she drove me to the hospital. Once the admission papers were signed the clerk at the reception desk pointed to the elevator.

"Second floor, maternity," she said, without looking up.

Sterile smells rushed in to greet us as the elevator doors banged open. The nurse on duty seemed to be expecting me. She pulled my file from beneath her stained coffee cup and walked me to my room, smiling and chatting all along the way. Just outside the door she turned to Joan.

"You will have to wait out in the hall dear," she said.

"Can't my friend please come in with me?" I begged.

"I'm sorry," she replied. "Hospital regulations."

Seeing the panicked look on my face, the nurse took me by the arm and ushered me into the room. She handed me a clean hospital gown.

"Here honey, put this on and get into bed. The procedure will be quick and fairly painless so try not to worry."

I braved a smile in response to her soothing words, but underneath my silence I was secretly drowning in an ocean of sorrow. All I had ever wanted was a baby to love and now I was about to kill it.

The nurse inserted a long, thick needle into the center of my stomach. After injecting several syringes of clear yellow liquid into my uterus, she clicked off the plastic tube but left the needle in place.

"I will be back shortly. Just lay still and don't touch this needle," she warned.

She pulled the sheet up to my chin and then went over to the sink to wash her hands. Before leaving she called to Joan.

"You can come in now dear," she said, and then turned back to me.

"Remember, no matter what, do not touch that needle," she said, and walked out the door.

Joan sat beside me while I waited for the baby to die in my womb. The impulse to scream and yank the needle out was strong, but I kept my mind focused on the ticking of the clock. When the nurse returned, she asked Joan to go back out to the hall. Turning back the sheet, she clicked the syringe back into place and withdrew some murky looking fluid from my uterus. Contractions began right away and like the nurse promised, the delivery was quick and not too painful.

"Take your time getting dressed," she said, while stripping the sheets from the bed. She hesitated at the door before leaving the room.

"I'm not supposed to tell you this, but the baby was a girl," she whispered.

The clock stopped ticking.

As soon as I was dressed Joan led me to the front desk to sign out. Unsure of what to say, she drove home in silence and my response was the same. Over the next few months, the nurse's words haunted me especially when I was alone.

"The baby was a girl. The baby was a girl. The baby was a girl."

Unable to cope with my grief, I welcomed the thick fog that was webbing its way into my mind. At night I would read my book *The Prophet* before going to sleep, but the misconceptions learned in early childhood were impossible to change on my own. I desperately needed someone to recognize my abilities and help me to grow, but that someone was not to appear for a long, long time.

The following week I went back to work at the nursing home, but my heart was not the same. Now that I was able to help with the rent, Joan suggested it was time to get another apartment. Over the next few months, we did little else but fix up our home and come and go from work. Our evenings were spent talking about our day and wondering about the future, but neither of us ever mentioned the past.

It was pouring rain one Friday afternoon when Joan came home from work. She had good news.

"Today in the lunchroom I overheard the janitor talking to one of the male nurses," she said, her face radiant with the prospects of adventure. "He told me there's a hippie hangout called the Chateau Regis in the Santa Cruz Mountains where several good bands come to get their start. Look," she said, pulling out a folded napkin. "I got the directions!"

Since both of us had been craving some excitement we went right out and bought the most fashionable hippie attire that money could buy. When we got home an unexplainable urgency nagged at my mind watching Joan put on her makeup.

"C'mon," I coaxed. "Let's get going! It's already 7:00 and it'll be another hour before we get to the bar."

Joan refused to hurry.

"Relax!" she said. "If we get there too early, we won't be able to sneak past the bouncers!"

Leaning close to the mirror she painted a metallic green line near the edge of her eyelids with a small makeup brush. After thickening her lashes with mascara, she ran her fingers through her shoulder length blond hair and gave herself a wink.

"All set!" she laughed and grabbed her purse.

It was dark when we finally left the house. The howling wind forced Joan's small car this way and that as the driving rain pummelled itself against the windshield. Holding the pencil-sketched napkin up to the light I tried to read the crumpled map.

"Take Highway 17 up to Summit Road and turn left," I directed.

Joan was having a hard time staying between the lines of the winding two-lane highway. Clinging close to the mountain, she made her way up to the top and then turned left onto Summit Road. After a series of wrong turns on the dark forest road, we finally pulled into the parking lot of what looked like an old saloon.

"HOT TUNA!" proclaimed a colorful banner tacked across the front porch of the rickety wooden building. A long line of young people anxiously crowded the front door.

"I'm leaving my purse under the seat," I said, shoving a twenty-dollar bill in the pocket of my new pants.

Joan followed my lead and then locked up the car. As we took our places at the back of the line, I noticed a dimly lit patio off to my right. The well-bleached cement had cracked over the years, leaving the barren swimming pool littered with dead leaves. A picnic table had been tipped over on one side and a faded umbrella lay on the ground beside an old plastic chair.

Since we were only eighteen, Joan and I waited for our chance to slip undetected past the bouncers. Pushed forward by the crowd, we ended up in a darkened dance hall with music so loud I wanted to plug my ears.

Black lights turned the gyrating dancers' white clothing purple and their waving arms created trails in the strobing bright lights.

"Let's go find the bathroom," Joan yelled, trying to make herself heard over the deafening music.

I had seen a few waiters carrying trays laden with beer coming and going through a door at the back of the room.

"You go," I called back. "I'll wait on the other side where the music isn't so loud."

When I got to the other side, I could not believe my eyes. There were more hippies than I had ever seen on the six o'clock news smoking pot right out in the open. Waiters carrying trays on uplifted arms hustled through the noisy crowd while bartenders filled pitchers of draft two at a time, promising their customers a cheap night's drunk and a painful hangover in the morning.

A lowered light hung directly over the pool table, spotlighting the balls as well as the girls as they bent over to take their shot. I was shocked to see these young women exposing their bare breasts beneath loose hanging blouses as they stretched out to display their skill. Feeling self-conscious in my new bell-bottomed dress pants and white lace blouse, I inched my way backward toward the wall.

It was easy to see that Joan and I were strangers in a strange land, but there was a mystique about the place that drew me in. Just when I had begun to relax in the hazy atmosphere of marijuana, patchouli oil, and male sweat, a man with long, wavy red hair reached out and pinched the nipple of my left breast. My face burned with embarrassment, but I refused to give in to the reaction he sought. Although my eyes stared straight ahead, I could see him leaning back on his barstool out of the corner of my eye.

What could be taking Joan so long to get back from the bathroom? I wondered, as I pretended to watch the game.

Suddenly, my friend came pushing her way through the boisterous crowd. Her voice was apologetic.

"The line-up to the women's bathroom went all the way to the back of the room!" she said. "Did you ever see so many cute guys?" she added, grinning with excitement.

Relieved to have her back, I scanned the room while she talked. I wanted to see how these people were dressed, because I knew I *would* be back, and these new clothes *definitely* had to go.

The glow of the fireplace flashed orange light across the faces of some very relaxed looking characters. Crowded together on a well-used sofa, they laughed and talked while one guy stood alone, warming his hands by the fire. An eagle feather poked out from his wide-brimmed felt hat, and the turquoise ring on his index finger seemed to guide his cigarette to and from his lips.

I liked the way the hippie girls adorned themselves with long beaded earrings and silver bracelets inlaid with turquoise, coral, and jade. A few wore paisley dresses that hung down to their ankles, while others had skirts so short you could see where their long legs began. Army issued trench coats, patched blue jeans, and tie-dyed t-shirts were in, bras and make-up were out, and nearly everyone had long hair. I liked this new world of sensuality that gave people the freedom to express and expose as much as they liked.

These people are truly free, I thought. *If I could just loosen up a bit, I could be just like them.*

After that Joan and I started going up to the mountain every weekend we didn't have to work. If Joan couldn't go, I hitchhiked alone, even after dark. After a while I got to know the people that lived in the cabins up the hill behind the bar. The mountain air was fresh, and the community of people gave me a real sense of belonging.

One of the guys flirted with me while I watched him play pool. I liked the nonchalant way he threw his poncho over his shoulder like Clint Eastwood in an old cowboy movie. The cigarette dangling from his mouth let long, curling streams of smoke wisp up past his squinting eyes when he leaned over to take his shot. Impressed by what I thought was self-confidence, I quickly became known as Ray's girl and wore his poncho like an engagement ring.

The first time I took LSD I felt like I was suffocating in the overcrowded bar. As the chemicals absorbed into my system, the strobe lights, loud music, and chaotic laughter magnified my fragile state. My feelings became fuzzy and I was unable to judge distances. When I started to lose touch with my bodily functions, I knew I needed to get away from the people and be alone in the forest.

Trying not to be noticed, I made my way out of the crowded bar. The fresh mountain air welcomed me as my yearning for silence drew me into the still, dark woods. With childlike innocence I took off all my clothes and hid them under a large rock. Climbing naked through the brush, the moon, big, white, and perfectly round, drew me forward into a well-padded grove of massive redwoods.

Great peace flooded my being as I entered the emerald thicket and a chorus of what sounded like a thousand angels singing held me in silent awe. Feeling connected with all of creation, I watched the night sky open up, revealing an intricate web of fine, glowing lines. Minutes or perhaps hours passed, as the knowledge of life revealed itself to me, and then I groped my way back to the edge of the forest to retrieve my clothes.

The following day I tried to tell my friends what I had seen and heard, but there were no words to explain my experience. I tried numerous times after that to recapture the same sights, sounds, and feelings of bliss, but all I did was take more LSD. Unable to sleep, I began hallucinating for several days at a time. As my reality became more and more bizarre, I swore that if I could only come down, I would never take acid again. Unfortunately, as soon as I returned to normal consciousness my vow was easily forgotten.

One night the Doobie Brothers came to play at the Chateau. At closing time, I piled into Indian Andy's van with the rest of the group to go to a party at one of the band member's home in San Jose. "Let It Bleed" by the Rolling Stones screamed from the speakers as we plunged down the dark winding road, smoking joints and drinking Red Mountain Wine from a gallon jug.

It was three o'clock in the morning when we pulled up to the house. I could hear rock and roll music drifting out from behind a front door that was painted like an American flag. Andy's girlfriend, Lily, had been sitting cross-legged on the protruding engine cover for the whole trip down the mountain. As soon as Andy parked, Lily slid the van door open and she and Andy jumped out onto the sidewalk. Without bothering to knock, they just opened the door and went inside and the rest of us followed right behind.

I recognized quite a few people from the bar talking in groups on the couches, chairs, and floor of the smoky living room. Tacked on the living room wall was a large poster of Frank Zappa licking a rolling paper filled with marijuana. The hash pipes and bags of pot scattered openly on the coffee table made me feel nervous, but these people blatantly defied the fact that drugs were illegal.

Over the next few weeks, I noticed something different about my new friends on the mountain. Their eyes were red and glassy with pupils the size of pinheads as they emerged from the bathroom in groups of five. With low, raspy voices they rubbed their noses until they were raw, calling Peter Leduc 'the Doc'.

One day I walked unexpectedly into Chuck and Charlie's kitchen. I was going to tell them I was pregnant with Ray's child, but Chuck's wife Charlie was gone, and Chuck was sitting at the table with his belt cinched tight around his arm. Holding one end of the leather strap between his teeth he injected a syringe of clear liquid into a bulging blue vein. When he pulled out the needle his head dropped to his chest. The belt fell to his lap as his eyes drifted upward and then closed.

After a few minutes Chuck regained consciousness and struggled to sit up. His pupils, now tiny black dots, seemed to float in the middle of his watery blue eyes. When he rubbed his nose and spoke to me in a low, husky voice, I recognized the same symptoms I had seen on the people emerging from the bathroom five at a time.

The following morning Chuck came into the bar looking like he had just seen a ghost.

"Little Jim was found dead this morning in his sleeping bag on the Doc's living room floor," he said. "When the physician examined him, he said his heart had exploded during the night from all the drugs he's been taking."

Seeing the puzzled look on my face one of the women whispered in my ear.

"Peter Leduc has been selling heroin to the mountain people," she said. "We call him the 'Doc' because he injects the people that don't know how or don't have their own needles."

Little Jim was only twenty-six years old. He loved his ex-wife and four-year-old son, both of whom he spoke of with great fondness. The bar scene, the hippies, and the drugs had seemed fun and exciting, but reality was beginning to rear its ugly head. The people I thought to be wild, creative, and free proved to be addicted to heroin or wanted by the police. Wanting a better life for myself and my child I quit going to the mountain and began focusing on my job at the nursing home. Ray occasionally came by to visit, but his behavior was becoming more and more erratic as his heroin addiction progressed. One day he sensed the coming separation.

"Please don't leave me, Sissy," he begged, his voice was raspy and low. Rubbing his nose, he said, "Here, I have six hundred dollars. If you stay with me the money is yours."

I looked at the worthless wad of paper. Wanting a responsible husband and loving father for my child, I accepted the fact that the baby in my womb would be mine alone to raise. I returned Ray's poncho and asked him to leave.

Little Jim's brother, Steve, was the wheeler-dealer type of person who was always on the move. The eagle feather poking out of his wide-brimmed hat made it easy for people to find him in a crowd. Since he was known on the mountain for selling drugs, I sensed he was using Joan for her car and a safe place to crash. One afternoon I came home from work to find Steve's copper headed friend lounging on the sofa reading the newspaper. I recognized him right away as the man who tried to humiliate me my first night up on the mountain. Seeing him alone in our apartment caught me by surprise.

"What are *you* doing here?" I asked, trying hard not to be rude.

"I'm waiting for Steve," he said. "He took Joan to work and will be right back."

As Joan's relationship with Steve continued, his friend Red began crashing on our couch for indefinite periods of time. Beneath his full beard and long wavy hair I could see the finely chiselled features of a good-looking man. Without coming on to me sexually, he made his way into my life by giving me pot to smoke and reading Winnie the Pooh stories in the evening before I went to bed.

In 1970 many of America's youth were coming back from Vietnam. They had a strange look in their eyes that I hadn't noticed before. One day Joey Elder came by for a visit. I remembered him from the early days at Joan's apartment before Diane the Snake and Doug Harrison came along. Since he had always been the enthusiastic one, I was not surprised when he pulled out a pound of Vietnamese weed which he had somehow smuggled into the country.

"Mind if I roll a joint?" he asked, as he proceeded to pour his bag of pot out on the table.

After inhaling the powerful drug into our lungs, the three of us giggled hysterically while listening to Joey's war stories. He talked about how the American soldiers paralyzed their brains on this potent marijuana and smoked heroin in their cigarettes both on and off duty. Even after Joey was gone, I was so stoned I could not stop laughing. Unable to get up off the couch I wondered how a bunch of laid-back soldiers hallucinating in a surreal jungle could survive the war and live to tell about it back home.

Early one evening Joan persuaded me to go with her for a drive. She acted strange, refusing to tell me what she was up to. When we got home, she had me follow her around to the back stairs.

"SURPRISE!" Susan, Liz, and Sue yelled when Joan opened the door.

The apartment had been cleaned and the overflowing ashtrays had been replaced by colorful balloons bobbing on either side of a large paper stork. A yellow plastic baby tub filled with gifts sat on the floor beside a new wooden rocking chair. The card taped on the back said, "Good luck, from your good friend Joan."

"Don't just stand there," Susan laughed. "Cut the cake!"

Ever since I started using drugs, I felt unworthy in the eyes of my family. The unexpected party made me feel part of them again and I was glad they were willing to celebrate the upcoming birth of my child.

By the second week in November the doctor said I was long overdue.

"Be at the hospital by nine o'clock Tuesday morning. We are going to induce your labor," he said.

As soon as I was alone in the labor room the sterile smells triggered the grief I had suppressed after the abortion. Efficient nurses without names poked and prepared my body while I stared at the ceiling, apprehensive and inept. When the doctor came into the room, he had a group of young male interns with him.

"Don't mind them. They will be watching the procedure as part of their training," he candidly directed.

I was nineteen years old and the open display before nine young men was more than I could handle. Separating my mind from my body so I would not have to think or feel, I split off from the experience until a push from deep inside pulled me back.

"Don't push!" warned the doctor, but it was too late; silent hysteria had taken control of my mind. Wanting to get the delivery over as fast as possible, I began to hyperventilate and push with all my might. One of the nurses recognized my distress and clamped a gas mask over my face. Feeling an odd sense of relief as I slipped out of consciousness, I realized it was professional people like these that I had needed all along.

When I woke up my father was standing at the foot of my bed holding a teddy bear. His beaming face and the vase of white roses on my bedside table told me he was sober. Just then the nurse came in and placed my son in my arms.

"His name is Joshua," I said, taking the child tenderly in my arms.

My dad kissed me on the forehead saying, "I have to get going, Sissy."

Although I longed for him to stay, to ask me what I needed, to tell me that he loved me, to say he would help me, I said nothing except, "Bye Dad. Thanks for the gift and the flowers."

After that I did not see my father again for several months. Like Diane promised, Welfare began giving me a monthly check and the day before Christmas I came home to Red shooting heroin.

"Loosen up and try a little sniff," he coaxed, as I watched him insert the needle into his arm. "Just sniffing it can't hurt anything."

As my usage increased Red's advice changed.

"You will use less and get off better if you inject it into your veins," he promised.

Sticking needles in my arms went against my high standards, but it didn't take long for those standards to change. Wanting to see what Red meant by a *really good high* I agreed to give it a try.

"Okay, but only once!" I said.

After the first shot I was mentally hooked and two weeks later I was physically addicted. I kept telling myself I could stop anytime, but the feeling was so great who would want to stop?

Through the process of buying and selling drugs, Red and I met a man people referred to as Big Johnny, but never to his face. Unlike those using heroin and smoking pot, Big Johnny's movements were quick and jerky. In the beginning he sounded concerned for our welfare, encouraging Red and I to get married. Our new friend promised to buy us any wedding rings we wanted; all we had to do was go downtown and pick them out. Being the smart man that he was, Big Johnny knew that heroin addicts don't go outside in the light of day, especially downtown to try on wedding rings.

Johnny Fernandez was a short, well-built Latino man who wore a black business suit even on some of California's hottest summer days. About forty years of age, he kept his body fit by lifting weights, and his new silver Cadillac appeared to be his mark of success. A large diamond ring sparkled from his pinky finger when he opened his briefcase to show us his wares. Assuring us that we could make a lot of money if we would start our own business, he spread a vast assortment of pills, pot, and heroin out on our kitchen table.

"You won't ever have to worry about the quality of my dope," he guaranteed.

It felt like Big Johnny was a great guy for helping us get started. He promised there would be no payment necessary until Red got on his feet, but Red was already taking so many drugs that he could not even get out of his chair.

Word got around fast that we were dealing. Because Big Johnny's drugs were such high quality, we became instantly popular with the drug crowd. People came and stayed all day, but no one did anything but more drugs. No games were played, or bright ideas mentioned. The only conversation exchanged was to say how good the drugs were, and did we have any more?

Red's friend Michael had long black hair and played a silver flute. Different from the other people who came to our apartment, Michael lit incense and decorated our walls with colorful tapestries from India. He never had money of his own and seemed to come and go in a flash. One day he hung a piece of yellowed parchment paper on the wall. It had a diagram of the chakra system drawn in gold ink. I would stare at it when no one was around but was too shy to ask Michael what it meant.

Just like the Doobie Brothers, we now had our own poster of Frank Zappa licking a marijuana-filled rolling paper on our living room wall. Mellow music by the Beatles, Pink Floyd, and Bob Dylan played night and day as an endless line of people came to buy dope. Sometimes there would be a drug bust in the city causing the flow of narcotics to dry up and a rush of paranoia among dealers.

It was during one of these times that Skip Spence, a guitarist for Moby Grape, heard that Red was dealing heroin. It was late in the afternoon when he came knocking on our door unannounced. When Red answered the door, Skip explained who he was and Red brought him inside.

"Man, I've got a gig tonight in San Francisco and I really need to score some dope," he said with an air of urgency about him.

"The town is pretty dry right now, but I'll see what I can do," Red promised.

Skip sat down on the couch while Red went in the bedroom to make a few calls. When he came out, he told Skip to wait at the apartment with me and he would be back in about an hour. After Red left, Skip paced back and forth in our small living room. Never one to idolize famous musicians, I turned up the music and went about my usual routine of taking care of the baby and tidying up the apartment. When the promised hour came and went, I noticed that Skip was becoming extremely anxious. I turned down the music and rolled a joint.

"What time did Red say he'd be back?" he asked after taking a long pull of the smoke into his lungs.

"He left at four o'clock saying he would be back in about an hour," I said, wishing Red would hurry up.

An hour passed and then another. Since I had no way to contact Red to see where he was Skip just had to wait.

"You must have some other drugs here. I am starting to get sick. I need something right now."

"Man, we're totally dry except some acid and weed."

"I'll take all the acid you've got," he said pulling out a wad of money.

I went into the bedroom and brought out some tablets of LSD. Skip asked if I had a spoon and some cotton he could use, as he wanted to inject it into his arm. I had never heard of anyone shooting acid but got him what he asked for. His pupils became completely dilated as he shot more and more of the psychedelic drug into his veins. With all the drug traffic that passed through our apartment I had never seen anything like this. In Skip's delirium he started calling me Sister Kate, saying he would not be able to make it to his gig that night. I could not imagine what would happen when the band's guitarist didn't show up to an arena filled with people waiting to hear him play.

When Red finally came home Skip shot up some of the heroin and then left the apartment. I never saw him again but years later I read an article about him. It said, "Skip Spence was one of psychedelia's brightest lights, but his musical career was plagued by drug addiction coupled with schizophrenia." I felt extremely sad for the part I played in providing him with drugs but at the same time, I was honored to have spent an evening with this brilliant star whose light went out far too soon.

Big Johnny began inviting us to his home in East San Jose. Looking forward to our visits, I made fresh bread and banana cream pies feeling like we were all good friends.

"It's a great privilege to know where the dealer lives," Red said one day after Big Johnny called. "It means we've proven ourselves worthy of his trust."

We now had more money than we could ever want, but never went to the park with the baby. When the car got a flat tire, it sat in the yard for months at a time. Josh never got new toys, we never shopped for clothes or furniture, and all our grocery shopping was done at the Seven-Eleven's frozen food section after ten o'clock at night.

I started to notice that Big Johnny's girlfriend was losing a lot of weight. Her movements were sharp and jerky, and she lit cigarettes one off the other. I thought it odd how she gritted her teeth when she spoke, and no matter how many layers of make-up she wore, she could not hide the fact that her skin was gray and haggard. One morning Big Johnny came by to tell us that Sharon was in the hospital.

"The doctor said she has been carrying around a decomposing fetus in her uterus for the past couple weeks," he said with utter disgust. "If I didn't get her to the hospital in time the dumb bitch would be dead."

Big Johnny sounded angry as he paced back and forth in our living room. He told us that Sharon's doctor said she could go home in a couple days, but she had to get off the speed if she wanted to live. Johnny cursed his girlfriend, saying she was stupid for taking drugs while she was pregnant. As his rage escalated, he said he would like to kill Sharon for murdering his child.

I wondered how anyone could be so blind. Big Johnny was the one supplying Sharon with all the drugs in the first place. He had influenced all of us by his example as an older person, but I didn't say anything. I just kept my thoughts to myself and continued to watch.

My heart went out to Sharon over the next few weeks. I wanted to see her get off the speed, but knew I had no right to talk. For months I had looked up to Big Johnny as if he knew what was going on, but now I was beginning to see him in a different light. He had begun sweating all the time and his movements were even faster than the first day we met. His once muscular body had become thin and his eyes constantly darted about the room.

One day Johnny showed us a pistol he was carrying in the back of his pants. I recalled the many times he remarked how he would like to kill certain people when they did not meet up to his expectations. It had been several weeks since Sharon stopped coming to our apartment with Big Johnny.

"What do you think happened to Sharon?" I asked Red one day after our dealer left.

Red shrugged his shoulders with indifference.

"It's not good to ask questions," he warned, and advised me to just keep quiet.

Red was getting slack with the dope dealing business. Small slips of paper indicating the large amounts of money people owed for drugs were scattered around our bedroom dresser. Sitting in the overstuffed armchair in our living room, he looked like a king who was well loved by his people. As the weeks passed, I began to realize he was not a king, but simply a poor, sick junkie saturated with the coffee, cigarettes, marijuana, pills, and heroin that coursed through his body like a never-ending river of pollution.

The continuous flow of drug traffic and late-night activity in our apartment insured an eviction notice every three months. When I used the toilet, I noticed that my urine was dark orange. I made no more homemade pies and Red's cosmic friend Michael with the silver flute never came around anymore. Like I had as a child, I began watching out the living room window filled with fear. The only difference was now the monster was approaching from outside the house and it was not the mummy from my brothers' afternoon matinee.

The last time we moved, Red put off telling Johnny our new address. Our dealer thought we had skipped out on him and flew into a rage. When his new girlfriend Sandy heard my name, she told Big Johnny that she remembered me from high school. She said she knew where my parents lived and offered to show him their house. As usual, Johnny ignored California's intense summer heat. Dressed in his dark three-piece suit, he parked his Cadillac up the street from my old house and waited while Sandy went to the door.

"Yes?" Sue said, when she heard the girl's knock.

"Hi," Sandy's smile looked innocent. "I was friends with Sissy in high school. We lost touch and I would really like to find her. I was wondering if you would give me her address."

Trying to be helpful, Sue went to get a pen and paper. Within half an hour the little man called Big Johnny was kicking in the front door of our new apartment.

"You son of a bitch," he yelled at Red. "You are trying to rip me off! Give me my money or my drugs NOW!"

Unable to do as he asked, Red sat waiting for Johnny's next move. Getting no response, Big Johnny screamed more obscenities and waved his pistol like a crazy man. His eyes were on fire as they darted about the room.

"You have until tomorrow morning to either come up with the money or get out of town. Remember my words. If you are here empty-handed when I come back, you are a dead man!"

Johnny went out and slammed the door. As his shiny silver Cadillac pulled away from the curb, I knew Red's days of pretending to be king were over. I went to the phone to call my brother Don.

"Hi Don," I said. "Red and I need your help. We are in big trouble."

I recalled the first time my brother found out that I was shooting heroin. He was appalled.

"My God, Sis," he scolded. "What are you doing?"

Wanting my brother to experience the drug so he would understand, I convinced him to try a little the same way Red had with me. What I didn't know was that my brother had already been addicted to morphine in the hospital after his accident.

"Come on Don, try some," I coaxed. "It's the best high ever!"

As soon as I injected the drug into his arm it awakened his latent memories and he quickly became one of our best customers. Now when he heard the desperation in my voice, he knew it was serious.

"I'll be right there," he promised and hung up the phone.

Feeling certain it was Red that Big Johnny wanted, I convinced the two men that Josh and I would be fine. When my brother saw that my mind was made up, he took Red to the bus station and bought him a one-way ticket out of California. Once they were gone an eerie silence took over the apartment. I cleaned up the mess of burned spoons, old syringes, and the other filth that comes with drug addiction. As the heroin left my body, I thought I was going to die. My back ached deep into my bones and my stomach cramped with pain. I could not eat or sleep but needed food and rest. Now that the "good high" was gone I was left alone to face myself.

When Big Johnny knocked on the door the following day, I was not prepared for the man who entered my apartment. There was no more talk of homemade bread or coconut cream pies, and the promise of wedding rings was long forgotten. His voice was low, and his face, dark and mean.

"Where's Red?"

"He's gone," I said.

He yanked the silver pistol from the back of his pants and pressed it hard against my temple.

"Where?" he demanded.

Realizing I was about to die, I knew I had nothing left to lose. I pointed to the door.

"GET OUT!" I yelled as loud as I could.

The back of Johnny's fist smashed against my face.

My waif-like body flew backwards, crashing into the coffee table.

"I said, where is he?"

I pulled myself up and once again pointed at the door.

"GET OUT!" I demanded again.

Once again, Big Johnny stepped forward and slammed his fist into my face. Each time I got up I yelled some more until he finally turned and left the apartment.

Since I had not seen Joan or contacted my family for a long period of time, I was ashamed to call them now that I was in trouble. Knowing my situation, guys came to offer their sympathy, drugs, and sexual advances, but not one offered to pay what they owed Red for all the drugs he'd fronted them in their time of need. My jeans and t-shirt hung loosely on my emaciated body and my face was badly bruised. As the withdrawals continued, I could not eat and taking care of my baby became extremely difficult. I vowed every day to stay off the drugs, but my will collapsed as soon as someone showed up with heroin or sleeping pills.

One night I saw myself in the mirror. I remembered the days at Joan's apartment when I felt superior to Diane and the young women I thought of as cheap prostitutes. As I lay alone on my bed I realized, I had become just like them. The only purity and sweetness left in my life was Joshua. His forgiving blue eyes and soft cheeks were to me what I must have been to my father in the depths of his sickness.

Feeling desperate, I got a ride to my stepmother's house in San Jose. When Sue answered the door, I was so loaded on sleeping pills that I could barely walk or talk. I needed someone to ignore my protests and get me to a hospital, but she just looked past me as though I were invisible.

Once inside the house I headed straight for the bathroom to take more drugs. Halfway down the hall everything blacked out and my body collapsed on the carpeted floor. Leaving me sprawled out the way I fell, Sue gathered up the pills that had spilled from my hand. No ambulance was called, and the kids stepped over my body the rest of the evening. As I came out of my stupor the following morning, I demanded to have my pills back. When Sue returned the drugs that were killing me I was crushed, for now I knew for certain, she did not really care.

That night one of my friends went off the road while driving up into the mountains on Highway 17. Passed out on the seat beside him, my head smashed against the windshield as the car plummeted off the steep cliff. When the car came to a stop, I crawled free from the wreckage, spitting blood and glass from my mouth. The night sky was so dark that I had a hard time figuring out which way was up until the lights of a passing car suddenly flashed on the road up above. As I crawled up the mountain on my hands and knees, I was glad I had left Joshua behind with my friends.

The next morning, we discovered that one lone tree had prevented us from falling to our deaths. The right side of my chest was badly bruised, and I could not lift my arm. Not knowing where else to turn, I phoned

Sue to see if she could take care of Joshua for a couple of days. When she agreed, we unknowingly drove down the mountain for the very last time.

A roadblock of five police cars waited for us at the corner of my old neighborhood. Their shrill sirens shredded my already fragile nervous system and fear threatened every fibre of my damaged body. The people I babysat for as a young teen came running out of their houses to see what all the commotion was. Embarrassed, I avoided their eyes.

Seeing Sue's son, Mike, in his police uniform alerted me that something was wrong. One of his peers came over and opened the driver's door.

"Both of you get out and stand over there by the squad car," he demanded.

Another officer did a quick search of the front seat. Within seconds he backed out of the car waving three perfectly rolled joints.

"Well, look what I found in the ashtray!" he exclaimed, grinning like he had just won the lottery.

Looking suspiciously at one another, my friend and I knew we had been set up. For the past hour we had stubbed cigarettes out in that same ashtray and besides, drug addicts know exactly where all the drugs are. Just then, Liz came walking up the street. Her timing was uncanny. Without a word, Mike grabbed Joshua out of my arms and placed him in Liz's embrace. Another officer pulled my wrists together and handcuffed them in front of my body. He pushed me into the front seat of his car and then joined the group of cops who were busy interrogating my friend.

I could not take my eyes off Liz who was lovingly caressing my son. When she raised her eyes and gazed at me with an impudent smile, my heart screamed betrayal. Like an animal separated from her young, I ripped my hands out of the cuffs and opened the door of the police car. Before anyone knew what was happening, I grabbed my baby and ran blindly up the street. The sound of the cops' holsters flapping behind me heightened my awareness that I was losing the race. Huffing and puffing, one officer gripped my shoulder from behind as my stepbrother once again grabbed Joshua out of my arms.

"Lock her in the back seat this time. And make sure you handcuff her wrists good and tight *behind* her back!" Mike ordered his partner.

My belief in justice soured as Mike handed my baby back to Liz. Ever since he joined the police force, I had listened to my stepbrother brag about how he used and sold a lot of the drugs he confiscated from arrests. I also thought of the times Liz showed up at my apartment to blackmail me for drugs.

"I'll tell Mom and Dad you're dealing if you don't give me some of those pills," she threatened.

Although I could not see it in myself, I knew my stepsister was a very troubled girl. Knowing she was too young to take drugs, I refused to succumb to her childish threats.

A couple days after the arrest a lawyer from the public defender's office came to see me at the jail.

"Where's my baby?" I angrily demanded.

"Your parents had your son taken to a children's shelter," he said. "If you want to have him back, you will have to go to court."

I bitterly recalled the many times I had fed, changed, and rocked my parents' crying babies late into the night when they did not come home from the bar. I had stopped the older children's battles and cooked half raw or burned chicken for dinner because I was a twelve-year-old child and didn't know how to do any better. Anger, hatred, and bitter resentment consumed my every thought.

Later that afternoon a guard came to my cell.

"You have a visitor," she said dryly.

Thinking one of my friends had come to bail me out, I hurried down the hall. When the guard raised the curtain, I was disappointed. It was my dad. Obscenities spewed from my mouth as tears streamed down my father's face. When he turned to walk away, the little girl he once called his crown jewel tried to yell out for help, but all that came forth was more profanity and rage. The following week another guard came to see me.

"All your charges have been dropped," she said. "You are free to go."

Knowing I had been set up, I began to argue.

"Shut up!" the other women demanded as they shoved me toward the door. "Don't be a fool! Get out while you can!"

"Do you want to call someone to come pick you up?" asked the guard at the front desk.

"No thanks," my voice bristled with contempt.

It was a scorching hot afternoon when the front gate slammed behind me. Wearing the same dirty jeans and t-shirt from the day of my arrest, I walked barefoot out to the main road and held up my thumb. I had no idea where Joan was and with Red gone, I felt all alone. Calling my family was out of the question and I no longer had any friends I could depend on. Memories of the humiliating strip search and being watched while having to shower with lye soap arose in my mind. A shiver ran up my spine thinking of the two mean-looking women who waited by my door that first morning after my belligerent entry during the night.

"Hey bitch!" called a big woman with a scarred-up face. "Who do you think you are comin' in here late at night makin' all that damn noise?"

Scared and too sick to respond, I lay curled up in fetus position on the dirty mattress on the floor. What Mike thought was a large drug ring in the Santa Cruz Mountains was in reality a few deluded young people trying to hold off the withdrawals of several different drugs. The so-called fun lasted only a short time before the insanity of addiction took over.

Since we did not understand what had caused us to use drugs in the first place, there was no way we could find a solution for our problem.

When a car finally pulled over, I gave the driver Margaret Burns' address. Now that Robert was in the Marines, I was sure she would be alone and happy to see me.

"Come in Sissy!" she said with a friendly smile when she opened the door.

The tattered pictures of saints in their cheap plastic frames now held new meaning. I no longer judged with disdain the faded blue walls, the worn sofa covered with a sheet, or the scratched hardwood floors. I was just grateful to be inside. After a couple of days, I decided to call my dad to let him know I was out of jail.

"Hi Dad," I said.

"Where are you Sis?" he wanted to know.

"At Margaret Burns' house in Saratoga," I said.

"Your court hearing is next week. Do you want me to go with you?"

Repressing my bitter assumption that he had helped to have me arrested I stubbornly refused.

"No thanks," I said, trying to keep the hurt out of my voice. "I can go by myself."

On the day of the trial I sat alone near the front of the courtroom. The woman from the children's shelter came and put Joshua in my lap. Holding my baby brought tears flooding to my eyes as feelings of tenderness welled up inside my heart.

"Joshua's father is sitting right across the aisle," she said.

Her remark was clearly a warning.

"He flew in from Texas last night with his mother and sister," she continued. "I just want you to know they are asking for full custody of the baby today."

My heart sank with dread as the judge entered the room.

"All rise," the bailiff's voice was monotone.

When it came time to hear our cases, he asked Joshua's father to stand up first.

"Are you working?" the judge wanted to know.

Known to be cocky when talking about his own good luck, Ray stood a little too straight, trying to impress the judge.

"Yes sir," he paused, stroking his chin hairs for effect. "I'm doing all right, if I do say so myself."

Ray went on to describe where he worked and all the money he was making.

"I'm living with my parents right now, but it won't be long before I will be building a house of my own," he boasted.

Without further comment, the judge asked Ray's mother to stand up. Unlike her son's slim frame and over-confident manner, Mrs. Ryan was a tall, hefty woman with an even voice.

"We have a beautiful home in Texas and our family will give Joshua the kind of life he deserves," she promised the judge.

Listening to all the good things they had to say made me sure I was holding my son for the last time. Lost in my thoughts, I began stroking Joshua's cheek. I knew I had no excuse for what had become of me. I was certain I would be deemed an unfit mother. The courtroom was suddenly too quiet. I looked up and saw the judge watching me with my child.

"Well, young lady," he said, peering sternly over the glasses resting on the end of his nose. "Do you have anything to say for yourself?"

Feeling uncomfortable in my borrowed dress and shoes I once again touched my baby's soft cheek.

"No sir," I replied sadly.

The judge called a short recess. When he came back into the courtroom my heart began to pound. The gruff-looking man shuffled through his papers and then defiantly folded his arms over his chest. Tipping his head off to one side, he raised his eyebrows the way Frank Mendoza used to do when concerned for someone's welfare. Keeping his gaze fixed firmly on me, the judge seemed to be challenging the people in his courtroom.

"I am releasing the baby to his mother," he said. After a pause he added, "Because I like her smile."

Somehow over the years I had forgotten the faith that had been such a vital part of my childhood. Now, as I walked out of the courtroom, I didn't even think to thank God for giving me a second chance to raise my son. As soon as I got to Margaret's I gave Red a call.

"I'm scared," I told him. "If I stick around here, I am sure to use heroin again. I don't know what to do but I want a better way of life for me and Josh."

Without hesitation Red said, "Come live with me. Things will be better now that I have a steady job."

I could tell by the sound of his voice that Red was off the sleeping pills and heroin.

"Go to the apartment and pack what you need," he said. "I'll wire you some money this afternoon."

I felt reassured knowing Joshua and I had a place to go where we would be welcome and safe. When I got to the apartment, I looked around at the furniture. Most of it belonged to Joan, but how could I find her? I thought about her boyfriend Steve with the eagle feather poking out of his hat. He had the reputation of being a drug dealer and I didn't want any more trouble. With no time to lose, I phoned a few people I used to call friends.

"I'm leaving town," I told them. "The furniture will be left in an unlocked apartment. It is free for whoever wants it because I won't be coming back."

Without saying goodbye to my dear father, Joshua and I boarded the plane that would take us to a new life.

CHAPTER THREE

Going through Sufferings

Red's two-bedroom chalet was easy to keep clean and I was able to heal in the stable atmosphere he provided. During the day, he worked as a carpenter with his old friend Michael. When he came home in the evening, he was content to smoke pot, lie on the couch drinking coffee, and watch the news. I went back to baking pies and cleaning the house, but a nagging feeling in my heart told me that things were still not right.

The people of the small town seemed to move in slow motion compared to the dramatic life I left behind in California. I was lonely for friends and my bitter resentments prevented me from contacting my family. I kept telling myself that I needed more time to adjust, but unless I was stoned, the unsettled feelings would not go away.

The rainy winter months dragged by until one morning, the weather turned oddly cold. Charged with anticipation, I peered out the window while washing the dishes. The sky was heavy with clouds and tension filled the air. Although I was twenty years old, I had never seen snow except far off in the distance atop Mount Diablo. When the white flakes began to fall, Joshua and I slipped on our coats and ran outside. Laughing happily, he danced around on the porch trying to catch the snow on the tip of his tongue. I smiled watching his innocent delight, realizing I was lucky to have a second chance to raise my son.

Every couple of days I saw a young woman across the field come out in her backyard to hang up her laundry. Since there were no fences around the houses in my neighborhood, I could see two small blonde children tagging along behind her, laughing, and playing while she did her work. Much too shy to go over and introduce myself, I would go outside to sweep my porch, hoping to catch her attention. The woman waved whenever she saw me and when the snow began to fall, she came over to invite Josh to go sliding with her kids. After several trips up and down the icy hill the children became tired and cold.

"Come on in by the fire!" Bonnie called, as she hustled her little ones toward her house.

Lifting Josh to my hip, I happily ran after my new friend. Once we were inside the house, Bonnie took off her kids' mittens and coats and hung them near the fire to dry. When she removed her own coat and laid it on the chair, I could see that her body was unusually thin. Her pale skin was blotched with purple and her hands shook so hard that her teacup rattled in its saucer.

Bonnie clenched her jaw when she spoke, and her smile revealed a pair of yellowing false teeth. Her children's baby teeth had already begun to rot, and their pale skin had the same purple blotches as their mother. As I removed my own son's wet clothing a deep longing to know the cause of people's suffering welled up inside of me.

I thought back to the patients at Beverly Manor Convalescent Home where I had worked as a young teen. Locking up a rape victim in a mental institution for over fifty years had seemed criminal and cutting out part of a violent person's brain, barbaric. I remembered my neighbor, Mary Patton, telling me I would make a good nurse but with no hope of medical training or schooling of any kind, I pushed away my desire to help people and went home to fix supper for Red.

The following week Bonnie introduced me to her good friend, Myrna, and the three of us got along well. As soon as the men left in the morning, we would hurry to do our chores so we could play cards in Bonnie's kitchen all afternoon. While my new friends drank their coffee, chain-smoked cigarettes, and shared the latest gossip, I sipped mint tea, smoked joints, and listened to what they had to say.

That spring I struggled to grow a garden in the small yard beside our house. The sun felt good on my back as I planted my seeds but unfortunately, the soil consisted mainly of clay. Whenever it rained the water gathered in puddles on top of the ground, and for every weed I pulled, ten more took its place.

Bonnie was out of town one afternoon, so I walked up the road to visit Myrna. Seeing two parked cars in the driveway I turned to go home. Myrna, who happened to be looking out her window at the time, quickly opened the door.

"Wait, Sissy! Don't go!" she called. "Come on in and have a cup of tea."

Her husband Mike had come home from work early that day and was standing in the kitchen talking with three of his friends. After introducing me to the men, Myrna carried our tea into the living room and turned on the TV. I tried to stay focused as my friend complained about the problematic affairs of people I would never meet, but my attention kept drifting to the long-haired man who was sitting at the kitchen table counting yellow capsules and placing them in baggies.

I had just turned twenty-one and was starving for fun and affection. Unlike the other men I'd met, there was a spark of life in Hippie Ron that attracted me. Occasionally, he looked up and made eye contact with me. When he picked up his guitar and went outside, I excused myself from Myrna's idle chatter and followed right behind.

Hippie's music was soothing, and I sat easily beside him without saying a word. While watching him strum his guitar I noticed a faded tattoo on his forearm. Since he did not appear to be gay, I found it odd that a man called Hippie Ron would have the name Henry with a trailing blue heart tattooed on his arm. He stopped a moment to rest his fingers.

"Whenever I'm in town I stay here with Mike and Myrna," he said, and then continued to play his guitar.

After listening to a couple of his songs I went back inside the trailer to finish my visit with Myrna. Hippie came in behind me and then went to his room to get his new pool cue. He seemed proud to show me the hand-carved stick and asked if I would like to come to the tavern that night to watch him play in the pool tournament. His long hair, beard, and association with drugs reminded me of all the good times I had in the Santa Cruz Mountains. Big Johnny, the frightening week I spent in jail, and the desperation of losing my son were all forgotten as my memories flooded in completely trouble free.

A familiar craving told me that it would sure feel good to get high again, now that my system was clean from heroin and pills. I wondered about Hippie's tattoo but after Sharon's disappearance in San Jose, I learned to mind my own business. I never asked who Henry was, or why a faded blue heart trailed behind his name. I just bought five dollars' worth of his pills and walked home to get ready.

When Red came home from work that evening, I was happy to show him the bag of pills I bought from Hippie Ron.

"There's a pool tournament at the tavern tonight," I said. "I've decided to go. Do you want to come with me? I know Maxine next door will be happy to take care of Josh."

"I'm tired of the bar scene," he said, popping a couple of the yellow capsules into his mouth. "Let's just stay home and watch a little TV," he said, and stretched out on the couch with a cup of coffee and his newspaper.

Refusing to change my mind, I got Josh to sleep, took a shower, and then swallowed a couple of the sleeping pills. Making sure the lacings on the front of my blouse were tied loose enough to reveal the cleavage of my firm, young breasts, I said goodbye to Red and left the house.

Walking up the road I felt sexy and free as my long, auburn hair blew gently in the wind. Whenever I thought of Hippie my step quickened and my heart pounded unusually fast. Due to the drugs in my system I felt lightheaded and brave when I knocked on the trailer door.

"Hey! All right! Come on in!" Hippie exclaimed when he saw me.

He included me into the party right away. When it was time to leave for the tavern, he put his arm around my shoulders as though I was with him. I was grateful for my drugged state, for I felt no shame as we explored every part of each other's bodies in the back seat of Mike's van.

When we got to the tavern Hippie and I were in a world all our own as we flirted, drank beer, and danced to the jukebox music. I was delighted to have finally found someone just like me, but there was a problem; I was already three months pregnant and the father of my baby expected me home at the end of the evening.

About four o'clock in the morning I awoke to someone pounding on the trailer door. There was a truck running in the yard and I knew it had to be Red. I quietly groped in the dark for my clothes and then slipped out the door without saying goodbye to Hippie Ron, who was passed out on the bed.

When I got in the truck Red didn't say a word, he just shifted into reverse and backed out of the driveway. Although we were only two minutes from home, the thick morning fog caused him to flick on the windshield wipers. Passing streetlights flashed across his white knuckles that were gripping the steering wheel a little too hard. The silence between us was daunting, and I welcomed the sound of the wipers clacking back and forth against the old truck's windshield.

When we got home, I checked on the baby and then took a hot shower. It was still dark when I climbed under the covers beside Red. Although he had still not uttered a word, his rigid frame spoke volumes about the disappointment and hurt he was experiencing. Although still drunk and stoned, my guilty thoughts prevented my escape into sleep as I tried to justify my promiscuous behavior. A vivid memory from our past life in San Jose flashed through my mind. I had come home from work a little late one afternoon and was surprised to see Susan there alone with Joshua.

"Where's Red?"

"I dropped by to see you this morning about eleven o'clock," she replied. "Red mentioned something about having to go see a girl named Linda. He asked me to stay with Josh and promised to be back before you got home."

Linda was a girl I knew from work. She lived up the street and had come to our apartment a few times to buy drugs. Feeling suspicious, I walked to her place and opened the door without knocking. She and Red were surprised to see me. Linda, who was wearing nothing but a black negligee, got out of bed and started to apologize. Red was so loaded on sleeping pills that he could hardly speak. I felt sick to my stomach like I had as a child seeing my father naked in bed with Sue. Without saying a word, I left and walked back home. Now, lying beside Red, I remembered how it felt to be betrayed. I became determined to forget Hippie Ron and be faithful to the father whose child I was carrying.

That February my dream to have a daughter was fulfilled but still, my heart was not at ease. I had a safe home to live in and my children were healthy, but my feelings for Hippie would not go away.

Hippie Ron was one of the main transporters of drugs in the small beach town where we lived. Unlike Big Johnny, he did not wear a large diamond ring or deliver his drugs in a briefcase. Instead of a suit and tie, he wore faded blue jeans, plaid flannel shirts, and drove around town in a pale green Cadillac he called mint condition.

I was delighted to see Hippie's car pull into the driveway one afternoon while Red was still at work. It had been several months since our night together at the tavern and I was happy to see him. Quickly smoothing my hair with my hands, I ran to the door to let him in.

"Want a beer?" he asked, cracking one for himself.

"Sure, thanks," I said, and sat down to roll a joint.

Sensing my determination to be loyal, Hippie never mentioned the first night we met, but we both knew the attraction between us was growing stronger.

As summer came to an end, I was disappointed with the results of my garden. None of the vegetables brought forth a harvest and my flowers were stunted, their blooms small and sparse. When Hippie stopped by to tell me he knew of a place for rent in the country I was ready to go.

"It will be cheaper if we all live together," he said. "I'll show you how to grow a real garden and we can raise our own chickens in the backyard."

I was delighted with the prospects of living in the country, especially with Hippie Ron. When Red came home that evening, I influenced him with my enthusiasm, and the following month, we moved into the dilapidated old farmhouse. Hippie and I got right to work cleaning while Red sat at the kitchen table drinking coffee and reading his newspaper. Following Michael's example, I lit incense and tacked Indian tapestries on the living room walls. When Hippie brought his large brass hookah pipe into the living room, I became extremely nervous.

Sensing my upset he said, "Don't worry. I have been living in this area for a while and the cops never come this far out in the country!"

It didn't take long for Red to quit his job as carpenter. The two men began investing their money on large quantities of dope and people came from all around to drink and smoke pot at our place. The steady flow of pretty girls wanting to be with Hippie Ron didn't bother me a bit. I knew deep inside that I alone was the one for him, but for a little while longer we had to lead separate lives.

Whenever the men went to the city to buy drugs, I cleaned, baked bread, and went for walks with my children in the forest next to our house. On the way home Hippie often stopped at auctions looking for good deals on second-hand appliances. One day he surprised me with a stove, gifts for the children, and one hundred baby chicks.

Conscious of our strong attraction, we were careful not to touch one another or remain in the same room together when Red was asleep or not home. The more I tried to be faithful to the father of my daughter, the clearer it became that I was living a lie. Red seemed to exist in a world of his own, far away from the rest of us. When he told me that he used to test LSD for drug dealers in college, I began to understand his spacey withdrawal.

"I took the chemical every day for weeks at a time, trying to kill my ego," he explained.

Lying beside me in bed one night he tried to describe his spiritual experiences, saying he and Michael often met in a cosmic dream. I didn't know anything about egos or cosmic dreams, but I was certain he wasn't killing anything except his own brain cells.

Hippie was a good businessman and he and Red began to make a profit. Our house quickly became known as the place to buy drugs until one day, I got a strong feeling that we were going to be arrested.

"We have to stop dealing right away," I told the men.

"Don't worry," Hippie said calmly. "If anything happens, I'll take full responsibility."

The following week Hippie and Red went to the city to buy several pounds of pot. When they got home, they bagged up the dope and then went to the pool tournament at the local tavern. Shortly after they left, three unmarked police cars pulled into the driveway. Dressed in dark suits, the federal officers flashed their badges at the front door and then held out a warrant to search the house.

"We are looking for a man called Hippie Ron," said one of the cops. "He has long brown hair and a beard and was last seen wearing a red and grey flannel shirt with faded blue jeans."

I tried not to look nervous.

"I don't know where he is," I lied.

"Then you are under arrest for the possession and sales of illicit drugs," said the officer in charge.

A knock sounded on the front door as he was reading me my rights. When no one responded, my neighbor opened the door and introduced herself.

"I will look after the kids until someone comes for them," she offered.

Since there were no lights or sirens, I realized that she was the one who had phoned the police. Hugging my children close I kissed them goodbye, telling them to be good and stay with the nice lady. As soon as they were gone, I followed the officers to the car in the numb state that was becoming all too familiar.

News travels fast in a small town and the tavern was soon buzzing with gossip. Afraid of a trap, Red went into hiding, but Hippie drove to our neighbor's house and sent a friend in to pick up the kids. In order to get out of jail on my own recognizance, I had to go to court and plead guilty. Once I was free, Hippie phoned to let us know he was in Ontario, the place of his birth. He explained that he had been illegally in the country and his real name was Henry. The faded tattoo on his forearm finally made sense, but I still didn't realize that I was the blue heart that would trail behind.

During the year we lived together, Hippie and Red had often discussed the prospects of homesteading in Canada. When Hippie called to say he was staying at an old summer camp on a lake in Ontario, Red decided it was a good time for us to go. I could not risk losing my children by going to prison, so I started packing for the trip. Our friends Frank and Rita heard we were leaving and unexpectedly stopped by for a visit.

"Rita and I are going on a fishing trip to Upstate New York in a couple of days," Frank said. "If you guys want to come along, we'll drive across Canada as far as Ontario and then cut back into the States after dropping you off."

A few friends came to help us clean out the old farmhouse and say their goodbyes. After storing our belongings in Bonnie's attic, Red and I headed up the road in Frank and Rita's Volvo station wagon. Four adults and three little children were crowded into the seats; our tents, food, clothes, fishing gear, and Frank's dog, Skylar, all had their places in the back. About a mile before the Canadian border Frank turned down the radio. Looking over his shoulder to make sure the kids weren't listening he spoke directly to me.

"Stay cool, Sissy," he whispered. "I have two pounds of pot stashed in the back with the spare tire."

In 1973 marijuana was highly illegal; an earring and long hair on a man were red flags of drug usage to any officer of the law. As Frank pulled up to the customs wicket, I glanced over at Red's long ponytail, bushy copper beard, and the small golden hoop piercing his left ear. Frank's unkempt, shoulder-length hair straggling out beneath the expensive cowboy hat that Rita gave him for his birthday, made my heart begin to thump. He casually rolled down his window and leaned his elbow on the sill.

"Good afternoon sir," the customs officer said, as he bent down to look inside the car. "Where are you folks heading and how long will you be staying in Canada?"

"Good afternoon. We're going on a two-week fishing trip," Frank replied easily, pointing at the rods and reels in the back of the car.

The officer looked over at Rita who was innocently holding up a well-padded wallet. Their three-year-old son, Yetsuh, sat sweetly in her lap.

"That's right. We're just going fishing for a couple of weeks," she said with a friendly smile.

Red, too, had all the right things to say, but when it came my turn to talk, my throat froze, and my chest began to heave.

"Your name?" the officer asked, pointing his flashlight directly into my eyes.

I stared at him like a mute woman. All I could think of was the pot stashed in the back with the spare tire. I was supposed to appear in court that morning but instead, I was a fugitive, crossing the border into Canada. If the customs officer decided to pull us over and search the vehicle, I would go to prison and lose my children.

"Your name?" the officer asked again.

My palms began to sweat. My mind, now consumed with fear, caused my pupils to reverse their nature and dilate in the intrusive bright light. Red nudged my arm.

"Tell the man your name," he whispered, and my lips began to move.

The officer stepped back and motioned us forward. Just then an eerie chill waved over my body.

"Enjoy your vacation," he said with a smile.

As Frank proceeded into Canada his nervous release was obvious.

"Wow, you almost lost it back there Sissy! Hey Reet', how 'bout rolling us a joint? It's time to celebrate!"

Holding baby Terra close to my chest, I laid my hand on Josh's face trying to help them relax in the confines of our cramped quarters. Since I was sure my friends would not believe me, I didn't tell them that I had seen it was God's grace that allowed us to cross into Canada.

The trip to Ontario was long and tiresome. Occasionally, I could hear my father's voice singing in the far reaches of my mind.

"Row, row, row your boat, gently down the stream; merrily, merrily, merrily, merrily, life is but a dream."

I thought about the dream life from my father's song and wondered why mine had turned out to be a nightmare.

Once we got to Ontario, we followed Hippie's directions to the summer camp on Lake Talon. When we pulled into the driveway he came out and threw up his arms as though glad to see us.

"Hey, far out!" he beamed. "You guys made it! Did you bring any weed?"

"Oh baby! Do we have some good shit, eh Reet?" Frank laughed.

Rita, although strong in character, was physically short and rather delicately framed. It never took much to get her stoned. She rolled her eyes and gave one of her 'Yes Frank, it's really good dope smiles' which seemed to satisfy her husband's inquiry.

"Alright!" Hippie exclaimed. "Let's smoke a joint and then I'll show you around. We can get your stuff out of the car after."

Hippie sucked one last pull from the joint and then popped the remains into his mouth.

"Don't want to waste it!" he laughed, walking toward a string of rustic log cabins.

"This place was built back in the 1920's," he said, opening the front door of the main house.

As we explored the room, the original families peered at us from their black and white photographs like ghosts from the distant past. Heavy green velvet curtains draped the windows, and three overstuffed sofas were crowded together in front of a massive stone fireplace. High above the mantle a hunter's pride followed our every move with its non-committal stare.

"Hey, look at this!" I exclaimed, heading for a large bookcase at the back of the room.

Seeing my delight in the ancient-looking texts, Hippie came and stood beside me.

"Some of these books are really old," he mused. "I read quite a few over the past several weeks. They kept me company as I sat by the fire at night while waiting for you guys to arrive."

A short well-trodden dirt path led us to a small cookhouse just across from the main building. An assortment of aluminum pots and pans hung from rusty nails pounded long ago into the yellowing logs. Mismatched plates and chipped teacups lined the wooden shelves. By the looks of the old wood-burning cookstove, someone had recently polished its chrome.

Overlooking the lake was a screened-in porch. It was just large enough for the two picnic tables that were pushed together in the middle of the room. Glancing out over the water Hippie's voice became quiet.

"It's kind of freaky being here alone at night. The loons' eerie wails echo across the lake and every time that ole north wind blows, the trees rub their branches against the screens. Yeah, it's freaky alright… real freaky."

After unloading the car, we took our clothes and sleeping gear to the bunkhouse. The cement caulking had eroded over the years, letting the mosquitoes come and go as they pleased. We pushed the iron camp beds together so each family had their own section of the room for privacy. Frank, Rita, and Yetsuh had their space on the far side of the room. Joshua and Terra slept together on the lower bunk next to Red and me, while Hippie claimed the top bunk, just above the kids. As soon as the others went to sleep, Hippie leaned over on his side and gazed deeply into my eyes. I was so happy to see him that I allowed his secret advances, but my conscience ached with guilt. The separation had not broken the strong bond between us, and our love was becoming difficult to conceal, especially to ourselves.

A few days after our arrival, Hippie took his sleeping bag and moved to another cabin. Feeling anxious that I would lose him forever, I felt like I had to do something right away. Once Rita and I got the kids to sleep that evening we joined the men in the porch off the main house.

"Game of crib[1]?" Hippie asked when I came in and opened a beer.

"Yeah sure," I casually responded.

Rita went to the other end of the table to study maps of New York with Frank and Red. Passing joints back and forth, Hippie and I seemed to be unconsciously stalling for time.

"Fifteen two, fifteen four, fifteen six, fifteen eight," we counted our points, until one by one, Frank, Rita, and Red all drifted off to bed. Now that we were alone the silence was awkward.

"Want to go for a walk?" Hippie asked, breaking the tension between us.

"Yeah, okay," I said, relieved to get out in the fresh night air.

I followed him through the woods until he stopped in a grove of young birch trees. I longed for him to take me in his arms, but he just stood there gazing at the moon's image reflecting on the ebony water.

I reached out and took his hand.

"What are you doing?" he asked, sounding young and naïve.

"I'm going to twist your arm," I answered with a mischievous smile.

He jerked his hand away as though he had been burned.

"What did you say?"

"I said I am going to twist your arm," I repeated, confused by his reaction.

"I thought you said you were going to break my heart," he said, and a loon wailed off in the distance.

---

[1]   Crib is short for cribbage, a card game using a board and pegs to keep score

"What was that?" I asked, jumping at the haunting sound.

Hippie laughed, amused by my innocent fright.

"A loon," he said, protectively taking my hand.

Leading the way back up the trail, he took me to his little cabin at the far end of the camp. After lighting the kerosene lamp, he stoked the fire in the small woodstove and then came over and held me close. Unlike the first night we had sex in a drug-induced stupor, this time we made love. Like a wild stallion unleashed from its coral, Hippie immersed himself in me again and again. Sensing his passion could never be sated, I got scared and wanted to run back to Red where things were safe, and I knew what to expect.

"I should go," I said, easing myself out of his arms. "It's late and Red will be wondering where I am."

Halfway down the trail I stopped at the cookhouse to wash. A lively pad of glowing embers heated the water in the cookstove's reservoir. The moon was so bright that I didn't bother lighting the kerosene lamp. I just filled a basin with warm water and slipped off my clothes.

Although I never knew my mother, I desperately needed to talk to her. I was alone in a foreign country with two small children. Do I follow my heart and stay with Hippie or do I go back to the States with Red? I wanted a nice home. I wanted to educate myself and participate in the betterment of society. I wanted a loving husband and father for my children. And most of all, I wanted her to explain why the lonely feeling in my heart would not go away. Unable to stop my thoughts, I poured the soothing water over my skin and watched in the moonlight as it disappeared through the drain in the middle of the cement floor.

The rusty hinges on the bunkhouse door announced my arrival. Groping in the dark, I slowly made my way over to the bed. I took off my clothes and the hum of the mosquitoes went quiet. When I realized they were feeding on my flesh, I brushed them off my skin and quickly slipped beneath the covers. Red rolled over to look at me. I was sure he could smell Hippie's scent still clinging to my body.

"Good night," he said, and then rolled back on his side.

"Good night," I whispered, wondering how long he had been lying there awake.

Early the next morning Hippie and Red went fishing. I didn't like the idea of the two men being out together, alone in the canoe. Hippie was bold and I was afraid he might tell Red our secret before I had the chance to do so myself. No matter how hard I tried, I didn't love Red like a husband, but I was still afraid to let go of the known for the unknown.

The air in the cookhouse felt oppressive as I got the breakfast fire going. Dusty cobwebs laced the window above the sink trying to distract me as I searched the lake for Hippie and Red. The early morning mist reminded me of the silent drive home I'd taken with Red nearly two years before. I needed to know Hippie's intentions, so I wrote him a letter and took it to his cabin. When I got back to the cookhouse, I searched the silver waters trying to catch sight of the canoe. When the boat finally pulled into the dock, the two men got out and climbed up the hill. There was no exchange of conversation and I could not read their faces.

During breakfast, the children were unusually quiet. The adults were reflective, like poker players contemplating a game of high stakes. When everyone finished eating, Rita and I stayed back to clean up the dishes. As soon as I was finished, I headed for the bunkhouse to tidy up and get the kids ready for the day. Red was coming up the trail. The look on his face warned me that something was very wrong.

He stopped and took a piece of paper out of his shirt pocket. When I saw my own handwriting, I realized it was the letter I put in Hippie's room while they were out in the canoe. My heart skipped a beat. I wanted to lie, saying it was all a mistake, but my face would not co-operate; it told him the truth. When Red finally spoke, his tone was condescending.

"Sissy, you're young, and you don't really love this man. We have two small children and our marriage to think of. Frank and Rita are leaving for New York tomorrow morning. Let's go with them and forget all about what happened between you and Hippie Ron."

As usual my mouth would not talk but the thoughts in my mind raced defensively.

We are not married, and I do love Hippie Ron! Only one of the children is yours, and we cannot just go away with Frank and Rita and make everything okay!

I needed time to think. My whole life had gone wrong because I could not speak up and tell the truth about who I was or what I wanted out of life. That afternoon I told Hippie that Red found the letter I left on his bed. He looked surprised.

"That's really weird," he said. "I hid it in the bookshelf in the main house."

Still unsure of his intentions I asked, "What should I do?"

"I love you, but the decision is yours alone to make," he said. "I don't want to say anything to convince you to leave Red."

That night a turbulent stream of thoughts raced through my mind. Just twenty-three years old, I was illegally in Canada with two small children to care for. I didn't have any friends of my own, and had lost touch with my brother, Bob. My father was traveling to the faraway places he used to watch on TV, and my brother, Don, had been strung out on heroin for several years.

Tossing and turning throughout the night, I wondered why Hippie hid my letter in the bookcase. It seemed impossible that Red could have picked the exact book he put it in. Battling with what was comfortable and what was right, I tried to think what was best for my children, but I was

Supriya K. Deas

too young and inexperienced to know what that was. By morning I was tired, but my answer was firm; I would be staying in Canada with Hippie.

The next day Frank and Rita waited in the car while Red and I said goodbye. It was hard letting go of my old friend and father of my daughter.

"Please Sissy," he pleaded, as I sobbed in his arms. "Won't you change your mind and come with us to New York?"

"No," I said, releasing myself from his embrace. "It's time I start living the truth."

An orange cloud of dust filled the air as the Volvo station wagon disappeared up the road. A loon's haunting cry wailed from the lake and I wondered if I had made the right choice. Taking a deep breath, I walked back toward the bunkhouse. Halfway there I met Hippie coming up the trail. His sleeping bag was slung over one shoulder and there was a victorious smile on his face. The camp suddenly felt very empty. Everything was moving too fast. I was not ready to move into Hippie's bed or to have him in mine. I needed time, but most of all, I needed guidance. Hippie sensed my apprehension.

"What do you say we take the kids and go for a canoe ride?" he asked.

Relieved, I brought the kids down to the dock. Hippie helped us with our life jackets and then pushed off to explore the lake. The quiet dipping of the oars soothed my raw emotions as he gracefully steered the boat near the water's edge.

"Look!" he exclaimed, pointing to the reeds. "A mother duck is teaching her five baby chicks to swim."

Joshua spotted a beaver floating on its back and then, without warning, a loon popped up right in front of the canoe. The kids and I laughed out loud when it stood up on the water and stretched out its neck. Yodelling and flapping its wings, it danced across the water and then dove back into the lake.

104

The day Red left with Frank and Rita, Hippie gave him his mother's address asking him to send us some pot from the United States. When our food supply ran low, he called his mom to say we were coming for a visit. Stuffing what we could carry into our backpack, we took one last look around. The lake seemed a little too quiet with the canoe sitting empty on the dock.

Our little group was silent as we walked up to the main road. I thought about the bookcase mysteriously revealing our secret the day before Frank and Rita left for New York. Had Hippie purposely put my letter in a book for Red to find? Doubts plagued my mind.

Rides came fast, making it easy to reach his mom's by mid-afternoon. When Ruth answered the door, she was overly exuberant, hugging and kissing me and the children like we were her own. A vase of fresh flowers sat on the table and she served us homemade soup in her best bone china. Before sitting down to eat, she insisted I open the gift-wrapped piece of Blue Mountain pottery that decorated my plate.

The next morning Hippie asked his mom to take us to Providence Bay, about an hour's drive from her home. Sensing we had no money, Ruth loaded us up with homemade bread and all the groceries we could carry. At the beginning of the lighthouse trail she kissed us goodbye, and then waved until we disappeared into the bush.

The view of Lake Huron was breathtaking and for the first time in my life I felt truly alive. Hippie took the lead, carrying our heavy pack on his back and bags of groceries in his hands. Terra rode in an aluminum-framed carrier on my back while Joshua, now four-years-old, picked up seashells and bugs along the rocky shore.

The beach was covered with round stones half the size of small cantaloupes. They moved as we stepped, making it hard to keep our balance. After several attempts to get Josh to go faster, Hippie kicked him in the seat of his pants. When my son fell to his knees, I gasped in silent horror. Cast backwards into the unresolved memories of my childhood, I heard my brothers' cries as I sat huddled behind my bedroom door. I never spoke about it as a child and still could not open my mouth as an adult but carried the trauma inside like an unlit explosive.

At the end of the lighthouse trail Hippie found a suitable place to pitch our tent. He gathered driftwood and dry twigs to start a fire while I organized a small kitchen. While rolling tortillas on a flat rock, my mind drifted back to Pola Mendoza's kitchen in San Jose. I cherished the memory of the shy elderly woman who held me close when I came home after school. She always asked if I was hungry and kissed me on the cheek saying words in Spanish that I knew meant she loved me.

Needing to be near her, I watched as she dipped small balls of dough in flour and then rolled them out, perfectly round. When she tossed a tortilla onto the steaming griddle, I suddenly remembered my own that was now bubbling up from the heat. My baby daughter stood beside me watching my every move. I smiled and took her into my arms. Like me with Pola Mendoza, I knew she had come just to be near me, and I had the feeling she was learning everything I knew.

The mid-June sun was warm, and we lived in the nude most of the time. While washing Terra's diapers in the stream one morning I got the strange sensation that I was being watched. I instinctively controlled my movements, showing no fear. Lifting my head, I saw the feet of three people, huddled together behind some bushes. Whistling softly, I tried to get Hippie's attention.

"Throw me a towel," I whispered when he looked my way. "We have company!"

As soon as I was covered, the visitors stepped forward with obvious curiosity.

"We wanted to see what was beyond the old lighthouse, so we decided to walk to the end of the trail," one said apologetically.

While eating supper that evening Hippie and I recalled the look on the people's faces and started to laugh.

"I bet our visitors did not expect to find a naked family living at the end of the trail when they set out on their hike this afternoon," I said, stoking the fire with a stick.

Our evenings were spent sitting around the campfire, listening to the waves lap against the rocks. I learned to watch the sky and occasionally, one of us would spot a shooting star. Somewhere along the way one of Hippie's friends had loaned him a silver flute. His inexperienced attempts to make music were soothing, and the kids went right to sleep listening to him play.

One morning Hippie's eyes squinted toward the horizon with obvious concern. A blood red hue was seeping upward where the water met the sky.

"Red sky at night, sailor's delight; red sky in the morning, sailors take warning," he said, moving fast to secure the plastic tarp over our tent.

Since I had no experience with the raw forces of nature, I followed his example of preparing for the storm. At dusk we were just finishing our meal when a loud crack sounded nearby. A jagged spear of lightening suddenly forked across the darkening sky.

"One, two, three, four," Hippie counted until thunder rolled off in the distance. "The storm is moving in fast," he said, gathering us and our belongings into the tent.

Like a sailor battening down the hatches, Hippie zipped up the flaps. Torrential rain began to fall as the wind whipped angrily at the thin walls of our tent. Playing cards, smoking pot, and sharing stories by candlelight, Hippie and I stayed up through the night stuffing clothes in the puddles to keep the kids dry.

When daylight finally broke, the rain stopped as suddenly as it began. I busied myself clearing out the tent while Hippie started a fire. I could tell by the look on his face that he was worried. He was not used to having a family to feed and our food supply was getting low.

"Don't worry, God will take care of us," I reassured him.

I picked up a bowl and was about to go into the forest looking for blueberries when Hippie put out his hand to stop me.

"Listen," he said, apprehensively glancing toward the bushes. "Something heavy is coming on the rocks."

We were certain it was a bear, so we gathered the children in close and watched with bated breath. Suddenly, the bushes parted, and Ruth pushed her way into our campsite. Relieved, we all started to laugh.

"Those rocks are slick!" she said, panting from the difficult walk.

Sitting down to catch her breath, Ruth scolded us with motherly concern.

"I hardly slept a wink all night knowing you were out in a tent with two small children during such a bad storm!"

She suddenly noticed our tired faces and her voice softened.

"I have some homemade biscuits and strawberry jam in the car if you would like to join me for a picnic," she coaxed.

Ruth didn't have to ask twice. We quickly abandoned the muddy campsite and followed her out to the public wharf. She opened the trunk and handed me a red and white chequered cloth.

"Spread this out on the picnic table over there will you?" she asked.

"Here son," she said, lifting a thick brown crock out of the trunk. "These baked beans are fresh out of the oven!"

Ruth placed a tin of her extra thick date squares on the table beside the biscuits and jam. Opening her thermos, she poured us a cup of tea and gave each of the kids a glass of milk. After lunch I sensed Hippie's need to speak privately with his mother, so I took the kids for a walk.

"It's a little wet in the tent right now Mum," he confided. "Do you think we could stay at your place for a couple of weeks until things dry out a bit?"

He neglected to mention there was a pound of pot coming to the post office near her home.

It was easy to see that Ruth had a soft spot in her heart for her son. Over the next several days, she cooked delicious meals while laughing and talking about the good old days when her mother ran the Old Mill Motel in Blind River. At Hippie's request, Ruth bought beer and rum and we all drank together starting right after breakfast. At first it felt like we were having a long celebration between mother and son, but after a few days Ruth's cheerful demeanor changed. Her face became set with tension and her voice whined when she spoke. She no longer spoke to me directly and I found myself watching her eyes to know what to expect.

It was about eleven o'clock one morning when we returned from our daily walk to the post office. Ruth was standing inside the screen door looking formidably pale. Her sky-blue eyes had turned gray like steel as they looked right through us without so much as a flicker.

"What's going on Mama?" Hippie asked, reliving the childhood anxiety that comes with an alcoholic parent afflicted with bipolar disorder.

"I don't want her or her children in my house ever again," Ruth replied coldly.

Shocked by her cruel detachment, I mentally scanned the checklist I had developed as a child trying to be accepted by the mothers that came and went. I did the dishes. I fed the children. I cleaned the house.

Hippie interrupted my thoughts.

"Would you and the kids wait in the backyard while I talk to my mom?" he asked.

Supriya K. Deas

"Yeah, sure, no problem," I said.

When he came back outside, he looked serious.

"When my mom drinks alcohol things can get pretty bad," he said, as though confiding a deep dark secret. "She has agreed to let me go in to cook our meals, but you and the children are not allowed in the house for any reason except to use the bathroom. We have one week to stay in the tent in her backyard but after that, we all have to go."

Feeling like unwanted refugees, the kids and I went into the house to use the toilet and brush our teeth before bed. The next morning, we waited in the backyard while Hippie went in the house to cook breakfast. After our meal we walked into town to check the mail. As we passed the well-manicured yards, I wondered how people afforded such beautiful homes with large, fragrant lilac bushes spilling over their white picket fences. Little birds twittered from their branches, giving us relief from Ruth's deadly silence at home.

"You and the kids wait here," Hippie warned, before crossing the street to the post office.

A few minutes later he came out holding the expected package. His face looked pale and grim. I was confused when he passed right by us and walked quickly up the street.

"Hey, wait up!" I called, as the children and I ran along behind him.

Hippie stopped. Pointing at the clean white tape covering the original smudged binding he began pulling on his beard. His breathing was fast and broken.

"This package has been opened," he said. "I'm going to throw it in the bushes!"

The little town with its white picket fences and neatly mowed lawns suddenly became too quiet. I thought of my pretty green jacket and Josh's new hiking boots that Red promised to send in the package with the pot. Feeling certain that such a small town would not have customs officers checking all the parcels, I begged Hippie not to throw ours away. I had no idea we were being followed.

When we got back to Ruth's we went straight to our tent. Hippie had me watch the street while he opened the package.

"I knew it!" he exclaimed. "This package is half stuffed with hay!"

Just then I saw two men running across the lawn with guns.

"Hippie look!" I cried.

In a flash Hippie jumped out of the tent to throw the package into the woods.

"Stop or we'll shoot!" yelled one of the men.

My thoughts raced with fear. I could not believe this was happening over a pound of pot through the mail. The two plain clothes cops tackled Hippie on the grass before he could toss the parcel. Clicking handcuffs on his wrists they shoved him in the back seat of a waiting squad car. Void of sirens or lights, the driver pulled out from the curb and sped off down the street.

When the two men came back for me, I was still sitting in the tent, holding my children. The scruffy one with the shoulder length hair opened the screen and held out his hand. A small silver roach clip[2] dangled from his neck by a thin strip of black leather. His faded blue jeans and t-shirt looked out of place.

"You and the children have to come with us," he said.

---

[2]   A small clip for holding the end of a marijuana cigarette so it can be smoked without burning the fingers.

Without saying a word, I took the children by their hands and quietly followed the men to their car. On the way downtown the man with the roach clip turned and leaned his arm over the back of his seat.

"My name is Roach, and this is my partner Larry," he said.

Sensing his kindness was just a ploy to get me to talk I stared straight ahead. At the police station, we were told to sit down while Roach and Larry spoke with the other cops. When no one was looking I whispered in four-year-old Joshua's ear.

"No matter what these men say I want you to keep quiet," I warned. "If you need anything speak only to me."

Concentrating on the ticking of the clock, I kept my mind empty and my stare blank. Sensing trouble, the children sat quietly beside me with stern looks on their faces.

"This is not the first time she's been in trouble with the law," Roach uttered under his breath, and then disappeared down a long, dim hallway.

It was almost an hour before he returned.

"You can see your husband now," Roach's voice bristled with contempt.

The undercover officer led the way down the tiled corridor. After unlocking the steel door, he motioned us inside where there were several small holding cells. I heard the key turn in the lock and then Roach's footsteps disappeared down the hall.

The kids and I ran over to Hippie. Tears ran down his face as he gripped the bars of his undignified cage. Spitting and wiping his mouth, he pointed to the putrid toilet behind him. I could see it was filled with feces and urine.

"That bastard cop shoved my face in this stinking toilet over and over saying, 'Who is your connection? Who is your connection?' I knew he wouldn't stop until I told him what he wanted to hear."

"What did you say?" I asked, sickened by Roach's cruelty.

"I said I had ten pounds of cocaine coming October 31st."

"Ten pounds of cocaine!" I gasped, shocked by the lie.

"Keep quiet," he cautioned. "I'll tell you all about it as soon as we're alone."

Hippie's well-honed survival skills got him out of jail that same afternoon. Gambling on the small city cop's desire for a sizeable promotion, he decided to string Roach along until he could think of his next move.

"You guys always blow it," he chided. "I will tell you when and where the deal will go down just before the coke is delivered."

When Roach heard there were ten pounds of coke on the way, he became anxious to keep Hippie content. He drove us back to Ruth's to pick up our belongings, and then delivered us to a youth hostel on the outskirts of Sudbury. After paying our month's rent, he gave us money for food and promised to come by to check on us. Of this we were sure he would be true to his word.

After a couple weeks of regular visits, Roach invited us to his home for a barbecue. Acting as though we were all good friends, he introduced us to his wife and then he and Hippie went to the backyard to fire up the barbecue. Our children played together in the living room while I helped Roach's wife in the kitchen. When everything was ready, I went to the backyard to see Hippie. Roach leaned back in his chair with an arrogant smile. Reaching into his pocket, he pulled out a small bag of pot and some rolling papers and threw them into Hippie's lap.

"Go ahead, roll a joint!" he laughed. "Just don't let my wife find out!"

Hippie pulled out a rolling paper and sprinkled some of the pot inside. Repulsive memories of his face being shoved in the filthy toilet arose in my mind. Roach's message was clear; the police have control of our lives. If you are on their side, it's okay to break the law. Otherwise, you will lose your family and go to jail.

After dinner I helped Roach's wife with the dishes. When we were ready to go, she gave me a bag of second-hand baby clothes for Terra. The undercover cop tried to be friendly with me on the way home, but my heart was not in it. *Justice is a sham,* I thought, and closed my eyes in utter disgust.

By the end of September, we were getting desperate. There was no cocaine on the way and our time was running out. We were certain the local police and border officials had been alerted to watch for a young couple hitchhiking with two small blonde children. I was sad to see Hippie under so much stress but had no idea how to help him. I just took care of the kids and waited for something to happen.

During our stay at the youth hostel we met a young guy named Billy Goodwin. Billy had lived all twenty-three years of his hapless life right there in Sudbury, Ontario. When Hippie found out that Billy had a car, he told him we were going to hitchhike to Florida to pick oranges. Billy lit up listening to the stories of the exciting night life and all the beautiful young girls he could meet at the beach. As Hippie expected, the young man was easily conned and quickly offered us a ride. Fearing I would try to discourage his idea, Hippie kept his plan to himself. He got himself a fake ID and when we were alone, he asked me not to tell Billy about our situation with the police.

When we pulled up to the border, our clean-cut young friend felt easy about crossing into the United States. Tipping his baseball cap back on his head, he rolled down the window. The disinterested customs officer asked him a few routine questions and then casually waved us through. Hippie nonchalantly turned and gave me a wink. Sitting in the back with the kids, I breathed a sigh of relief. We were home free.

On the way through Kentucky Hippie directed Billy to stop at his friends' home. Although they were surprised to see us, Fran and Dale invited us to stay the night. When Billy got tired of listening to them reminisce, he excused himself and went to bed. As soon as he was out of earshot Hippie explained our predicament.

"You can stay here with us. We have plenty of room!" Fran offered.

The next morning it was hard telling Billy that we would not be going to Florida with him. Hippie waited until after breakfast to break the news.

"Man, I'm really sorry, but we have decided to stay in Kentucky with my friends. If you still want to go to Florida, I can give you the directions to some really great beaches and orange groves."

"Naw," Billy muttered. "I think I'll just head back to Ontario."

Tossing his bedroll onto the backseat of his car the young man was obviously disheartened by the sudden change of plans. We waved as he backed out of the driveway and watched him go back the way we had come. Extremely tired of seeing innocent people hurt, I yearned for the day I could begin telling the truth.

Dale Jarvis was a retired minister who liked to clean his rifles and go hunting with his dogs. His wife was a born-again Christian who spent her time cooking and talking about Jesus. I didn't feel comfortable going to her church, but Fran's kindness was a living example of her words, so I listened to what she had to say. While chatting over a cup of tea one afternoon, I told her that Hippie had asked me to marry him just before we left the youth hostel.

"I was sitting on an old tree stump by the lake when he got down on bended knee. He said from the first day we met he knew I was the one he would marry. Hippie had no money, no house, and no diamond ring, but because of his sincere heart, I smiled and said yes."

Delighted with my story, Fran began making our wedding arrangements right away. She called her minister, arranged a date for the church, and even brought out several patterns for my wedding dress. After spreading them out on the dining room table, she encouraged me to pick the one I liked best.

"I'm a seamstress," she laughed. "Take a look at some of these dress designs. I will make you into a beautiful bride!"

I was excited until we got to the fabric store. Fran picked up a bolt of pure white satin and I shyly withdrew.

"What do you think?" she asked enthusiastically.

"No thanks," I replied. "White is for virgins and I have two children. If I walk down the aisle in a pure white dress, I'll feel like a hypocrite."

"Sissy, for most of your life you've been a hurt and confused young person with no spiritual direction. In the eyes of the Lord all his children are pure and worthy of love," Fran consoled.

She quickly exchanged the fabric for a bolt of white satin intricately laced with tiny pink, yellow and blue flowers. She placed it in my arms with a mischievous glint in her eyes

"What about this one? The flowers can represent your children!"

Since I trusted her knowledge on spiritual matters, I allowed her to buy the material for my dress. Now that we had a wedding to pay for, Fran agreed to keep the kids while Hippie and I stripped tobacco every evening in Mr. Deever's barn. The young farmer paid us each two dollars an hour plus all the homemade sweets we could eat in his wife's kitchen after work.

One morning I got a letter from my father saying he was driving from California to walk me down the aisle. I was excited to see his car pull into the driveway, but as soon as we hugged, my happiness began to fade. There was no mistaking the familiar pint bottle inside the breast pocket of his rumpled jacket. His sour breath and sombre look told me he had been drinking nonstop for several weeks.

"Are you getting married because you're pregnant?" he whispered before releasing me from his hug.

My heart sank. This was not the greeting I needed to hear.

Over the next several days my father became embarrassingly obnoxious. The night before the wedding, he took Hippie aside for a man-to-man talk.

"It is customary for the father of the bride to take the groom out on the town the night before the wedding," he said. "What do you say you and I go downtown and shoot a few games of pool?"

When Hippie told me of my dad's request, I knew it was not a night out for the groom that pulled my father to the tavern.

"We won't be late," Hippie promised, and kissed me goodbye.

My childhood memories told me different. As soon as I was alone, Fran came to my room to say goodnight. By the remote look on her face I knew there was something on her mind.

"I spoke to your father about your fervent love for God this afternoon," she said. "He told me your religious aspirations are only a scam for a place to live."

Refusing to defend my spiritual longing, I responded with silence. Fran wished me good luck with my wedding and kissed me goodnight. As soon as she was out the door, I wept like a little child. Trying to justify my anger I paced back and forth, rehashing my resentments. Finally exhausted, I vowed never to reveal my spirituality to anyone else for a long, long time.

About two-thirty in the morning I awoke to the lights of my father's car pulling into the driveway. When I heard his drunken conversation out in the hall it triggered my long-suppressed rage which suddenly erupted with venomous force. Forgetting where I was, I opened the door to confront him.

"You are a poor example of a father!" I yelled. "All those nights you spent at the bar drinking with your friends your children endured hunger, terror, and shame because of your neglect."

Dad's drunken indifference only added fuel to the fire of my rage. Frustrated and powerless to evoke tear or woe from my intoxicated parent, I went back in my room and shut the door.

Hippie sheepishly came in and took off his clothes. Picking up a Playboy Magazine he climbed into bed and flipped through the pages. This was unlike any of the weddings I had seen in the movies. Feeling disappointed and betrayed, I silently turned over and tried to get some sleep.

The next morning Hippie looked handsome in his rented tuxedo, but his face was drawn and pale. He sat beside me in the back seat of Dale's car on the way to the church. His breathing was anxious, and he nervously pulled on his beard. When we arrived, Fran and Dale took the kids up to the altar while I waited in the front hall with my father. As soon as Hippie took his place beside Dale, the pianist began to play the familiar wedding song, *Here Comes the Bride.*

Even though my father was badly hungover, his presence at my wedding was important to me. Walking down the aisle beside him I suddenly became aware of the empty seats in a church I didn't know. I missed having my brothers, friends, and other relatives there to bless our marriage. Swallowing hard to hold back the hysteria hiding just beneath my smile, I moved along slowly, holding my father's arm. Sensing my distress, Dad tightened his grip. I could feel his warm breath as he bent down and leaned in close to my cheek.

"Your mother would be so proud of you today, Sis," he whispered softly.

Tears spilled down my veiled cheeks for he had finally said exactly what I needed to hear.

Three months after the wedding, I became pregnant for the fourth time. The atmosphere at Fran and Dale's had become tense, and I was certain it was because we had overstayed our welcome. Although everyone interacted with polite smiles and casual exchanges, none of us were brave enough to voice the truth: our children's futures looked bleak with parents always running from the law.

I understood that if we were to raise our children in a safe environment, we needed to take our rightful places in society. After so much deception and heartache I no longer believed Hippie when he said everything would be okay. Spells of loneliness overtook my mind as I began finding fault with everything my new husband did.

One night after putting the kids to bed, I came out to join the others in the living room. The dim lamplight covered us like a shroud. Fran knitted in her rocking chair, the two men played chess, and I sat alone on the loveseat. Feeling like I was suffocating in the silence, I wondered how it was possible that I was the only one who could see the elephant standing in the middle of the room. Taking a deep breath, I went into the kitchen to put on my boots.

"I'm going for a walk!" I called, desperately trying to disguise my wavering voice.

"Where are you going?" Hippie called back.

Secretly wishing he would come after me, I did not answer but closed the door without making a sound. The looming black trees magnified the darkness as I made my way up the winding country road. The familiar chirping of frogs reminded me of the crickets in California on a hot summer night. Memories of my family tugged at my mind.

Was Don still alive? How was Dad? What was Bob doing now? Where was Joan?

Shaking my head, I walked a little faster. The blinding lights of an occasional car threatened my imagination with thoughts of men with rape and murder on their minds. Refusing to revisit the terror of my childhood I tried to ignore my thoughts, but there was one that would not go away.

It had first appeared the night Dorrie found lipstick on my father's collar. It came a second time when the women who shared my father's bed had no intent to be my mother. The morning I saw my father in bed with Sue, it emerged as deep sadness, and when I had the abortion, it ravished my spirit with shame. Now the same thought arose every night I put my children to bed without their own fathers.

Tears were coming fast. I stopped in the middle of the road and folded my hands in front of my chest.

"Please God, take this child if I cannot stay with its father," I prayed.

The night became oddly still. No more cars passed, and a strange weakness flooded my body. I turned and went back toward the house. Off in the distance I heard Hippie calling my name. When he saw me coming down the road, he rushed out to greet me.

"Where have you been?" he asked with great concern. "I've been worried about you walking on the road all alone in the dark."

Wrapping his arms around me, he searched my face for answers that would not come. He wanted to know what was wrong, but I was still afraid to tell the truth, so I kept my feelings to myself.

The next morning, I announced that I was going to find a place for our family to live. Sensing my newfound strength, Fran offered to watch the kids until I got back. Tucking the last of our savings in my pocket I kissed the children and headed out the door. Hippie jumped up and followed close behind, wanting to know my plan.

"I have no plan," I replied, and kept on walking.

My firm resolve silenced his questions, but the look on his face told me that doubts bothered his mind. I knew one thing for certain; I was being guided from within and it was time to listen.

The early morning sun was hot as we made our way up the two-lane country road. Feeling small and insignificant, I looked up at the sheer-faced cliffs towering on my left. Off to my right a few lazy heifers grazed the sparse, dry grass of the rolling Kentucky hills. Somewhere far below, a stream rushed unseen through a hidden gully.

I stopped at the front gate of a rundown farmhouse. A heavyset man was out in the yard feeding his chickens. Hippie was embarrassed by my bold stare and began to fidget as the large figure shuffled toward us with a definite limp. His clothes were shoddy, and he obviously needed a bath. Extending his right hand, the friendly man introduced himself.

"Hi there. My name is Ted, but most people around here call me Chicken Man."

Hippie stepped forward and shook his hand.

"Hi, I'm Hippie and this is my wife, Sissy."

The walk from the chicken coops seemed to weary Ted. Cocking his head to one side, he leaned on the rundown fence and then raised an eyebrow with suspicious curiosity.

"What are you folks doing up in this neck of the woods?"

"We need a place to live," I said, refusing to back down from Hippie's controlling glare.

"Move in with me!" Ted said. He painfully shifted his weight to the other leg before leaning back against the fence. "I live here alone with my thirteen-year-old daughter, Candy. It ain't much, but we have a spare room you're welcome to use. And besides, I could sure use a little help around here."

We talked about the weather and I told him of our children. As the lumbering man led us through the house, I noticed right away that the place lacked a woman's care. Although there was electricity, there was no indoor plumbing. Since Candy was in school, we peeked in her door as we passed. Discarded clothes and tangled blankets lay strewn across her slumping dirty mattress. Hippie motioned with his eyes for me to look beneath her bed. Two restaurant-size ketchup cans were filled to the brim with urine and the air reeked of the young girl's savings.

Stained from long-ignored leakage, the kitchen ceiling sagged in several places. In one corner flies swarmed an outdoor garbage can that was overflowing with trash. The floor was filthy, and a heap of dirty dishes were piled in the sink.

"Thanks Ted," I heard myself saying as if the words came from someone else's mouth. "We would love to live here with you and your daughter."

In my mind's eye I could see the house scrubbed from top to bottom. A fresh coat of paint covered a new kitchen ceiling, and the garbage can was outdoors where it belonged. Curious to see the chickens, Hippie headed for the backyard.

Walking slowly beside Ted, I noticed that his right hip caused him a great deal of pain. His breathing was labored, so he stopped to rest about halfway to the coops. After many years of habit, his dirty, nicotine stained fingers automatically searched his pockets for tobacco and a package of rolling papers. With smoke billowing from his lips, Ted joined Hippie who was now examining the rickety pens. Three mean looking birds perked up their heads as their owner approached.

"These here gamecocks are worth thousands of dollars," Ted bragged like a proud father.

His wide, childlike grin revealed two missing front teeth. Spitting a piece of tobacco through the gaping hole, Ted explained how the chickens had been raised with the intent to kill.

"For several generations, the trainers have taunted these birds to make them mean," he said. "Feeding them raw bits of chicken has given them a thirst for the blood of their own kind."

As Ted came closer, the birds' vengeful eyes seemed to glare at him. Taking one last pull on his cigarette, our new friend threw the unfiltered butt on the dirt and ground it with his boot.

"This highly illegal sport brings rich gamblers from all over the South," he admitted, his eyes now gleaming with excitement. "On the morning of the fight, private jets deliver their feathered champions in air-conditioned cages. Men, drunk on local moonshine, gather in the designated barn and place their bets. Hollering and jeering, they watch while thick-gloved handlers strap razor-sharp steels on the fighting cocks' legs."

As though they had a mind of their own Ted's fingers once again fumbled through his pocket.

"Yessir, the fight goes on until one of the chickens is dead or mortally wounded."

When the Chicken Man offered to give us a ride back to Fran and Dale's I readily accepted.

"You folks go ahead and get in the car," Ted called, as he trudged back to the house to get his keys.

The bumper of his old brown station wagon hung down on one side and the floor was filled with trash. The engine coughed and sputtered when Ted turned the key. White clouds of exhaust filled the air as we drove up the road, but for some reason, my heart was finally happy.

When we got back to the house, I quickly packed our belongings. After thanking Fran and Dale for letting us stay, we took the kids outside to meet Ted. As we drove up the road, I had no idea how soon we would need that marriage certificate that Fran had moved so fast to attain.

Since I was an American citizen, I was able to receive public assistance, and things finally began to look up. Like I had seen in my vision, Hippie repaired and painted the damaged kitchen ceiling while I tended the children, cleaned the house, and cooked delicious meals for us all.

After a couple of months, we rented our own place a little further up the road. Hippie helped the landlord harvest his hay and in return, Mr. Deevers plowed us a garden right beside our house. Friendly neighbors donated beds, dressers, and a sofa plus all we needed to start our own kitchen. While the children played in the shallow creek beneath the trees, I cooked, baked bread, and sewed quilts from some of the second-hand clothes we'd been given.

By the middle of August, I was six months pregnant. I spoke often to the child in my womb, calling him Isaac right from the start. With Hippie's hard work and natural skill, the garden flourished, but once again, he ignored my warnings, and planted marijuana behind the corn. We had just finished breakfast one morning when a police car pulled into the driveway. Seeing me out in the garden, two officers rushed over flashing their badges.

"You and your husband are under arrest for the illegal propagation of marijuana," they said, as they walked me to the house.

While I was watering the garden, Hippie stayed inside the house to watch the kids. When he heard a car pull into the driveway, he ran to an upstairs window to see who was there. Watching from behind the slightly parted curtain, he saw two police officers get out of their cars and show me their badges. Hippie suddenly remembered that his real name was on our marriage certificate. In a panic, he ripped the document out of its frame and hid the torn pieces behind the bed.

The two cops ushered me around to the back door. With warrant in hand they entered the house to search for drugs. Finding nothing in our closets and drawers, one of the cops dumped our flour and sugar out on the kitchen floor. The other went outside to get the marijuana that was growing in the garden.

"You have the right to remain silent," the officer said, as I bent down and took my children in my arms.

"Be good and go with these nice men and Mum will come for you in just a few days," I reassured them.

Unfortunately, the kids knew the routine.

The Frankfort County Jail housed both men and women who were waiting for trial. Hippie was taken upstairs to the men's unit and I was put in a holding cell with two other women on the main floor. One sat quietly on her bunk, while the other paced back and forth with the exaggerated walk of an arrogant man. Her eyes stole quick glances at me while combing her oiled, short hair straight back. It was easy to see she had something on her mind.

Although I wore shorts and a light cotton maternity blouse, the hot humid weather left me drenched with perspiration. When I gathered my long hair into a braid, the pacing woman stopped and plopped herself down on my bed. Sliding her comb along the length of my bare, outstretched leg she said, "My name is Savage, and I just *love* pregnant women," in an intentionally slow, sexy voice.

Something cold surged up inside of me. Ready to protect the baby in my womb, I glared fiercely into her eyes.

"Get off my bed and don't ever touch me again," I commanded, and Savage quickly backed away.

After that, I kept my eyes to myself. Ignoring the passionate groans coming from the bed across from me at night, I turned toward the wall and tried to get some sleep. Early the next morning one of the male guards came by to wake us up. His face was unshaven, and his smile grotesque.

"Lookie here ladies," he said, waving two frozen hot dogs in front of the bars. "Weenies for supper! Now don't y'all go gettin' excited, cause I'm gonna make sure the chef cuts them into itsy bitsy little pieces so ya'll can't pleasure yerselves in the middle of the night!"

When I went to take a shower, the grimy stall had no curtain. To my distress, the opening was right across from Savage's bunk. Unsure if the male guard would return to taunt us, I got inside before taking off my clothes. I didn't know which was worse; the guard's crude suggestions or the blatant stares of the woman called Savage.

I missed my children terribly but trained my mind to stay calm for the sake of my baby. On the afternoon of the third day, a new guard came on duty.

"They say you're the farmer's wife," he said, without even a hint of sarcasm.

I responded quickly to his kindness.

"Yes, we were arrested for growing marijuana in our garden."

Unseen by the others, he slipped a note between the bars.

It said, "I'll be seeing your husband this evening after delivering your meal. If you want me to pass him a letter you can't tell anyone, especially those two in the cell with you."

The guard seemed sincere, so I put my letter in his hand that evening as he passed my dinner tray through the slot in the bars. When he came back to turn off the lights, he had a reply from Hippie.

"Don't worry honey," he said. "Everything will be okay. I am going to get us out of this mess, just you wait and see. I love you, Hippie."

At the end of the fourteen days we were taken to court. When Hippie was called up to the stand, he told the judge I was pregnant, and made a plea for my freedom.

"The pot in the garden was mine," he admitted. "She's pregnant and needs more than white bread and beans to eat. Let her go free and I'll take her sentence on top of my own."

With no further questions, the judge dismissed my case. He directed the county clerk to phone social services on my behalf, and then scheduled Hippie's sentencing for the following week.

Hot air blasted me in the face when I stepped outside the air-conditioned building. As I walked along the side of the road, I could see heat waves radiating off the cars that were caught in afternoon traffic. Ignoring the scorching heat that penetrated my thin leather sandals, I hurried to get my children before the welfare office closed at five o'clock.

A ceiling fan clacked overhead in the overcrowded reception room, churning hot, sticky air down on the people waiting for their welfare checks. I was exhausted and needed time to rest, but it was getting late and we had a long way to go before we were home. I approached the front desk and gave the tired-looking woman my name.

Stifling a yawn, she mumbled, "Take a seat ma'am. The social worker has gone to get your children and should back in a few minutes."

It was quarter to five when a young woman came through the door with my two little children. She pointed in my direction and Joshua and Terra raced across the room with open arms. Their clothes were new, and Joshua's shoulder-length hair had been cut short.

"Mum, you're out of jail!" he exclaimed, hugging me tight.

The people in the room turned to stare. Embarrassed by the truth, I tried to control the tears welling up in my eyes. After thanking the woman, I took the kid's hands and headed for the highway. The glaring heat caused their fair-skinned faces to flush bright red. At the onramp I put up my thumb and within minutes, a black, four-door sedan pulled over and stopped.

"Where ya'll goin'?" the driver asked with a strong southern drawl.

"Up to Bald Knob Hill," I answered without one.

"Come on," he said. "Git in."

I put the kids in the back seat, and then climbed in the front beside the driver. Without signaling, the man pulled out in traffic and pressed down hard on the gas pedal. Turning to check on the kids, I glanced around the car. The floors were spotless, and a plastic rosary swung from the rear-view mirror. The driver's oily hair had been recently cut and his simple clothes were clean and neatly pressed. He took a long swig off the beer he was holding between his legs and then turned up the radio a little too loud.

A country tune began to play as he pulled a new pack of cigarettes out of his rolled-up t-shirt sleeve. Removing the cellophane with his teeth, he peeled the foil back from one side and then smacked the package against the steering wheel, making a cigarette pop out. Looking back at the children, I rolled down the window. The driver pushed in the dashboard lighter. When it popped out, he lit the cigarette that was dangling from his lips.

"Want a beer?" he asked, taking another pull on his.

"No thanks," I responded evenly.

I just wanted to go home.

Once we were on our way, the driver reached over and put his hand on my bare thigh. Keeping my gaze straight ahead, I picked up his hand and put it back on the seat. A few minutes later, he placed his hand back on my leg and once again, I returned it to the seat. Knowing better than to indulge in the fear screaming in the back of my mind, I kept the conversation casual.

The driver pulled into a gas station and got out to pump his fuel. I waited until he went inside to pay the cashier, and then quickly took my children into the women's bathroom. Trying not to frighten them, I nonchalantly peered through a crack in the bathroom door. The man came out of the station, looked up and down the road, lit another cigarette, and then got in his car and drove away.

I walked the kids back to the highway and put up my thumb. Even though our next ride came pretty quick, it was starting to get dark by the time we got home. Holding Terra in one arm, I unlocked the back door and flicked on the kitchen light. Two large rats were feeding on the flour that the police had dumped on the floor. When they heard us come in, they scampered beneath the fridge. Exhausted and weak, I fixed the children a sandwich, and then got them ready for bed.

"The people cut my hair and bought me and Terra new clothes!" Joshua reported happily when I kissed him goodnight. "Their house was really nice, and they took us to the park to feed the ducks!"

My relief mixed with jealousy. I had always wanted to provide my children with the kind of home my son described but couldn't seem to make it happen. Lying awake until late in the night I strained to see the future, but no vision would come. Although I felt healthy, it weighed heavily on my mind that I was in my seventh month of pregnancy and I had not been to see a doctor yet.

The wind whistled through the hills and I could hear an owl hooting off in the distance. Fear tried to weave its way into my mind as I wondered how many local men knew my husband was in jail. Over the next few days, I stayed focused on cleaning the house and playing in the yard with the kids. One morning the mailman handed me a letter. It was from Hippie.

"Hi honey, I'm sorry about all this," he said. "I miss you and the kids something terrible. One day you'll see; I'm going to make all of this up to you. As soon as you were free, I admitted to the judge that I'm a Canadian citizen with charges pending in my own country. My deportation trial is in Covington next week. Put only what you need in the backpack and leave the rest behind. Material things can be replaced, but our love cannot.

Meet me at the courthouse and be prepared to take the bus to Ontario right after the trial."

The night before Hippie's trial I prepared enough food for the long journey ahead. After filling the backpack with our clothes, crayons, and the children's coloring books, I climbed into bed with joyful anticipation of going to be with Hippie. Our dawn departure was unceremonious as the kids and I walked up to the main road. Without looking back, we once again left our house, furniture, and friends behind. I held up my thumb and the little ones followed suit. They grinned triumphantly when a car pulled over and offered us a ride.

When we arrived at the courthouse the receptionist was friendly. She showed me where I could leave my backpack, and then led us to a room with a long oval table. Hippie was already there seated beside several official looking men. After reviewing my husband's lengthy police record, the deportation officer gave him a warning.

"If we ever catch you trying to cross the border into the United States again you will be sent to prison for a minimum of two years."

Once the papers were signed the meeting was adjourned. I got up to leave and one of the officers approached me with a soft, friendly voice.

"Hi, I'm Officer Kinnon. I will be driving your husband to the airport this afternoon. If you want to come along, you and the children are welcome to ride in my car."

"Thank you very much," I said, returning his smile. "I would like that a lot."

As our family huddled together in the back seat of the unmarked car, Hippie tried to assure me that everything was going to be okay.

"When you get back to the city, have the officer drop you off at the bus station," he whispered. "Buy a one-way ticket to Sudbury, Ontario. When you arrive, tell the driver you want to get out downtown. From there you and the kids can walk up the street to the county jail."

Just as we approached the flight pad, another unmarked squad car pulled up behind us. Hippie looked worried as he kissed us goodbye.

"Please be careful, honey," he warned. "And put your money in a safe place. You and the kids will need it for food."

A police officer in casual clothing opened Hippie's door.

"I will be escorting you back to Canada," he said, as he locked the silver handcuffs into place.

Mr. Kinnon got out of his car and came over to stand beside me. About halfway up the ramp Hippie turned to wave. When he raised his arms, the sun glinted off the metal that bound his wrists, and then he disappeared through the open door of the waiting airplane.

Sissy's parents' cutting wedding cake

Sissy on her way to Doreen's dance recital. Shown with brothers Bobby (left) and Donny (right), 1957

Sissy with stepsisters, Liz and Susan, and baby brother,
John, in Santa Clara, California, 1962

16-year-old Sissy with co-worker and nursing home residents. (Ch. 1)

Sissy's graduation from Lynbrook High in San Jose, 1969

Sissy is now a fugitive living in Canada (Ch 3). This is the campsite at the end of the lighthouse trail in Providence Bay, Ontario, 1974

After Hippie's temporary release from jail he and Sissy escape back to the USA. This is their wedding day in Akron, Ohio, 1974

Sissy in the garden with Terra and Josh the day before being arrested in Kentucky, 1975. She is 7 months pregnant

Sissy decides to change her name to Kate upon arrival in Nova Scotia in 1977

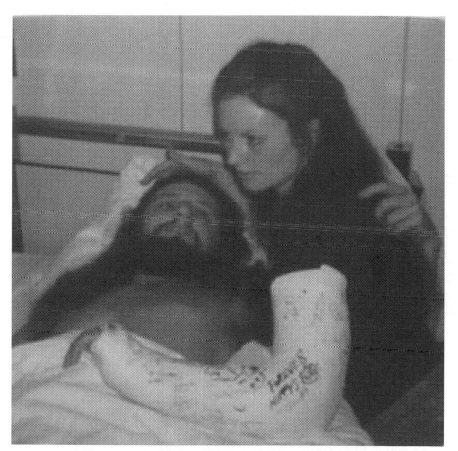

Kate visiting Hippie in the Halifax Infirmary after the accident in 1979

Hippie digging the well on the new land in Woodstock, NS.
Josh is inside passing buckets of mud up to his dad.

Kate's store on Main Street after separating from Hippie.

Kate has now accepted the spiritual name, Supriya, from her Yoga Master, Baba Hari Dass, at the Salt Spring Yoga Retreat in 1997

CHAPTER FOUR

Turning Point

Joshua and Terra were content with their storybooks and crayons until they fell asleep. The steady drone of the bus engine helped me to relax as the child inside my womb shifted from side to side. Throughout the night I drifted in and out of sleep, waking just long enough to check on the children, and touch the money pinned inside my bra. About two o'clock the next afternoon the bus pulled over on a busy downtown street. Trying not to bump the other passengers with my backpack, I struggled to get the kids up to the front of the bus.

"Can you tell me how to get to the county jail?" I asked the driver.

"Only six blocks to go," he said, pointing up the street.

The driver looked sympathetic as I set the heavy backpack down on the sidewalk long enough to help my children down the steps. I was sure it was my face that told him the truth; my life had gone wrong. Longing for a safe place where I could wash my children and tuck them into clean beds, I hoisted the pack onto my back, took their little hands in mine, and began to walk. Disapproval leered at me from the oncoming cars. I thought about my family back in California. I had broken all the rules in my attempts to live and love the way my heart knew was true, and still, I refused to accept defeat.

When we got to the jail, we were taken to a small cubicle to wait for Hippie. Joshua explored every inch of the visiting room while Terra, who was now two, climbed up on my lap and pressed her face against the glass.

After a few minutes, a guard brought Hippie into the small room directly across from us. He motioned for my husband to sit down and then he moved back against the wall and folded his arms across his chest.

The thick barrier between us was deeply etched with foul words and lovers' initials. After a short conversation over telephones, Hippie realized I was tired.

"Go to the YWCA," he whispered.

The fog of my exhaustion made it difficult to understand his direction.

"Where?" I asked, shifting Terra to my other knee.

"The Y," he repeated a second time. "They will take care of you. That's what they do. They help people in need."

The guard unfolded his arms and motioned to the door with his head.

"Visit's over," he commanded.

The YWCA was situated in a large building downtown, about seven blocks from the city jail. Too tired to climb the stairs, the kids and I rode the elevator up to the second floor. As we entered a spacious living room, I saw several women, young and old alike, sprawled comfortably on the well-used couches. The two receptionists were busy talking, so I set my backpack on the floor and waited. After a few minutes I cleared my throat to get their attention.

"Yes?" one responded as her eyes scrutinized our clothing.

"I don't have much money and we need a place to stay," I said, close to tears.

The receptionist gave a disinterested toss of her head.

"I'm sorry, we aren't taking any more women with children. We're already full."

With no further direction or concern for our welfare, the woman turned back to her previous conversation. A wave of horror flooded my thoughts as I looked down at my children.

Where will we sleep? I worried. *I don't know anyone to call. I'm in a foreign country. Where else can I go for help? Motels are expensive, and I need to keep our money for food. The park is dangerous at night, and besides, the grass will be wet and cold once the sun goes down. If I were alone, I could sleep anywhere and go without food for a long period of time, but I have two small children and they need care!*

I thanked the woman and went back to the elevator. Fighting with my fear, I pressed the downward-facing arrow. The doors suddenly flew open and out came a nun all dressed in white.

"What is the matter sweetheart?" she asked.

My words tumbled out in broken sobs.

"My husband is in jail," I cried. "We just took the bus all the way from Kentucky to be near him. We are so tired and the lady at the front desk said the YWCA can't take any more women with children. I don't have much money and we have no place to sleep tonight."

The kind woman got down on her knees and gathered us into her arms. "My name is Sister Frances," she said. "You are welcome to stay with me if you like. I have a room on the third floor. It just opened this morning. I call it La Paix. It means 'A Place of Peace' in French."

Politely concealing my emotions, I followed Sister Frances past the reception desk. I was sure the women who had not concerned themselves with our plight saw us pass. The anger and bitterness I had kept bottled up for so many years wanted to cry out saying, *Ha! We have been given an even better place than yours to stay!* but I remained quiet and hurried to keep up with the fast walking nun.

Understanding our need to clean up after the long, weary journey, Sister Frances took us straight to the bathroom. She handed me a stack of towels, ran a bath for the kids, and showed me how to regulate the shower. When we came out, she was sitting in the kitchen reading a magazine. Seeing the kids hungrily glancing at the basket of crackers on the table, she got up and went to the stove.

"I always have a little something to eat before bed," she said. "Would you and the children care to join me with a bowl of my homemade soup?"

After the meal, I got up to wash the dishes, but Sister Frances stopped me.

"I can do these later," she said. "It has been a long trip, and you and the children need to rest. Come with me and I'll show you to your room."

About halfway down the hall Sister Frances stopped and opened the door of a small, well-kept room. The clean beds I had longed for earlier that day had their covers turned slightly back. Against one wall was a desk with a small golden lamp. I felt safe seeing the familiar cross above the door, but when I opened the closet, my heart began to sink. The room was only meant for a short stay. The nun's hand was gentle on my cheek.

"Don't worry," she said, as though reading my mind. "You can stay just as long as you like."

The next morning Sister Frances took me to the welfare office. After explaining my situation to the receptionist, she helped me to complete the forms for public assistance. The following afternoon she took me to the doctor and when it came time for Hippie's trial, she sat beside me in the front row of the courtroom. Cupping her hand over her mouth she whispered like a mischievous teenager.

"I went to school with this judge," she confided. "When he sees you're with me, I'm sure everything will work out just fine."

After a few minutes Hippie came out and took the stand. The bailiff crossed the room and handed him a Bible.

"Do you swear to tell the truth, the whole truth, and nothing but the truth so help you God?"

"I do," Hippie swore, and then took his seat.

Occasionally, I caught the judge looking at me sitting beside Sister Frances. The small reading glasses perched on the tip of his nose reminded me of the kind judge in San Jose who had trusted me because of my smile. After the last testimony was in, the judge hit the podium with his gavel and called a short recess. When he re-entered the room, the bailiff stood up.

"All rise," he commanded, and a guard escorted Hippie back to his place beside the judge.

Once everyone was seated, the public defender paced back and forth and then flashed my husband a confident wink.

"I'll have you out of here by this afternoon!" he whispered a little too loudly.

Overhearing his flippant remark, the judge gave the enthusiastic young lawyer a reproachful glance.

"Five days in the county jail plus time already served," he said, and once again, he struck the podium with his gavel.

That evening Sister Frances had good news.

"My friend Mr. French called this afternoon," she reported, while pouring a little milk into her tea. "He said the tenants who were renting his apartment just moved out. If you and your husband are interested, it will be cleaned and ready in five days."

When I went to see Hippie the next morning, he also had good news.

"I can be released a day early if someone is at the front door five minutes after midnight to sign me out," he proudly announced. Lowering his head, he dropped his voice to a whisper. "Reserve us a room at the nearest motel," he winked, casually stroking his beard. "And pick up a bottle of whiskey. We'll celebrate!"

During my stay at La Paix I made friends with two young women from the second floor. When I told them Hippie's news they seemed to understand.

"Go spend the night with your husband!" they encouraged. "The kids can stay with us and you can pick them up in the morning."

On the evening of the fourth day, I waited until Sister Frances went to bed before taking my children downstairs. As soon as they fell asleep, I shouldered my bag and headed downtown. Discourteous drivers rushed by as I walked, splashing my clothes with gutter water from the previous day's rain. An early September frost had turned the maple leaves red, and the crisp night air made me wish I had worn a heavier jacket. The traffic lights at the main intersection flicked yellow, then red, cautioning me to stop so my conscience could be heard.

Sister Frances has been good to you and this is the way you repay her? it scolded.

I spotted a liquor store and crossed the street.

"A quart of Jack Daniels please," I said, handing the proprietor a twenty-dollar bill.

When I got to the jail the front office was dark. Peering through the window, I tried to see the time. It was only ten o'clock. I had two hours to wait. I sat down on the cement steps and looked up. Billions of stars shimmered across an otherwise black northern sky. Off in the distance I could hear the swish of traffic.

People with somewhere to go.

I began to shiver. My hands automatically reached beneath my shirt to hold my large, round belly. The child inside my womb had become my best friend. Isaac, I called him right from the start. He was the one who listened when I spoke and understood my desire to know the truth.

At exactly five minutes after midnight someone flicked on the light. The door opened and a uniformed guard came out and handed me a clipboard. Feeling guilty about the alcohol, I discreetly pushed the bulky shoulder bag behind my back.

"If you will just sign this form, your husband is free to go."

I could see Hippie peeking anxiously over the guard's shoulder. As soon as the paper was signed, he stepped through the door.

"I can't believe it!" he cried when the door shut behind him. "I'm free! I'm free!"

Linking his arm through mine, Hippie walked enthusiastically toward the motel. I was so happy he was free, but I felt awkward with my determination to tell the truth.

What will happen if I tell him who I am and what kind of life I want for our family? I worried. *I already have two children by different fathers. What will I do if my husband doesn't want a woman who doesn't want to drink alcohol or scam people anymore?*

As soon as we got to our room, Hippie poured two shots of whiskey into each glass and then opened a can of Coke. Adding just enough of the fizzy brown liquid to color the alcohol, he plopped in a couple ice cubes from the machine out in the hall. Without hesitation he removed his clothes and threw back the covers on one of the beds. A slight smile formed on Hippie's lips as he stretched out on the clean sheets.

"Come 'ere, honey," he said, patting the space beside him.

Feelings of self-betrayal raged in my heart as I sipped the intoxicating drink. Trying to act like my old self I sat down on the bed beside my husband, but all I could think of was Sister Frances and the loving atmosphere of La Paix.

The following month I went into labour. In the delivery room several nurses huddled around the bottom of my bed. "I see feet!" one cried and ran to the window looking for the doctor's car in the parking lot. Another nurse got on the intercom.

"Dr. Armstrong? Dr. Armstrong! Please come to the delivery room. Dr. Armstrong? Please come to the delivery room."

Controlling my breath, I tried to stay calm. The double doors suddenly flew open and the doctor pushed his way through the chattering nurses to assess the situation.

"We have to work fast," he warned. "It's a footling breech and the child's life is in danger."

The doctor pointed to a round ceiling mirror at the foot of my bed.

"Watch the birthing process if you like, but try to stay calm," he directed as my body wrenched and struggled, trying to release the child.

After several minutes, a high-pitched cry pierced the air. I fought to stay awake when the nurse placed my newborn son in my arms, but it was no use, I was exhausted. Looking gratefully into his eyes I whispered, "Isaac," and then drifted off into a long, deep sleep.

That evening I awoke to the sound of babies being delivered to the other mothers in my room. Anxious to see my son I sat up in my bed, but the nurses passed me by. When they returned to take the infants back to the nursery my heart seized with fear.

"Excuse me," I meekly addressed one of the nurses.

She continued her work without response.

"Nurse?" I raised my voice a little louder, but she did not seem to hear me. She just straightened my blankets, turned out the lights, and left the room. Like I had as a child trying not to be heard, I covered my face with my pillow and cried myself to sleep. The following morning the doctor noticed my red and swollen cheeks.

"Hey young lady," he comforted. "What is the problem here?"

"I haven't seen my baby yet," I said, as tears welled up and spilled down my cheeks.

The doctor went out into the hall and asked one of the nurses to bring me my son. He came back and took my hand.

"Whenever there is a difficult birth the newborns are kept in the incubator for twenty-four hours. Everything is fine," he assured me. "Your baby will be here in just a few minutes."

On the way home from the hospital, I directed the cab driver to stop at La Paix. While the family visited upstairs with Sister Frances, I excused myself to go down to the chapel to pray. Humbly kneeling before the altar, I watched as two well-protected candles flickered from their rack.

"Hail Mary full of grace," I began, but the Catholic prayer of my childhood sounded hollow and rehearsed. I bowed my head and tears welled up in my eyes. "I just came by to say thank You," I whispered, and then went back upstairs to see Sister Frances.

After graduating from nursing school, Henry's[3] mother, Ruth, worked at the hospital in Sudbury, Ontario. Living alone in the woods six months of the year, his father, Henry Sr., tended fire towers for the Department of Lands and Forests. When he was off duty, he rarely came home but stayed in town, drinking, and carousing with the loose women at the tavern.

Ruth's mother had the reputation of being a shrewd businesswoman. Widowed young in life, she took the small inheritance from her dead husband and bought the Old Mill Motel just up the road from Ruth. Unlike her mother, Ruth was poor. Her small house had no telephone, electricity, or indoor plumbing. Struggling to make ends meet, she often worked extra shifts at the hospital, leaving Henry and his two older sisters alone to fend for themselves.

Ruth suffered from bipolar disorder. Drinking alcohol severely aggravated her already manic-depressive behavior. When she realized she was pregnant for the fourth time, she was unable to cope with the responsibility of raising another child by herself. After the birth, Ruth gave baby Edwin to her mother who raised him as her own son.

The absent relationship between Henry's parents magnified his already troubled life. Unable to tolerate the boy's disruptive behaviour, his eighth-grade teacher sent him to see the principal one morning. When the disobedient lad walked into his office, the large angry man took out his strap.

"Hold out your hands young man. Palms up," he sternly demanded.

After two lashes, Henry grabbed the strap and threw it out the window. To escape the principal's rage, he dashed out the door and ran all the way home.

After that Henry refused to go back to school. Instead, he spent his days alone on the beach behind his house gathering driftwood and pulling rusty nails from sodden logs. When he had enough wood to work with, he

---

[3]   Hippie's name as a child

set about scavenging odds and ends of rope to secure it all together. Seeing the young boy's earnest attempts to make a raft, an old fisherman took pity on him, and donated enough canvas to make a sail. One day a concerned neighbor called Ruth at work.

"Your son is out on the lake again," she warned. "You'd better do something before he drowns!"

A truant officer summoned Henry's mom to court the following afternoon. She was noticeably shaken when called to the stand.

"There is nothing I can do with this boy," Ruth told the judge. "Go ahead and put him in reform school. He is an uncontrollable child!"

When Henry was finally released from the juvenile detention center, he walked into town looking for his father. Standing outside the tavern door he tried to catch a glimpse of his dad in the darkened pub. Henry senior was delighted when he saw his boy, and decided it was time to teach his son about sex. He rented a motel room and paid a prostitute to instruct the boy on the finer pleasures of life. Henry was only fifteen years old.

Henry's grandmother knew the beneficial value of hard work. She taught little Eddie responsibility by letting him help around the motel. Every year before the weather turned cold, she would shut down the business and take the boy with her to Arizona. Although the youngster had everything he wanted, he was constantly pestered by a nagging feeling that something was missing from his life. No one had ever told him the truth; Ruth was his real mother.

Henry spent most of his time on the First Nations reserve near his home. Accepting the small white boy as one of their own, the indigenous people fed him and let him play freely with their own children. One afternoon, Henry left the reserve and went home early. When he opened the front door, he saw his mom in a compromised position on the couch with a man he did not recognize. Grabbing a blanket off the nearby rocking chair, he tried to cover his mother's body.

"Get out!" Henry yelled at the man while pointing toward the door.

"Stop it!" Ruth screamed.

But the boy did not stop.

"I said get out!" Henry shouted at the man once more.

Grabbing a pair of scissors off the coffee table, Ruth stabbed her son in the leg. Henry was shocked by his mother's betrayal. He dropped the blanket and ran out the door. Hiding in the bushes across the street, the disconcerted boy waited for the couple to leave. As soon as the way was clear, he went back to the house to get his clothes.

Henry knew that the best place to hitch a ride was in front of his grandmother's motel on the outskirts of town. Determined to get away from the insanity at home, he walked up the street and stuck out his thumb. Ten-year-old Eddie was playing in the front yard.

"You are my brother!" Henry yelled, trying to set the record straight.

Seeing Henry was about to leave town, Eddie began to cry.

"Take me with you!" he called, but Henry knew the boy was too young.

"I can't!" he yelled back and got in the first car that came along.

The clever fifteen-year-old made his way to Toronto, Ontario's largest city. Like the troubled runaways in San Francisco's Haight Ashbury, Ontario's vulnerable youth gathered in the crime-infested area called Cabbagetown. Sleeping in back alleys and abandoned cars, many of the homeless kids learned to steal and prostitute their bodies, while others sold drugs to get what they needed to survive.

One afternoon Henry heard a girl calling out from behind some bushes. Running toward the sound, he found a young girl struggling to get away from an older man. Without hesitation, he jumped in to help her while someone else called the police. Within minutes a squad car came screaming to a halt. Henry was still on the ground fighting with the man.

"All right, all right, that's enough," the police officer demanded, pulling the two apart. "Let's start with you sir. What's going on here?"

Wiping the dirt off his pants the aging man feigned innocence.

"This young punk jumped me from behind," he lied. "He was probably trying to get my wallet."

Terrified of her violator, the teenage girl went along with his lie and Henry was charged with assault. Already bristling with resentment, he no longer trusted his elders and his instinct to protect women was wearing thin.

With nowhere to go on the day of his release, Henry hitched a ride to the rail yard just outside the city. Crouching down in the shadows, he saw a boxcar with a partly open door. Unseen, the boy ran across the yard, and climbed aboard the train. After a long and arduous trip across the country, the young stowaway found himself right in the heart of Vancouver's fast emerging hippie generation.

Over the next ten years Henry spent his time honing his skills as a drug dealer. Traveling back and forth between Canada and the United States, he tried to make sense of his so far uneducated and useless life. After being deported to Ontario, he scammed a false ID and then hitched a ride right back to the West Coast. In order to cross the border from Vancouver to Washington, Henry pretended to be a roadie by carrying a guitar for a group of musicians on their way to a gig. He showed the officer his ID that said Ron Gere, and easily passed through customs. A few months later Myrna introduced him to me as Hippie Ron.

The birth of Isaac brought with it a growing hunger for spiritual knowledge. When a social worker offered Hippie the chance to upgrade his education, he enrolled in night school in Sudbury, Ontario. His capacity to learn showed in his high marks, but his new friends were much the same as the old, only now they were married with children.

It wasn't long before my husband started bringing home expensive pens and craft supplies, stolen from the campus bookstore. When he asked me to sew a large pocket inside his jacket, I convinced myself that we deserved nice things, and quickly did as he asked.

That winter one of our friends offered Hippie a good deal on a pickup truck. When we went to check it out, he told us about a place for rent in the country.

"The house is in pretty good shape and the rent is really cheap," Marty assured us. "There's a great swimming hole nearby and big open fields all around the house. The landlords' names are Lanie and Richard Kempf."

The elderly couple had emigrated from Germany twenty years before the morning we walked into their sunny kitchen in Field, Ontario. Lanie, was stocky in build and course in manner. Wearing dirty wool pants and knee-high rubber boots, she spent her mornings milking her cows and shovelling cow manure out of the barn. Her husband, Richard, on the other hand, was thin and more refined. He wore clean khaki pants and pressed flannel shirts while driving his tractor through his hay field, quietly puffing on his pipe. When we told him we wanted to rent the house next door, Richard insisted we come in for a cup of coffee.

"Ah, gud morning!" Lanie called as we entered the kitchen. "Cuppa kaf?"

Richard gave Josh and Terra each a piece of candy and then took them into the living room to watch cartoons. Chatting nonstop, Lanie filled Hippie's cup with her strong, bitter brew and then put the kettle on to boil for my peppermint tea. An earthenware crock of sauerkraut fermented behind the wood stove and a small cotton bag of soured cream hung from a hook on the side of her cupboard. The combination of putrid smells made us wince with disgust.

"Have a leedle taste of zis gud cheese!" Lanie insisted.

She untied the cotton sack and tenderly removed a spoonful of the smelly curds. Proudly heaping them onto a small plate, she set it before us on the table. Lanie's generous smile displayed the remnants of breakfast, still wedged in her false teeth. Trying to be polite, Hippie picked up a cracker.

"Thanks, Lanie," he said, reaching for the butter knife. "How about a little of your fresh cream for my coffee?"

The elderly woman was easily distracted. As soon as she turned toward the fridge, Hippie scraped the cheese onto a napkin and shoved it into the pouch I had sewn inside his jacket. Just then Richard came into the room and caught Hippie's play. Methodically stuffing his pipe with tobacco, he explained what it was like to be a German soldier after World War II.

"Many uv us vere exiled to zuh salt mines in Siberia," he recollected. "Eet vas so cold und hundreds of men starved to death een zuh verk camps. Vee ate ze raw onions like dey ver apples."

Holding a lit match over the bowl of his pipe he took a few long, concentrated pulls. When the tobacco finally caught fire, the fragrant smoke hovered close to his face before it streamed upward and disappeared. Richard picked up a cookie and poured some thick cream into his coffee. His glazed over eyes seemed to peer into his unforgotten past.

"Eet's all vee had to stay alive," he said.

That September Joshua was finally old enough to start school. Five days a week the bus picked him up at the end of our driveway and took him into Sturgeon Falls. The small French community was Catholic, and the nuns were placed in charge of the children's education. Before leaving for school, we often warned Josh that if he talked about the drugs in our home the police would take Hippie and me to jail. Our son's patched jeans, long hair, and beaded necklace sparked questions from the curious nuns. Wanting to protect his family, Joshua answered their questions with a shrug and endured our secret in silence.

The sun flooded the spacious upstairs bedroom one morning as I sat down to nurse my baby, Isaac. When I flicked on the television an attractive-looking blonde woman came out and introduced herself as Kareen Zebroff. Dressed in a black leotard and tights, she spoke to her audience about the importance of keeping the breath calm and the body supple. As soon as my son had his fill, I laid him on the bed so I could practice the stretches along with my new yoga teacher.

Seven years had passed since Big Johnny threatened to take my life in San Jose. Fortunately, I had withdrawn from heroin, but my brother's heroin addiction got progressively worse. We lost touch over the years until one day, a letter came in the mail.

"Hi Sis," he wrote. "Dad and I are coming to see you. We are driving across the country in his Volkswagen station wagon. We should be there in about ten days. I hope you are up for a visitor because I am in a lot of trouble and need your help. Love, Don. P.S. Dad doesn't know."

Afraid to tell our father what was really going on, my brother spent every waking hour of their trip drinking whiskey to mask his painful withdrawal from heroin. Now that Dad was sober, he could not tolerate Don's obnoxious behavior. As the sun set on the fourth day of their trip, he pulled over at a rest stop. Ignoring my brother completely, Dad pumped up the Coleman stove and prepared dinner for them both. After cleaning up the dishes he took Don's sleeping bag out of the car.

"Well Donald," he said, as though stifling a yawn. "I am a little tired tonight. I think I'll hit the hay and get an early start in the morning."

Don had no idea of the truth behind our father's words!

The desert sun was not quite overhead when my brother rolled over and looked at the morning sky. Purging his body of chemical toxins, the morning sweats made Don kick off his sleeping bag and come to sitting. His throbbing head and parched mouth told him he needed a cup of coffee. As his eyes began to focus, he noticed his backpack on the ground beside him. Dad and his green Volkswagen were gone.

That's odd, Don thought. *Dad must have gone into town for supplies. But why did he leave my backpack here?*

An hour passed and my brother began to worry.

Would my own father really go off and leave me alone in the middle of the desert? he wondered.

Two more hours passed and then, off in the distance, my brother saw a car coming toward him on the long-deserted stretch of highway. Grabbing his backpack, he ran out to the road.

"Where is Dad?" I asked as Don waved goodbye to the car turning around in my driveway.

"Isn't he here?" he asked, looking haggard and sick.

"What do you mean, isn't he here? He's supposed to be with you!"

During supper that night I listened to my brother's woeful tale of unfortunate events. Although sorry for the strain in his relationship with our father, I refused to let it deter my happiness. When Dad's car pulled into the driveway the following day the kids and I ran out to greet him.

Taking us into his arms, my father hugged us as though he were sincerely glad to see us. We showed him our goats and walked about the land talking and laughing. Over the next few days, I could see that Don's drinking irritated my father. I also sensed that our relaxed hippie lifestyle went against everything Dad believed in. To escape the awkward situation, he spent most of his time outside working in the garden or playing with the kids. On the fourth morning of his visit, Dad came over and kissed me on the forehead while I was washing up the breakfast dishes.

"Well, Sissy," he said tenderly. "I have to get going."

"So soon?" I asked, tears welling up in my eyes.

"Yes, it's a long trip back and there are a few other places I want to see along the way," he said.

Right before he left, I had Don take a picture of Dad with my family. Still resentful from being abandoned in the desert, my brother snapped the photograph and then retreated to the front porch to drink a beer. Hippie, the kids, and I waved goodbye as Dad's car made its way out the long driveway and then turned onto the main road. Many years later my father told me about his experience with my husband at the hardware store.

"We went into town one afternoon to buy some nails," he confided. "At the store Hippie went off by himself to get what he needed while I spoke with the owner who was tending the cash register. As soon as people got in line for the checkout, I stepped out of the way and went looking for Hippie. Just as I came around the corner of the aisle he was in, I saw him steal an expensive tool. My heart went out to the proprietor because I used to own a liquor store and people were always stealing from me. As soon as we got to the truck, I told Hippie I forgot something and went back inside the store. After relating the incident to the store owner, I paid for the stolen tool.

"I don't steal Sis, and I can't stand being around people who do," he said, still upset by the incident. "When I saw Hippie take that wrench, I knew it was time for me to leave."

After Dad left, Don continued to detox and slowly regained his strength. I felt bad that our father could not understand what was going on with his son, but felt it was not my place to interfere.

I was canning tomatoes one afternoon when Hippie came in from the garden. With an air of excitement, he wiped his hands on a rag and then walked straight over to the large school map on our living room wall. Like a man with a mission, he examined it closely and then circled a small province on the East Coast of Canada with his index finger.

"What do you say we move to British Columbia?" he asked. "We can drive around this little province of Nova Scotia first and then head west before winter sets in."

When I looked at the map my second-grade classroom flashed through my mind. The clear childhood memory showed me sitting at my desk with the assignment of coloring a map of Canada. Leaving all the other provinces untouched, my little hand colored only one and then carefully traced its letters N-o-v-a S-c-o-t-i-a with a purple crayon.

After returning to normal vision I said, "Sure Hip', let's go!"

The following week Hippie bought a flatbed trailer and a vinyl cap for the back of the truck. Over the next several evenings he checked the engine and built cages on the trailer for our animals. He also rigged up a little battery-operated TV inside the camper and made beds for the kids and our German Shepherd, Luna. I packed our belongings into boxes, cleaned the house, and prepared enough food for the long trip ahead.

When it was time to leave, we loaded up the furniture and then put the goats, chickens, and turkey in their cages at the back of the trailer. Once the kids were settled into the camper with their toys and snacks, we said our goodbyes to our friends, Lanie and Richard, and began our journey east. Like it had when I was a child, the drone of the engine quickly made me feel drowsy. I drifted in and out of sleep until the sound of Hippie's voice woke me.

"Sissy?" he called, turning down the stereo. "Hey, Sissy, how about rolling us a joint."

"Oh, sure," I said, and reached into the Playmate cooler at my brother's feet. It was packed to the brim with expensive Colombian weed.

"Where are we?" I asked, carefully spreading the pot on a rolling paper.

"We're just on the outskirts of Quebec," Hippie said, taking a long pull on the joint.

About three o'clock that afternoon we stopped in a wooded meadow to rest and have something to eat. On my way to get the children out of the back of the truck I heard Hippie calling my brother's name. I could tell by the tone of his voice that he was up to something.

"Hey Don! Come here for a minute!"

Ever since my brother's car accident his legs were stiff, especially after sitting for long periods of time. Having been raised in the city, Don admired Hippie's survival skills and delighted in his spontaneous nature. Periodically touching the truck to keep his balance, Don made his way to the back of the trailer where Hippie was scattering grain on the grass for the turkey, he called Christmas Supper. Leading our two goats off the makeshift ramp, he tethered them to a nearby tree and then grabbed one of the chickens by the throat.

"Grab the hatchet," he instructed my brother.

"Ah, Hip'," Don moaned, disgusted by the very thought of taking the bird's life. "You're not really going to kill that bird, are you?"

"Where do you think the chicken at the grocery store comes from? Now come on, are you going to help me or not?"

Without further argument Don followed my husband into a nearby grove of trees. While my brother held the bird, Hippie chopped off its head and then turned the chicken upside down and tied its claws to a branch. Once its bloody entrails were out, he proceeded to strip off its feathers.

"We can't cook it until all the blood has drained out," he advised.

Disgusted by the stench, my brother went to find the quart bottle of whiskey he had stashed beneath the front seat of the truck. Smiling fondly, I watched the children playing nearby on a sunny patch of grass. It was hard getting off heroin by myself I recalled, and I was glad that my brother could be with us during this difficult time in his life.

It was late September of 1977 when we took the ferry from New Brunswick to Nova Scotia. The changing colors of the maple leaves triggered Hippie's concern.

"It's getting too cold to take the kids through the Rockies in the back of the pickup," he said. "We'd better stay in Nova Scotia for the winter and then head west as soon as the weather breaks in spring."

As usual, I trusted Hippie to know what was best for our family.

Nova Scotia is one of the five Maritime provinces of Eastern Canada. Located on the Atlantic Ocean, it is a peninsula that is connected to New Brunswick. Besides the small fishing villages dotting the rocky coast, much of its pristine landscape is untouched by human beings.

Due to the heavily loaded trailer, Hippie carefully steered the truck up the steep, curving highway. Peering out the window to our right, Don and I observed six eagles soaring above the vast stretches of miniature trees climbing the stony mountains that rose one, and then another.

"Look!" I said, pointing past my brother.

Far below in the middle of the fetching landscape was a thin blue line. Etching its way through a thick forest, the winding river reflected the majestic blue sky. Hippie suddenly reached over and turned off the music.

"What's that smell?" I asked, pinching my nose.

"Burning rubber!" Hippie responded, sounding worried. "The electric brakes on the trailer aren't working. The line must have broken which means the brakes on the pickup are carrying all the weight. The truck's brakes will never make it down this steep mountain. As soon as I can find a spot I'm going to pull over and check it out."

I looked once more at the thin blue line far below us which I knew was a large river. Suddenly afraid for my children's lives, I held my breath until the truck had been eased to the side of the road. Hippie turned off the engine and reached behind his seat for a ground cover. Within minutes I heard him mumble from beneath the trailer.

"Just as I suspected! The brake line is broken."

Hippie stood up and pulled on his beard.

"It will be about half an hour before the brakes are cool enough to drive," he cautioned. "We might as well have some lunch and let the kids walk around a bit while we wait. Be careful and keep them away from the road but not too close to the edge of the cliff."

As soon as the brakes had cooled enough for travel, we continued our hazardous trek down the long, curving mountain. I held my breath knowing that one slip of the brakes could plunge us all to our deaths. I looked anxiously at our children through the small window behind my head.

"Don't worry, honey," Hippie said, trying to comfort me. "Everything is going to be okay. As soon as we get to flat ground, we'll go straight to a gas station and buy the part I need to repair the brakes."

Once the brakes were fixed, we continued our journey along the scenic coastal highway. Awed by the natural beauty of the ocean, my brother rolled down his window. A frosty mist permeated the air as turbulent waves crashed against the rocks. Flocks of seagulls screeching for handouts drew our attention to the incoming boats painted crimson red, canary yellow, or paint-sale green, all designed to match their captain's house. On the side of each lobster boat was the name of a loved one or an unrealized dream.

Fishermen could be seen mending their nets on rustic wharves and occasionally, we would glimpse a lighthouse flashing through the fog. The long drive to this simple land gave me time to think about the troubles I had experienced so far in life. The best I could figure was that it had something to do with my name. Wanting a better life for myself and my family, I asked Hippie to respect my wishes, and introduce me as Kate to our next circle of friends.

Although there were a variety of scenic villages to choose from, we ended up on Nova Scotia's southernmost tip, just outside of Yarmouth. Up and down the back roads we drove, searching for a place to live. At last, Hippie spotted a vacant house in a field of dry, yellow grass. Pulling up to the curb he slowed to a stop and then pulled into the driveway to have a better look around.

"It's empty," I said, wiping spider webs from a dusty window.

"I wonder who owns it," Hippie said, kicking over a rotten piece of lumber, perhaps the remains of an old barn.

The wooden shingles on the house needed painting and the roof was in desperate need of repair. Every time the wind blew, the outhouse door creaked and banged on one rusty hinge.

Don stayed with the kids while Hippie and I walked up the road to the nearest farmhouse. THE MILLERS was stencilled on the mailbox in blocked red letters. A dog came out of the barn and barked. When its master stepped out on the porch it cowered back inside. The large man's stance was that of a person in charge.

"We're looking for the owner of that deserted white house up the road on the right," Hippie said.

The man didn't speak but waved us inside the house. Hearing voices in the kitchen, his wife came timidly into the room to make us some tea. Her tightly permed silver hair was cropped close to her head and her painful-looking ankles swelled over thick-soled shoes. When Mrs. Miller reached into the cupboard, her silky flowered dress rose just above her knees, showing the same knots in her nylons that Zola Karr taught me to tie when I was just a girl.

Mr. Miller's tight swollen belly bulged through his suspenders and his fat bottom lip protruded like that of a pouting child. He took a seat at the table before motioning for us to do the same. His breathing was labored, and white spittle gathered on his lower lip as his eyes feasted indiscriminately on my braless young breasts.

"The house rents for $60.00 a month!" his voice boomed.

Mrs. Miller flinched. Her eyes darted nervously toward the hall where two boys, about twelve and fifteen, peeked out from behind a half-closed door.

"Great! We'll take it," Hippie said, pulling out his wallet.

Two months had passed since my brother arrived dope sick and hungover, a mere rack of bones. Repairing the roof with Hippie was good for him and he happily consumed the healthy meals I prepared. I was delighted to see him playing with the kids after supper instead of drinking so much whiskey, but we were both aware of the harsh winter that was on its way. The cold north wind caused Don's stiff body to contract, and when the snow began to fall, my brother knew it was time to go back to the warm California climate.

One evening a local fisherman came by to invite us to his party. With Isaac on my hip, and Josh and Terra by my side, I followed Hippie into the smoke-filled kitchen. Paxton welcomed us to the party with a friendly smile and then offered us each a beer. I could see a blonde woman with red cheeks in the living room singing and playing her guitar while a dark-haired man with a big grin sat beside her, strumming his banjo. I liked the bluegrass music they played and the subdued group of people who were talking and smoking pot seemed open and friendly.

Paxton introduced us to his friends and then went back into the kitchen to boil some lobsters. His rustic seaside home was decorated with the taste of a cultured person. A beautiful young woman in a red poncho stood smiling at me from across the room. Small golden hoops glistened from her ears and her thick, dark braids hung nearly to her waist. There was something familiar about the glint in her eyes, and she seemed to stand alone, even in a crowd.

Gwen Corning had lived in Yarmouth, Nova Scotia all her life. Her father was a retired jazz musician, and her mother made the best cheese cookies in the whole Yarmouth county. Gwen and I became best friends right away and when Hippie started lobster fishing, she came and kept me company on the weekends. As the long hours dragged by, I confided my fears of losing my husband to the churning sea, while Gwen tried not to eat too many of the sweets I prepared for his return.

In Nova Scotia, lobster fishing season begins in November and finishes the end of May. All through the heart of winter Hippie was up before dawn and returned well after dark. At night he would be tired from bouncing around on the ocean all day. After supper he liked to stretch out on the living room couch and fall asleep while watching TV.

Once I got the kids to sleep, I spent my evenings practicing yoga postures in the warmth of the crackling woodstove. I preferred the quiet but every time I turned off the television, Hippie woke up, saying he was watching his show. After a couple of tries, I learned to leave the TV on and turn down the sound as soon as he fell asleep.

Our bay windows had no curtains, but I didn't worry about being nude because we lived so far out in the country. There were no houses directly across from ours and our neighbors were too old to go strolling about after dark...or so I thought.

I became anxious one evening as the eerie blue television lights flashed across my naked body while doing yoga. Slipping on my bathrobe, I opened the front door to investigate. Directly across the road was a man standing beneath the streetlight. His stance was unmistakable; it was Mr. Miller.

"Can I help you?" I called.

"Is your husband home?" he yelled back.

A shiver went up my spine, but not from the cold.

"Yes, my husband is home," I replied. "Would you like to speak with him?"

"No, that's okay," he called, and turned back toward his house.

The next day I asked our only other neighbors, an elderly couple who lived up the road, what they knew about John Miller.

"He's a butcher," the woman spoke out first.

"He raises cattle for his livelihood," her husband added. "But it's an awful thing to see him get angry. During his fits of rage, he's been known to beat his cows over the head with a sledgehammer until they are dead."

I thought about the dog cowering off to the barn the day we stopped to rent the house. Mrs. Miller's frightened glances and his two young sons peering nervously from behind the door was upsetting. Thanking the couple for their honesty, I went back to the house to make curtains for all our windows.

Hippie's lobster fishing career was short-lived. Still trying to find his place in the world, he decided to try a boatbuilding course near Cape Breton. As soon as we were settled, one of the other students called to invite us to a party at his Uncle Lloyd's. When we pulled into the driveway, Marcel spotted our lights, and came outside to greet us.

There is a custom in small Cape Breton villages that family and friends always enter by the side or back door. After removing our winter boots, mittens, and coats, our family went in and gravitated right over to the woodstove to warm our hands. Marcel offered Hippie and me a beer and then introduced us to the others.

Marcel's Uncle Lloyd spent most of his seventy years mining coal. Whenever his nephew's friends needed a place to gather on the weekends his door was always open. Looking around, I noticed that the clean, well-kept home was sparsely decorated, but the living room was equipped with an expensive stereo system and two large speakers. According to my upbringing, it wasn't normal for an elder to allow a bunch of young people to play loud rock and roll music while drinking and smoking pot in their house. Confused, I went over and sat down next to the old man who was sitting alone at the kitchen table. Uncle Lloyd seemed to be reading my mind.

"The stereo and speakers belong to Marcel," he said. "These young people don't have anywhere to go in this small village except the gas station, the corner store, or the tavern. I welcome them in my home on the weekends because it keeps them inside and safe especially during the winter. Besides, I like my nephew and enjoy getting to know his friends."

It was already eight o'clock when we arrived at the party. Before leaving home, I had bathed the children and dressed them in their pajamas. Understanding my need to put them to bed, Uncle Lloyd took me to a carpeted stairway leading up to the second floor. He calmly flicked on the light and directed me to a spare bedroom on the left side of the hall. There was a familiar gentleness in his presence, so I gladly accepted his offer.

Once the kids were asleep, I closed the door and headed down the hall. In passing, I noticed that the room on the right was empty except for a wooden chair sitting mysteriously in the middle of the floor. Finding that odd, I clicked on the light to look around. The pale blue walls were unadorned by picture or poem, and the floor was clear of distraction. I never asked Uncle Lloyd about it, but I had the strong sense that he sat in that chair to pray and meditate.

I returned to the kitchen to find Hippie and the others watching Marcel brew a pot of tea.

"I picked these magic mushrooms myself," he proudly announced as he poured us each a cup of his steaming brew. I drank mine right down.

"Oh, that's terrible!" I said, my face puckering from the acrid taste.

Shortly thereafter, I went back upstairs to check on the kids who, fortunately, were sound asleep. A strong urge from within pulled me over to the wall. Although the room was dark, a tunnel of vision opened showing a brilliantly lit city of dome-like structures far below. Closing as unexpectedly as it opened, I had the distinct feeling that the inhabitants had to stay inside the futuristic buildings in order to stay alive.

When I came back downstairs Marcel's Uncle Lloyd was sitting at the kitchen table drinking his cup of regular tea. His penetrating dark eyes watched with dispassion as the young people around him drank their beer and smoked pot in his noisy kitchen. I pulled up a chair and sat down beside him.

"Are the kids okay?" he asked.

"Yes, they're sleeping. Thanks for letting me put them to bed in your spare room. Do you mind if I make myself a cup of mint tea?" I asked.

"Don't you drink alcohol?" he sounded surprised.

"Not too often," I said. "Besides, I had some mushroom tea earlier and I don't want to ruin the high."

The old man explained that he was a healer who could cure anything, even cancer.

"I'm the seventh son, of the seventh son, of the seventh son," he said, recounting his lineage.

"Do the townspeople come to you for healing?" I asked.

"No, most of them don't believe in me," he said. "They just think of me as Marcel's crazy old Uncle Lloyd."

Holding out my hand I said, "I believe in you. Can you take away this wart? It bothers me a lot!"

His sparkling eyes were friendly. As he placed his hand over mine the drunken laughter suddenly dropped away, leaving the two of us alone in a quiet void all our own.

"The wart will be gone in nine days," he said, as he released my hand.

Just then someone snapped a picture.

"Thanks a lot," I told him, and went over to make my tea.

I forgot all about the incident until Marcel's girlfriend stopped by our house one evening. She had a photograph she wanted to show me.

"Look at this," she said, handing me the picture. "There's a large ring of light around your head."

"Over exposure," I said casually, and went to the kitchen to put on the kettle.

As I picked up the teacup, I noticed that the wart on my finger was no longer there. The old man's penetrating gaze emerged clearly in my mind. I glanced at the calendar.

"Just like he promised," I remarked quietly.

"What?" the girl looked puzzled.

"My wart is gone. Marcel's Uncle Lloyd said it would be gone in nine days. Today is the ninth day."

Gaetanne tossed her dyed blonde hair over her shoulder with a flick of her hand.

"The people in our village say he's kind of crazy."

"The people in your village are crazy for not believing in him!" I replied.

After the boatbuilding course ended, we moved back to Yarmouth to tend Paul Gillen's land while he was away in the United States. Since we only had three months to live in his house, Hippie bought an old school bus from a guy he knew in town. He removed all the seats, installed bunk beds for the kids, a bed in the back for us, a small bathroom, and a kitchenette, complete with counter, cupboards, sink and fridge.

Late one afternoon, a couple and their two children came by to visit. Shortly after their arrival, we got the call that our friend, Trudy, had given birth that morning. Since our friends also wanted to congratulate Trudy and Joe, we decided to drive into the Yarmouth Hospital in Donnie's work van. Trying to make Linda and me more comfortable, Hippie installed one of the bus seats right behind the driver. There were no seatbelt laws in 1979, so the five children played in the back of the van on a blanket on the floor. On the way home from the hospital I became extremely uneasy.

"Come sit near me," I warned. "You never know when there will be an accident."

Without hesitation, all five kids came and huddled at my feet. Donnie stopped at the light and then turned left onto the main thoroughfare, Starr's Road. Just as he was shifting into second gear something crashed into the back of the van. Linda and I quickly exchanged fearful glances.

"Cover your face!" my inner Voice warned.

Without hesitation I raised my left arm and once again, something rammed into the back of the van. In a flash, I was hurled through the windshield. Remaining fully conscious but feeling no pain at all, I watched as tiny squares of glass exploded in slow motion. The next thing I knew I was sitting outside on the pavement, sitting straight up. Seconds later, the van hit a telephone pole causing it to come to a sudden stop directly behind my back. Like an exhausted horse, the vehicle trembled, hissed, and went quiet.

I could hear the children screaming inside the van but could not move to help them. Off in the distance a siren wailed louder and louder as a swarm of curious bystanders pushed in close to gawk at our misfortune. I looked around and realized I was sitting in the parking lot of the local shopping mall.

The driver's mother suddenly pushed her way through the crowd to get to the van. With no concern for my welfare, she bent down and frantically shook my shoulders.

"Where's Donnie? Where is my son? Where is Donnie?" she cried.

Excruciating pain shot up my left arm as the woman's knee pressed against it. Two paramedics saw my distress and lifted Donnie's mother to her feet. It was then that I noticed my hand dangling loosely from the end of my jacket sleeve.

I suddenly remembered how odd it was that Paul Gillen had unexpectedly come home for the weekend. Right before we left for the hospital, he insisted I wear his leather jacket. Not wanting to take a chance at messing up his favorite coat I passed it back.

"No thanks, Paul," I said. "It's a warm evening. I don't need your jacket."

"Come on," he persisted. "It's my lucky jacket from back in the day when I owned "Funky Records" in New York City. Wear it tonight and if you like it, it's yours."

When I realized I was unable to move my arm, I understood that Paul's lucky jacket had probably saved my life.

The same two paramedics who took Donnie's mother away now squatted beside me to prevent me from lying down on the pavement.

"I just want to go to sleep," I said weakly.

"No, no," they said, patting my face. "You've got to stay awake. Come on now, stay awake!"

Although Paul's coat had protected my body from being cut, my left elbow was badly broken. At the hospital I was given an anaesthetic so the doctor could set my arm. My body became numb as the drug took effect, but I remained conscious, floating in a dark liquid void.

"Hippie! Hippie!" I cried, frantically searching for my husband.

Space and time disappeared, making it impossible to find Hippie's body or mine. Unable to lose consciousness I thought, *this must be what it's like to be insane!*

The lights and images of the emergency room came into view as the nurses' voices crackled in my ears. As soon as I was able, they helped me into a wheelchair, and then rolled me down a long, darkened corridor to where Hippie was lying on a stretcher bed, covered in soot. Rivulets of tears streaked his blackened cheeks as I moved in close to his bed.

"Kate, I can't move my legs. The second time we were hit, Donnie's industrial vacuum flew forward and slammed into the back of my seat."

The nurse stepped away to give us some privacy.

"I can't be a husband to you anymore," he whispered, cringing at the thought of losing his manhood.

All I could think of was our children screaming in the van.

"Don't worry about that right now, Hippie," I soothed. "You're safe and alive. That's all that matters to me. How are the kids?"

"The doctor said Joshua walked away without a scratch, but Terra's leg has a deep gash, and she's in shock."

He paused, searching my face.

"And Isaac?" I asked with an edge. "Where is Isaac?"

Hippie's eyes dropped and I detected a slight tremble in his voice.

"The doctor told me he died twice in the ambulance on the way to the emergency room. He had to be resuscitated each time by electric shock. They say he may have brain damage because of the time spent without oxygen. They rushed him to the children's hospital in Halifax for rest and observation."

My husband's words squeezed at my heart. The blind faith I had depended on throughout my life was spent. The death of my child was the death of me, and nothing made sense anymore. I looked my husband square in the eyes.

"There is no God," I whispered, and the nurse wheeled me to my room.

The next morning Hippie was transferred to the neurology ward in Halifax. Gwen came to visit me that afternoon, bringing news of Josh and Terra. Without my knowledge she called my father to let him know I had been in an accident. I was surprised when he phoned the hospital later that evening.

"Jesus sister, what happened?" Dad sounded worried.

I was thrown through a windshield. My husband may never walk again. My baby might have brain damage. My daughter is in shock. I need to see Josh. I lost my faith in God...

My heart choked with emotion, but as usual, my words would not come out of my mouth. All I could say was, "I love you Dad."

"Yes, well Sissy, life goes on," he responded matter-of-factly.

With a sinking heart, I hung up the phone and went back to my room. During my week-long stay in the hospital, rumors wafted into my room like smoke from an unwanted fire.

"The driver was drunk and speeding when he hit you!"

"The driver threw a whole case of beer into the ditch because he didn't want to get caught with it in his truck!"

"The driver tried to flag down a taxi to help him flee the scene of the accident!"

My visitors' remarks fell on deaf ears. Instead of getting caught up in bitterness and blame, I reflected on the many times I was saved from long jail sentences and near-death experiences.

After my release from the hospital, Gwen and I were on our way into the grocery store when a couple of strangers approached me. They said they witnessed my flight through the windshield and expressed their sorrow for me and my family. The following week I was coming out of the bank when a man passing on the sidewalk noticed the fresh cast on my arm. He stopped and introduced himself as the ambulance driver who had saved my baby's life. While we were talking, a woman came up to me and pointed across the street.

"That's the man who hit you! His name is Rodney Paquet. The judge gave him weekends at the county jail. He didn't even lose his license!" she said with an angry, hushed voice.

All I could think of was the many times I had driven intoxicated or coaxed someone into having one more drink before getting in their car to drive home. I knew what Rodney did was wrong, but I understood that I, too, could have harmed or killed someone's family. Instead of focusing on his misdeeds, I took a solemn vow that I would never drive under the influence of drugs or alcohol again.

After a week of tests and close observation, the neurologists in Halifax sent Isaac home with a clean bill of health. The specialist caring for Hippie said one of his vertebrae had been crushed, causing the temporary paralysis in his legs. After twelve weeks lying flat on his back, Hippie was told he could go home if he had a hospital bed to complete his rehabilitation.

Although I was still deep in shock, I rented a house and furnished it for Hippie's homecoming.

Ever since I left California I had kept in touch with my father through the mail and occasional phone calls. No matter what happened, I always informed him of my travels, and tried to keep up with his. Although my language was foul, I wrote to him exactly the way I spoke to my friends. I wanted him to know the truth about my life, and to accept me the way I was. One afternoon Terra came running into the house with a letter from my dad. I was excited to hear from him and went straight to my room to be alone while reading what he had to say.

"My dear daughter," it began. "I don't like stealing, foul language, or the using and selling of drugs. I am tired of your broken promises to change and prefer you do not write to me anymore, Dad."

As I replaced the letter in its envelope I felt as though all the wind had been kicked out of me. No matter what obstacles arose, I always had my dad to turn to and now he was gone. I was disowned, a player without a home base. My sadness quickly turned to anger.

He has his nerve judging ME after the way he lived HIS life! my thoughts screamed as I tried to justify my irresponsible behavior.

A small group of people were drinking, laughing, and smoking pot in the living room with Hippie. I just wanted them to go away so I could be alone to think. All the anger and bitterness I had stuffed back for so many years was now raging inside my heart but for some reason, it felt like the madness was almost over.

Most people thought our friend, Bud Pitman, was an eccentric old fool, but for those of us who watched him work it was easy to see that he was a genius in his field. A welder by trade, there was not much Bud couldn't do from designing bush buggies to baking apple pies. When he found out we had an insurance settlement on the way, he came by to offer us three acres of his lake frontage land for only three thousand dollars.

His snaggletooth grin lit up as he pushed his welder's cap back and forth on his balding head while trying to sell us on his idea.

"Like the feller said, fer next to nothin' you folks could build yerselves a nice little house down by the lake. And if you buy yerselves a cow and grow a garden well, by Jesus, when this ole world goes to hell in a hand basket, you'll be fixed for life."

We were excited! We had long dreamed of the day we could build our own home in the woods and live off the land. As soon as Hippie was strong enough, he bought a chainsaw and cut a road through the woods. We worked together as a family hauling brush and stripping bark from the trees that would be used as lumber for our house. To prevent the voracious little black flies from swarming our faces and biting our flesh, we wore green head nets and taped our pants and long-sleeved shirts around our ankles and wrists. Once the road was passable, the backhoe came to dig out the foundation. Our family had fun gathering truckloads of rocks at the local beach. When we had enough, Hippie rented a cement mixer and put the foundation stones into place.

At the end of every day we stopped by Bud's to report our progress. Telling stories with the rhyme and reason of a Newfoundland yarn, our friend occasionally stopped to poke the fire. As the flames in his kitchen cookstove expanded, so did his imaginative tales.

"Well, there I was walking through the woods one evening just about sundown, when an owl with a seven-foot wingspan flew right at me. It had a head the size of an alligator's and if I hadn't jumped out of the way, it would've damn sure killed me!"

Hippie's brother Ed came from Ontario that summer to help frame out the house and get the roof in place. Thin sheets of oiled fiberboard were nailed onto the green lumber studs and large recycled windows were inserted for light and a view of the lake. Hippie installed an old barrel stove for heat and when it came time to build our chimney, Bud convinced him not to purchase an expensive liner. His hand automatically reached up to rub his greasy welder's cap back and forth on his head while he spoke.

"Yessir, just go to the dump and get the inserts out of five hot water tanks. You bring them to me, and I'll weld them together to make you fellers a fine chimney liner for next to nothin'."

Of course, Hippie was all in. He loved scrounging at the dump to see what kind of treasures he could recycle. As directed, he got the inserts and delivered them to Bud's yard. When we stopped in to see him the next day, Bud was fully masked and bent over his welder's torch. He suddenly realized we were standing behind him and turned off the gas. Placing his hands on his hips, the tall, lanky man stood up and stretched his aching back. His near toothless grin lit up his weathered face.

"Yessir," he proudly announced. "I'll just cut a trap door in the bottom for cleaning out the soot and you'll be all set to go. Once it's installed you can rock this baby up, giving you a fail-safe liner that will last a hundred years!"

When the insurance settlement came through, we took Bud his three thousand dollars.

"Why not stay here with me?" he asked, stuffing the wad of one hundred-dollar bills into his pocket. "You fellers spend all yer time drivin' back and forth to town when you could better spend yer time workin' on the house. And besides, I could sure use some of that good home cookin' from the little missus here!"

On the way home Hippie and I discussed Bud's offer.

"Maybe he's right," I urged. "Ed has gone back to Ontario and there is enough room for our family to sleep in Bud's loft. And besides, the money we would save on gas could be better used on supplies."

Bud's two-story house was a work in progress. A hillbilly at heart, our friend was most comfortable with the simple things in life that his greenhouse and the woods around him could provide. After cleaning out our home near Yarmouth we stored our furniture in Bud's shed, except the mattresses, which we moved upstairs to his unfinished loft. Wanting to create a comfortable space for our family, I hung cloth tapestries over the unfinished walls, arranged the kids' clothes and toys in their own boxes, and covered the mattresses on the floor with soft flannel sheets and colorful handmade quilts.

In the beginning, we shared all our meals with Bud. After supper, Hippie would play his guitar while Josh read his books, Terra played with her dolls, and Isaac drew detailed pictures of bush buggies by the light of the kerosene lamps. Once the dishes were done, the kids had their baths in a large, galvanized pail in the warmth of the kitchen woodstove. As soon as they were asleep, Hippie and I joined Bud in the kitchen to talk about the next day's work and listen to his tall tales by the fire.

One morning while the men were at work, I started my morning chores of sweeping, washing dishes, and baking bread. Joshua and Terra were in school, and Isaac was out playing in the yard. While greasing my bread pans, the bottle of cooking oil slipped out of my hands and spilled all over Bud's new plywood floor. His strict warning the first day we arrived arose in my mind.

"The new plywood base for my flooring needs an undercoat of paint to preserve it. Whatever you do, don't spill anything on the unprotected wood!"

Watching the greasy liquid ooze out on the forbidden territory, I began to panic. Just then Isaac came through the door. He was only four years old.

"Bud asked me to be careful and not spill anything on his new plywood floor," I cried. "Now look! He is going to *KILL* me when he sees what I've done! I'm running away. That's what I'll do. I will just run away before he comes home."

"Where will you go Mum?" Isaac asked innocently.

"Far into the woods," I said, helplessly wringing my hands.

"Maybe you should just clean it up and tell him what happened," the wise little boy advised.

"You're right," I said, calming down. "Yeah, okay. I guess I can do that. Thanks son, thanks a lot."

"It's okay Mom. Everyone makes mistakes sometimes."

Building our house took longer than Bud expected. His icy withdrawal made it clear that our family was invading his solitary lifestyle. Knowing I was anxious to be in our own home, Hippie went down to the cabin one morning and tacked a thick canvas tarp over the hole that would be our front door. He fired up the barrel stove and then went back to Bud's to load our belongings onto the bush buggy.

Excited to be moving, the kids and I followed Hippie down to the land to help unload the bush buggy. To keep our feet warm in the frigid climate, our indigenous friend, Fast Eddie, helped me caulk the gaps between the unfinished floorboards with toilet paper and a butter knife. When it was time to blow out the kerosene lamps that night, we were all extremely grateful to finally have a home we could call our own.

One morning, after bundling up in our warmest winter gear, the kids and I followed Hippie down to the lake. Having grown up in the sub-zero winters of Northern Ontario, my husband was an experienced ice skater. I, on the other hand, spent my warm California childhood roller skating on solid cement sidewalks. Terrified of falling through the ice, I cautiously skated close to the water's edge.

"Wait for us!" the kids yelled as they chased after their dad, who turned backward and forward, and then raced ahead like a pro.

It was the first of April and new life was emerging in the brittle forest around our cabin. Songbirds twittered from the budding trees while butterflies dipped and fluttered among the daffodils now peeking out from the melting snow. The rising temperature suddenly caused the ice to shift and crack. The splitting sound echoed across the eerie frozen lake, bringing my skates to a paralyzed halt. Up ahead where Hippie and the kids were skating, I could see large pools of water on top of the ice.

Ever since my arrival to Canada I had listened to stories about skaters falling through the ice in spring. Although a few were saved, many froze to death while desperately trying to find and get out of the hole through which they had fallen.

"Come back!" I yelled into the frigid atmosphere. "The ice is too thin!"

Unconcerned with my warnings, Hippie and the kids skated a few more laps around the lake. Every time he whisked by, he would laugh calling, "We'll be fine! Don't worry so much!"

Our small cabin had no electricity, indoor plumbing, or telephone. The barrel stove kept us warm, and the golden glow of our kerosene lamps lit up the forest around us every evening after dark. While I cleaned up the supper dishes, Hippie would roll us a joint and rest his back while playing guitar. As soon as the kids finished their homework, we all played cards or read books until time for bed.

As soon as the snow was gone, Hippie tilled the soil and together, we planted a garden. Having grown up in a warmer climate, I wasn't used to the harsh winters and rainy springs of Eastern Canada. Because we were so poor, I looked forward to canning the vegetables from our garden to feed our family during the long winter months. Worried that our seeds might rot in the cold, damp terrain, I went out every morning to part the soil to see if the seeds had begun to sprout.

My friend Elizabeth also lived in a small cabin in the woods, about forty miles from our place. Her partner, David, was a boat builder who sailed to Florida every spring looking for work. It was during that time that he met a wealthy young couple whose sailboat was in desperate need of repair.

"Limp it to my place in Nova Scotia," David coaxed. "I'll sail along beside you just in case there's a problem. You can stay at my place on

Surette's Island. I have a private dock where I can fix your boat for half the price these expensive Florida docks are charging."

Rico was a short, good-looking Italian man who loved to drink wine and flirt with pretty women. His wife Gita was one of Sweden's top five models. Her long shining hair fell easily to her waist and her tall, svelte body swayed gracefully when she walked. Although extremely wealthy, she and Rico dressed in faded blue jeans and baggy t-shirts. While the men worked in the boathouse, Gita squatted in the yard, deftly mending the massive sail by hand. She prepared healthy vegetarian meals and had a strong sense of who she was.

One day, I will be just like Gita! I assured myself.

When the weather turned warm, I often went down to the lake to meditate. I felt safe on our land and watching the sun glisten like diamonds on the rippling water made all my troubles disappear.

Every morning except holidays and weekends the postman delivered our mail to a box at the end of our long driveway. Trying to avoid the muddy ruts I would stick to the high ground as I walked, picking flowers, and watching for deer along the way. One morning, the mailman drove up and handed me a letter from my father. Excited to hear from him, I sat down on a rock and opened it right away.

"Hi Sis," the handwriting was warmly familiar. "I have been traveling around the world and haven't touched a drink in over two years."

Not only was I happy to hear from my dad, but I was proud of his accomplishment. On the way home, I considered my father's strength.

If Dad could free himself from alcohol, maybe one day I can get clean from drugs.

The following morning after setting my bread to rise, I got to work cutting out a stained-glass window on the kitchen table. Without previous warning, the sky clouded over and off in the distance I could hear the roll of thunder.

"One, two, three, four," I counted, the way Hippie had done in our campsite so many years before.

As the storm moved overhead its downpour beat hard against the cabin roof. I put down my tools and opened the door. Pelting rain bounced off the little rivers that were now flooding down the sloping road leading to our cabin. Mesmerized, I got a glimpse that one day, Hippie and the kids would not be coming back. Suddenly nothing around me seemed real, and a deep sense of sadness pervaded my mind.

Over the next few months, I continued to fight my losing battle with drugs. One morning, I smoked a joint and then went outside to meditate near a large pile of rocks we had gathered for our house.

Please God, I begged, tears rising close to the surface. *Please help me to stay off drugs. I can't do it by myself, and I want to know You with all my heart.*

Everything suddenly, became still. A large orange cloud mushroomed up over my head, and the quiet Voice inside began to whisper.

"You don't need drugs to reach Me." And then, "You don't need that anymore."

A wave of peace washed over my body and mind and I knew, the war was finally over. When Hippie came home, he sounded excited.

"Take a look at this good dope I scored. It's some of the finest red-hair this town has seen in a long time!" he reported enthusiastically.

I went over to see what he had in his hand.

"Go ahead, roll one up," he said.

I looked dispassionately at the tightly woven marijuana buds.

"No thanks," I responded easily. "Not right now; maybe later."

Hippie continued to smoke and sell pot. Every time he offered some to me, I would repeat the same reply as a mantra, "No thanks. Not right now, maybe later."

After a year or so the fog began to lift. Now thirty-two years old, I thought back to my favorite childhood television show, *Leave It to Beaver*. Mr. and Mrs. Cleaver dressed well, kept their hair cut short, and taught their teenaged son, Wally, to be kind to his younger brother, Beaver. They were a good example to their children, and when problems arose, they worked them out as a family. Wanting a better life for my kids I decided it would help if I cut my hair and wore better clothes.

Now that I was off the drugs, I felt safe writing to my dad. Certain there had to be more to life than being born, experiencing the world, growing old, and dying, I asked my father to please help me understand life's deeper meaning. His reply left me empty.

"Go to the library, Sissy," he advised. "I don't know what you're searching for. There is a book called *Siddhartha* by Herman Hesse. Maybe it will help."

Disappointed with his response, I began to weep. No matter what happened I had always looked up to my father, thinking he knew all the answers. *Go to the library?* I didn't even know the questions, let alone where to look for the answers.

After that I began slipping out of bed at four o'clock every morning to go downstairs by the fire to meditate. One morning Hippie was roused from his sleep. Seeing me heading downstairs with my blanket and pillow sparked his curiosity.

"Where are you going?" he asked sleepily.

"Downstairs to stoke the fire," I replied, not knowing how to explain my intense spiritual yearning.

Ever since I was a child, I had loved Jesus and wanted to be pure like him. I was sure there were spiritual masters in India that could teach me to be holy but unfortunately, their high mountain abodes were too remote and inaccessible from our little cabin in the backwoods of Nova Scotia.

"Please Lord, send me a Guru. I can't do this on my own," I prayed one morning just before dawn.

Since the road to our cabin was not yet paved, Hippie blocked off the entrance for the duration of the spring thaw. Due to the long muddy walk, we had very few visitors at that time of year. One morning I was working on a stained-glass window when I heard a knock on the cabin door. It was my friend Elizabeth Shannon.

"Come in out of the rain!" I laughed, surprised by my good fortune.

Sporting a mysterious grin, Elizabeth stepped inside and handed me a book.

"I was doing my housework when I kept getting the nagging feeling that I needed to bring this book to you," she said.

I read the title out loud.

Silence Speaks from the chalkboard of Baba Hari Dass.

When I flipped open the front cover the picture on the first page took my breath away. It was him! The porcelain sage of my childhood who advised me not to worry. Now just a couple days after my soulful prayer he had come to me as an adult with the questions and answers I needed in simple words I could understand.

"Purify the body and mind in order to realize your true nature," he directed. "Life is a means for raising the consciousness, not the indulgence in sensual pleasures."

The silent monk explained that samskaras are impressions in the mind from past births, as well as the mental conditioning of our environment. He said the purpose of life is to work out our samskaras and develop dispassion for the world. When one attains samadhi[4] through the process of meditation, the seeds of their samskaras can be wiped out completely. At that point, one attains liberation from the cycle of birth and death.

This was exactly what I was searching for! While cooking, cleaning, and lying in bed at night, all I could think of was my Guru, Baba Hari Dass. Being young and inexperienced, I neglected to read the information on the back of the book that said he was teaching classes in Santa Cruz, California.

One day my inner Voice urged, "Go to Santa Cruz. You'll find him there."

Having grown up in San Jose I knew Santa Cruz quite well. I never thought to go to the local health food store to inquire about the saint's whereabouts and traipsing through the mountains searching for my Guru seemed a bit far-fetched. My prayers continued.

The following week I spotted the book, *Autobiography of a Yogi*, by Paramahansa Yogananda, while visiting my neighbor Ellen. Seeing my avid interest in the guru's life she handed me the book.

"Go ahead, take it home," she encouraged. "Just don't forget to bring it back when you're finished reading it."

Paramahansa Yogananda's autobiography extolls the lives and teachings of several of India's greatest spiritual masters. Within two weeks after begging God for a guru, India's great saints were coming to my cabin in

---

[4]   samadhi : super consciousness

the form of books. I absorbed their wisdom like a starving person. Before going to sleep one night I read a few passages from *Silence Speaks* to Hippie. Seeing the blank stare on his face I realized he did not understand the ancient truths.

"You are going to leave me one day and go to an ashram," he sadly predicted, fearful of the prospects of losing his wife.

"You can come with me," I assured him, knowing anyone can change if they have the desire.

Now that I had found my Master, my thoughts were tortured by my desire to study with him.

Was the book old? Was the silent monk still alive? If so, how could I find him?

"Write to the address on the back of the book," the guiding Voice tried again.

I had seen publishing companies in the movies. They were large, busy offices filled with worldly-minded people smoking cigarettes, answering phones, and tapping away at typewriters.

Impossible, I replied, and never gave it a try.

Inside Yogananda's book there was an application for membership. Secretly cutting corners on groceries, I saved enough money for the spiritual lessons he wrote before his death. As soon as the package arrived, I practiced the energization techniques and studied the lessons as directed. Shortly thereafter my life began to change in a way I did not expect.

I was sitting outside near my favorite pile of rocks one morning when I saw Hippie go into the woods to clear some land. When he fired up his chainsaw the trees began pleading for my help. I jumped up and ran as fast as I could to stop him, but it was too late, Hippie had already cut down a tree. A blood-red substance poured into the sunlight and I began to sob uncontrollably.

"What's wrong?" Hippie asked, turning off the saw.

Ignoring his irritation, I begged for the lives of the trees.

"Please don't cut down any more trees," I cried. "They are our friends. They have protected us from the wind, provided lumber for our home, and gave us wood for our fire. We have a house, garden, and road. Why kill the trees just to make more space?"

Although it was clear that my husband did not understand, he sensed my sincerity and put away the saw.

Hippie worked several jobs over the years, but they were all short-lived. Our financial state was generally poor, so we would steal what we could not afford to buy. It was like a game when we went grocery shopping. Hippie would go off and take the most expensive steaks he could find, while I headed for the dairy department to get the butter and cheese. One day I was about to slip a pound of butter under my poncho when the quiet Voice began to whisper.

"There are mothers who would watch their children starve before stealing from another human being."

I put the butter back. The Voice was right. What was I doing?

"Did you get it?" Hippie asked, as he came up the aisle with the steaks tucked in the back of his pants.

"No, I'm not stealing anymore," I replied, feeling strangely courageous.

The following week I was out watering in the greenhouse when I noticed several large marijuana plants off in one corner. Remembering the heartache of being arrested and losing our children, I plucked the plants out by their roots and took them deep into the forest. When Hippie came home and saw what I had done he just stood there looking lost. For the first time, I saw the hurt behind his anger.

"Our family has had too much trouble," I explained. "That is finished now. We are not doing or selling any more drugs in our home."

Hippie was a hard worker but his lack of education and inability to keep a steady job kept him from being a good provider. I was fed up with being poor and realized that if we were ever going to have a decent home for our children I would have to go out and earn the money myself. The following week my friend, Adrienne, came down to the cabin to offer me a job.

"I'm looking for an assistant gardener. The work is extremely hard, and the boss only pays $3.75 an hour to start," she said apologetically.

Since I had nothing more than a high school education, I felt fortunate just to have a job.

"I'll take it. When do I start?"

"Come first thing Monday morning at 8:00," she directed.

While hauling water, pulling weeds, and mowing lawns I thought of the good home, plentiful food, and new clothes I would buy for my children. After two months of dirty, exhausting work for very little pay, I noticed the waitresses arriving for their evening shift. Thinking it would be better to work inside where I could wear a clean uniform and make a lot of money in tips, I decided to apply for a waitress job when the inn reopened in spring.

The owner of the country inn was a hot-tempered little man who was known by his staff to cheat on his wife. When the restaurant got busy, none of the workers moved fast enough to please him. One evening Mr. Munroe shoved a busboy in the hall trying to make him hurry up on his way to the kitchen. The young man stumbled but did not drop his large tray full of dirty dishes.

"The owner's behaviour is intolerable!" I remarked to the other waitresses, but each one just looked in the other direction.

Later that night one of my customers needed change to pay their bill. The restaurant was quite busy, and I had to wait for the cashier at the front desk. I didn't notice the boss come up behind me. Without saying a word, he seductively leaned in and pressed his hand into the small of my back. I thought about the man in Kentucky who had given the kids and me a ride when I was pregnant.

"Take your hand off my back," I said, gazing evenly into his eyes.

His charming smile quickly disappeared, and I knew it was time to look for another job.

When I told Adrienne what happened she said, "The manager of the fruit and vegetable stand is looking for help during the Mother's Day rush. If you apply right away, you're sure to get the job."

After a quick interview, the manager handed me an apron.

"You're hired," Sharon said with a smile. "When can you start?"

My new boss gave me several plant and tree catalogues to study and showed me how to use the cash register. She taught me all about the shrubs and flowers in the greenhouse and explained which trees were best suited to Nova Scotia's cold climate. I quickly became friends with the other women, and by the end of the week the manager wanted to know if I would stay for the rest of the summer. I loved working with the plants and looked forward to my job until one day, Sharon insisted I push the chemicals.

"That's how we make money," she said. "Selling chemicals."

Familiar words!

Work became drudgery. For easy distribution, a fifty-pound sack of wireworm poison was placed on the floor beside my checkout counter. The fumes gave me headaches, and I was certain the chemicals had to be harmful to the environment.

"Birds will eat the poisoned worms and cats will eat the poisoned birds," I said, trying to enlighten the farmers. "The rain will wash the chemical into the water table and our families will also be poisoned."

Furadan[5] sales mysteriously dropped and then one day, the manager overheard my whispered warnings.

"Come see me as soon as your customer leaves," she said in passing.

I was not afraid. As soon as I had the chance, I went directly to her office.

"Here," I said, handing her my apron with determination. "I cannot sell your chemicals and live with a clear conscience."

Clara Harris was one of Yarmouth's success stories. The eldest daughter of a local fisherman, she was raised in a small, seaside village about twenty miles south of Yarmouth. As a young woman, Clara opened a small take-out stand selling fresh fish chowder and homemade bread to tourists. Believing in her ability to succeed, one of her customers from the United States loaned her enough money to start her own seafood restaurant. Over the years her restaurant was written up as one of the best seafood restaurants in North America. When I applied for work Mrs. Harris shook her head.

"I don't have any openings right now dear," she said. "My waitresses have been with me for twenty-five years." Before turning away, she grinned and shrugged her shoulders adding, "For some reason they don't want to leave!"

"Thank you," I said, and headed for the door.

---

5   Granular Furadan was banned in the United States in 1991 as one of the most toxic carbamate pesticides directly responsible for the death of one million birds. In 2009 the Environmental Protection Agency banned the application of its liquid form on crops for human consumption.

When I came back a week later Clara said, "You certainly are persistent dear, but like I told you before, I have no work for you."

"Okay, thanks anyway," I said.

Feeling disheartened, I returned home. When I came back the following week the parking lot was empty, and the front door locked. I went around back and climbed the steps of the rickety old porch. The kitchen door was open, and I could see Mrs. Harris through the screen. She was alone, kneading her bread.

"Mrs. Harris?" I called out so as not to frighten her.

"Oh, yes dear, come on in. I'm just here by m'self a makin' some bread," she responded in her quaint, friendly manner.

I could no longer hold back.

"Your workers love you," I said. "And your restaurant has a good reputation. I don't want just any job. I want to work here, with you!"

Mrs. Harris looked pleased as she placed a portion of her kneaded dough into one of the many oiled pans lined up on the counter.

"Come back next week. I'll train you as a hostess for the dining room," she laughed.

Over the next few months Mrs. Harris taught me to work as a team player. I fit in well with the other workers and the following summer someone left, allowing me to have my turn as waitress.

It had been just four years since we moved into the cabin and it already looked like an impoverished shack. The green lumber studs were never boarded in, so they warped in the hot sun causing the temporary walls of oiled fiberboard to pull away from their nails. When my co-workers offered to drive me home after work, I was ashamed for them to see where I lived.

Although I had to walk a half mile through the woods late at night, my pride kept me from accepting their good-natured help.

"You can just drop me off here," I'd say. "I really enjoy the quiet walk through the woods late at night. And besides, the fresh air helps me sleep!"

During freezing winters, muddy springs, hot summers, and windy falls our family took turns hauling buckets of water up the hill from the lake.

"As soon as we get enough money, I'll hire someone with a backhoe to dig us a well," Hippie promised.

Enough money never came. One morning while reading *The Mother Earth News,* I came across an article about the women who dowsed for water and dug their own wells while their men were away fighting in World War II. Inspired, I put down the magazine and went over to the closet. Taking out two metal coat hangers, I cut off the hooks and bent the hangers into right angles. Without saying anything to Hippie I went outside to see if it really worked.

Holding the makeshift dowsing rods loosely in my hands I walked slowly through the grass near the house. An electrical current flowed through my body causing the rods to turn right and left of their own accord. Following their lead, I continued to walk until the hangers crossed. Trusting this to be the convergence of two underground springs, I marked the spot with a rock and went back inside to get the shovel.

Unbeknownst to me, Hippie had been watching from inside the cabin. When I picked up the shovel, he could no longer suppress his curiosity.

"Where are you going with that?" he asked.

"I'm going to dig a well," I replied, determined not to be dissuaded by his elusive promises.

To my surprise my husband followed me into the yard. Protectively taking the shovel from my hands, he dug until well after dark. The next morning, he got up early to continue the job. When water started seeping in, Joshua climbed into the hole to pass buckets of mud up to his father. I was tired from waitressing the night before, so I sat in the shade watching them work. While Hippie and Josh dug the well, Terra and Isaac washed gravel for drainage. When it finally came time to rock up the inner walls, the whole family went to the beach to load up the truck with stones. After four years of waiting for enough money, we now had water pumped to the kitchen sink with only two weeks of hard work.

In 1981 fishing was still one of Nova Scotia's main industries. One night I overheard two of the busboys talking about all the money they were making at the fish plant during the day. I had always felt above working in such places, but when they bragged about the exorbitant prices the Japanese were paying for herring roe, I decided to give it a try.

My strong desire to have a nice home, decent clothing, and good food for my children drove me to work so hard that I rarely saw my family anymore. Throughout the week I left early in the morning to cut fish until three o'clock in the afternoon. As soon as I got home, I ran down to the lake to relax and scrub the fish scales from my arms. After tidying up the house and making supper for Hippie and the kids I would kiss them goodbye and dash off to work at Clara's restaurant.

Upon arrival, the waitresses generally ordered their meals and then sat in the kitchen eating and talking before the long evening shift. One of the young women heard about my second job at the fish plant and made fun of me whenever I came to work.

"Here fishy, fishy, fishy," Caroline teased in passing, or "Ooh, what's that smell?" while pinching her nose and turning away with a disgusted look on her face.

Throughout my life I tried to please other people. Trying to be part of them and their groups of friends, I would laugh at jokes I didn't think were funny or compromise my morals by following along with what seemed popular at the time. But this was different; I was working long, tedious hours trying to build a home for my children. The last time she made fun of me I stopped and looked her square in the face.

"That's money you smell honey!"

I could hear the other waitresses snickering and cheering me on as I left the kitchen to check on my tables. After that, Caroline's highly competitive nature caused her to ask me how many boxes of roe I filled that day when I came into work. She wanted to know how much each box was worth, and if the fish plant was still hiring. Although I didn't encourage her to work with me, she ended up cutting fish the rest of that summer at a plant near her home.

Tourist season brought so many customers to Clara's restaurant that it was often midnight before I could go home. Hippie always left a kerosene lamp turned down low on the kitchen table so I wouldn't have to come into a dark house. After washing the restaurant sweat from my body, I would go upstairs to check on the kids. Although dead tired, I liked to read a few lines from Silence Speaks or Autobiography of a Yogi before going to sleep. I no longer had time to meditate and Paramahansa Yogananda's energization techniques were completely forgotten.

While browsing through the local newspaper one day, Hippie noticed that the small piece of land at the top of our driveway was being sold for back taxes. On my next day off we took a walk out to the main road to check it out. Our neighbor, Enos Ringer, was out in his yard. When he saw us looking at the charred remains of the old foundation, he came over to see what was going on.

Enos was a simple man whose friendly demeanour allowed him privy to everyone else's business. His wife, Betty, would have been shunned as a dullard had she lived anywhere other than the Woodstock Road.

"Hello Katie!" she called from her porch as Gwen and I walked past her house. "Come on in and see my bathroom!"

Unable to refuse her innocent request, we entered the humble yellow shack.

"Look here Katie!" she said, her dentures slipping from their shrinking gums. "I cleaned it up real pretty don't you think?"

The rough chipboard walls had been whitewashed with a thin coat of paint and faded plastic flowers decorated the scratched enamel shelf beneath the mirror. With childlike excitement, the sixty-year-old woman held up a large, crocheted doily that Mrs. Gilford gave her in a box of second-hand clothes.

"That's real nice Betty," I said, knowing her mental capacity was not quite up to par.

Whenever Enos spoke about the personal affairs of his neighbors, the deep creases in his face seemed to take on a life of their own. With his thumbs hooked in his suspenders, he insisted that the previous owner had set fire to the house to collect the insurance money. Shirking off all thoughts of bad omens, Hippie and I went into town to pay the seventy-five dollars that the government was asking for the land.

Hippie's mother died that summer, leaving him an inheritance of five thousand dollars. With his money from Ruth and the wages from my two jobs, we bought enough supplies to build a small house close to the road. Hippie hired a friend with a backhoe to dig a hole for the foundation. He worked all through the night mixing and pouring cement into the footings he built. Ignoring his chronic back pain, he spent the next several weeks boarding in the frame, installing windows, and lining the walls with insulation. From time to time he tried unsuccessfully to stop using drugs.

"It's impossible to change in a small town where everyone knows me!" he exclaimed one morning, when I walked in on him smoking a joint.

My own experience told me it was hard, but not impossible.

The fish plant paid their workers by the box, so I purposefully stood next to the most experienced cutter whose example impelled me to work faster and faster. Filling the boxes with roe became a game for more money, until one day, I saw the fish. Seeing their glazed-over eyes staring up at me from their murky bin of bloody water, I realized the foul smell of the fish plant was the stink of my own greed. Unable to continue, I said goodbye to my co-workers and told the boss I would not be back.

While I had been consumed with making money, Hippie was spending his evenings at his friend's barn, playing pool and smoking pot. Left alone at the cabin to fend for themselves, the kids were showing signs of depression, violence, and promiscuity. After picking up my last check from the fish plant, I stopped in at the credit union to cash it. The manager saw me in the lineup and called me into her office.

"Did you ever think about working here as a teller?" she asked with a slightly hushed voice.

Her question caught me by surprise.

"No, I don't have any experience working in a bank."

"Well I've already spoken with the rest of the staff. We like your smile and think you would fit in well here. Give me a call by next Friday if you want the job," she said, as she passed me her card.

On the way home I considered her offer. If I gave up my position at the restaurant, I would make a lot less money, but I had to admit, working nine to five with weekends off sounded pretty good. At work that evening I asked Mrs. Harris what she thought of my new opportunity.

"The restaurant will be closing for the winter soon," Clara explained. "If the new job doesn't work out, your position as waitress will still be available when we reopen in spring."

That fall our new house was finally ready. The floors were tiled, and the walls sanded and painted to perfection. Electric heaters lined the baseboards and beautifully handcrafted cupboards showed Hippie's natural talent as a carpenter.

Now that I was clean from drugs, I didn't want to associate with our old friends anymore. Trying to look professional for my new job at the credit union, I cut my hair and wore stylish dresses with matching high heels. My friend Jackie invited me to join her meditation group and I went back to practicing the energization techniques from Paramahansa Yogananda's spiritual lessons. On the way home from work one day, I stopped in at the detox unit on the second floor of the hospital. Helping troubled people to find peace when everything around them seemed hopeless or cruel was something I had vowed to do in early childhood.

I approached the front desk to ask if I could speak to the supervisor. When Sandra Noah came out of her office, I told her I had conquered my drug addiction all by myself. She listened as I proudly announced that I had been off all drugs for over five years and wanted to help other drug addicts free themselves from the compelling urge to get high. For some reason, Mrs. Noah was not impressed.

"Hmmm, you got clean all by yourself, did you?" she asked.

"Yes, all by myself," I replied, feeling proud of my accomplishment.

Sandra Noah had worked too many years in addiction treatment to let my denial slip by undetected. Knowing that abstinence does not equal recovery, she leaned back against the wall and folded her arms across her chest. Rubbing her chin, she seemed to be looking for just the right words.

"All alone," she repeated a second time.

"Yes, all alone," I said, beginning to feel a bit irritated.

Her arms dropped to her sides as she pulled herself away from the wall.

"Listen dear," she said, as though speaking to a child. "I recommend you go to AA meetings for the next six months. If you are still interested in helping others after that, come see me."

I was shocked.

AA? I didn't belong in a program for alcoholics! I was a drug addict!

"Okay, thanks," I said, carefully masking my wounded pride.

Defensive thoughts screamed from behind my solemn face as I walked through the corridors and out to the car.

Who does she think she is telling ME to go to AA? My FATHER was the ALCOHOLIC! I had a problem with DRUGS, and I stopped without anyone's help but my OWN!

Tears blurred my vision as I pulled out of the parking lot and onto the highway. Deliberately passing my exit, I drove to Port Maitland and pulled into the driveway of my ninety-year-old friend, Leta Delaney. Our meditation group had been scheduled to meet that afternoon at one o'clock and I was already an hour late. When I knocked on the door the elderly women were patient with my soulful interruption.

"Well you know Kate," Jackie advised in her wise-owl voice. "Angels are known to take things lightly. That is why they can fly! How about a cup of tea and a cookie? I bought them fresh this afternoon!"

Her kind offerings were appreciated, but my aching heart refused to be comforted.

The following week I started my job at the Yarmouth Credit Union. My new position gave me a sense of self-esteem and I found the company of my co-workers refreshing. When we were invited to their homes, Hippie felt uncomfortable. A new battle began to irritate my mind.

Do I stay with my husband and hope things will change on their own or do I get a divorce and try to make a new life for myself and the children?

The guidance by Baba Hari Dass in *Silence Speaks* said, "Marriage is very important. If two people love one another, then they must tolerate a few of the other's weaknesses. Living with another person is a hard austerity and much sacrifice is needed."

I thought of my own situation when Babaji explained it can sometimes become impossible to live together if a person goes crazy or develops bad habits like drug addiction or gambling. Not clear on the right thing to do I explored different churches, searching for the truth. I quit going to the homes of people who were using drugs and tried to fit in with what I considered a higher class of people. Sensing the coming separation, Hippie tried to save our marriage by cutting his long hair and shaving off his beard. He promised to stop using drugs and even suggested we see a marriage counsellor.

I didn't know how to make him understand; his long hair and beard were not the problem. Although I appreciated his efforts for better personal grooming, I knew it would not last if there was no inner change. What I wanted was to live a virtuous life and be healthy parents for our children to emulate. I was certain Hippie was only looking for a temporary fix, so I told him it was too late; we were getting a divorce.

"You stay in the new house with the kids," he said, as a protective gesture. "I've been offered a job out of town and can fend for myself."

After packing all his belongings into his truck, Hippie kissed the kids and told us goodbye. We didn't hear from him again until two months later when I heard a knock at the door. Wondering who would be out so late in such a terrible storm I opened the door just a crack. It was Hippie.

"I need a place to stay," he said.

The moisture from his warm breath froze in little beads on his newly growing beard. My heart filled with compassion seeing him standing alone in the cold with no family or home to go to. I remembered the many times we had been together in the same predicament and now I was to turn him away? I just couldn't do it. The next morning the kids were confused.

"Why is Dad sleeping on the couch?" they asked.

I told them the truth: "He was cold."

After a couple of weeks, I asked Hippie if he had been out looking for a place to live.

"You're the one who wants a divorce," his voice bristled with contempt. "If you want out of our marriage then let it be you who leaves because I'm staying right here."

I was shocked. Had he played on my sympathy as a ploy to get the house back for himself? When I spoke with my women friends, one of them offered me a place to stay. Joshua, who was now sixteen, had left home a few months before so I felt like my responsibility with him was finished. I knew Terra and I could share a room at my friend's house, but Isaac had just turned thirteen and needed his own space.

Deep inside I was afraid that if I took my youngest son with me, he would lose his dad, or worse, resent my new way of life and run away to be with Hippie. Instead of openly discussing my fears with Isaac, I told him he had to stay with his dad. Hugging him goodbye, I promised he could stay with me on the weekends as soon as I got a place of my own.

For several years I earned my Christmas money by selling homemade crafts at the Farmer's Market. Since my customers returned year after year, I thought it would be a good idea to open my own gift shop. Nova Scotia's unpredictable weather meant a short tourist season, which meant I had to get moving right away if I were to have a successful beginning. My lunch hours at the credit union were spent driving around town looking for the perfect location. One day a friend stopped in to tell me about an empty shop right up the street from the ferry terminal.

"There's a vacancy on Main Street," she said, sounding excited. "You would be smart to inquire about it right away. It's the perfect location for your store, and I'm sure it will rent pretty fast."

After negotiating a lease, I met with the bank manager to discuss my financial options. When the estimate for my sign was ready, I went to see the town advisor about a small business loan. After reading my proposal he tried to dissuade me.

"We already have too many gift stores and not enough customers," he warned. "The Bluenose Ferry between Yarmouth and Bar Harbor, Maine, has been redirected causing tourism to drop significantly. And most of our local people do their shopping at the mall, causing our established downtown merchants to struggle just to make ends meet."

My mind was already made up and I refused to listen to his advice.

"My store will be different than the others!" I assured him. "I'll be using the theme of the loon and make my own crafts. I even have a catchy name, *The Looney Bin Curiosity Shop*. You'll see, people will love it!"

With no further discussion, the loan officer handed me a check and wished me good luck.

Every once in awhile Hippie got dressed up and stopped in at the credit union to invite me out to eat. Although I was still unable to talk to him about my need for an honest and responsible lifestyle, I was touched by his efforts to dress better and accepted his invitations. Using some of the money I received from the loan I hired Hippie to remodel the interior of my store. By the first of June, my inventory was on the shelves, the sign was up, and the doors were open.

I was proud to have Terra working with me after school. She knew how to dress for work and was polite and helpful with the customers. We had fun laughing when we were alone and when I had to go out, I trusted my daughter's ability to tend the store.

Sunday mornings were reserved for Isaac. We had doughnuts and hot chocolate at the local pastry shop, and then walked down to the wharf to look at the boats. I was not skilled at talking with my thirteen-year-old son and he was careful to hide the truth: he felt abandoned by me and was often left alone and afraid at night.

One morning on my way to the bank, a tall handsome man stopped me in the middle of the sidewalk. I knew him as one of the men who used to come to our house to buy drugs. Flashing an attractive smile, Drake wanted to know what I was doing now that I was single.

"I'm leading a straight life, staying away from drugs and trying to run my store," I told him.

"I've been trying to stay clean too, but I'm not having much success," he admitted.

Recalling my own inner battles, I thought I could help.

"Stop by the store if you ever need to talk," I said, and continued my walk to the bank.

Over the winter Drake dropped by my store several times to talk about his struggles with staying clean. I was happy to encourage him and looked forward to his visits. One day he came in and wrote down his address.

"Come up to my place after work," he said with a teasing smile. "I have a surprise for you."

The apartment Drake shared with his father was a five-minute walk from where I lived on Cliff Street. Feeling unsure of my reason for being there, I climbed the dimly lit staircase and rang the bell. Drake opened the door looking happy to see me.

"Come on in," he said with a gentlemanly air.

I followed him into the living room where he pointed at a large comfortable chair.

"Sit down and close your eyes," he said.

I settled into my seat as his footsteps faded down the hall. When he came back, he laid a gift-wrapped box of flowers in my lap.

"Okay," he laughed. "Open your eyes!"

Drake had been clean from all alcohol and drugs for three months which according to him was a huge accomplishment. He started calling me at my store every morning that he wasn't lobster fishing and often popped by for a surprise visit in the afternoon. One evening he greeted me with an unexpected kiss on my cheek when I opened my apartment door.

"Come on, let's go for a walk and get some fresh air!" he urged.

On the way home we stopped at the Dairy Queen for a milkshake, talking and laughing about everything and nothing at all. It didn't take long before I completely forgot about being his sobriety coach, and the fact that he was ten years younger seemed like no big deal at all.

I started to look forward to Drake's visits until one day, he completely disappeared. The phone didn't ring in the morning, he didn't stop by my store in the afternoon, and there were no unexpected knocks on my apartment door after supper. I could not understand what happened. We had so much fun! The sex was good. We enjoyed each other's company. Where did I go wrong?

I became obsessed with wanting to see him again. Scanning both sides of the street on my way to the bank, I tried to get a glimpse of his red wool bomber jacket among the people walking on the downtown sidewalks. Every day after work I went out of my way to drive past his apartment to see if the light was on in his upstairs window. In passing one evening I saw his car in the driveway. When I got home, I dialed his number.

"Hello?" his father's voice sounded unusually quiet.

"May I speak with Drake please?" I asked, unsure of what I would say if he came to the phone.

"I'm sorry," his father lied. "He's not here right now."

After separating from Hippie, I realized that becoming a responsible member of society was not enough. Outwardly I appeared as though I had it all together, but inwardly I felt fake and emotionally immature. Although I had done well selling my crafts at the Christmas Farmer's Markets, I had no experience with managing a real store. Professionally inept, I became stressed about ordering stock, creating window displays, advertising, and paying taxes. The extreme loneliness I felt for family and friends magnified my obsession with Drake, causing the untreated hurts, resentments, and misconceptions from my childhood wounds to sabotage my life.

Frustrated by the sudden turn of events, I booked an appointment with Edna Aker, a well-known psychic woman from Kentville. While parking my car outside her trailer, I reminded myself to keep quiet just in case her spiritual abilities were not real. Edna must have noticed my stiff demeanor because she laughed as she closed the door behind me.

"Relax honey!" she gently admonished. "Take a seat at the table. I'll be right with you."

The friendly, middle-aged woman returned with her tarot cards.

"Shuffle these cards while thinking about your problem," she directed, and then handed me the deck.

I did as she asked and then set the cards back on the table. Edna cut the deck into three piles and then picked them up in their reverse order. One by one she laid out a circular spread of thirteen cards. After studying the images for a few moments, her voice became subdued and her gaze blurry, as though she could see right through me.

"You're gonna meet an older man who will be very good for you," she prophesied. "He has silver hair and he's gonna help you a lot."

Her face suddenly clouded over, and her voice dropped to a raspy whisper.

"This man you're with right now, he's no good. Stay away from him!"

Flipping over a few more cards, her face once again took on its previous glow.

"I like this silver haired man. He has hair on his face and he's a good man. Yes, he is a GOOD man! He's gonna help you a lot."

She shuffled the cards and then fanned them out face down in front of me.

"Pick one," she said.

I chose The Sun.

"What does that mean?" I asked.

"It is the highest outcome," she said. "And it will be yours!"

A few nights later the telephone startled me awake. It was Drake. He had been drinking and wanted to talk. I was glad to hear from him but knew that talking to a drunk person is useless.

"Call back when you're sober," I said, and hung up the phone.

The next day he came over to apologize.

Looking sheepish he said, "I don't know what got into me last night, calling when I was drunk. No wonder people call me Drake the Snake!"

Ignoring the psychic woman's warning I let him in. The following week a friend dropped by the store. Looking concerned for my welfare he folded his arms across his chest and leaned against the counter.

"I was talking to Hippie the other night," he said. "He told me he can't stand seeing you with other men and has decided to move to British Columbia."

My heart sank as my thoughts raced ahead.

Hippie can't leave! He is the only one who loves me more than life itself. And what about Isaac? He can't go to British Columbia. He's too young! Who will love him like his own mother? When I gave Hippie custody, I thought they would live on our land and Isaac would come stay with me on the weekends!

The next day Hippie came into my store looking tired and pale.

"I'm going to British Columbia to look for work," he said. "I can't take Isaac right now, but I'll send for him in a couple of months."

My inner Voice prodded me to speak.

"Tell him you care. Ask him not to go. Encourage him to get counselling and stay off drugs for his sake and that of his family. Remind him he has a home. Tell him to finish the house on the lake and to build it well. Guide him to get involved with the community and go on vacations like healthy people do. Tell him you don't have to go to an ashram. You can love God wherever you are. Speak up! Say I love you, say anything, but don't let him go without trying!"

Choking back the truth I said, "Goodbye Hip'. And good luck!"

As soon as Hippie's truck disappeared around the corner I went to the back room of my shop and closed the door. Thoughts of heroin raced through my mind as I took the picture of my smiling family off the wall and turned it face-down on my desk. At precisely five o'clock I locked up the store and got in my car. Like every other day I drove past the tavern on my way home. For some reason I noticed some familiar looking vehicles parked out front. Unlike the quiet, guiding Voice of my childhood, my mind began to chatter in a loud, coercive dialogue.

What's the harm in just stopping by for a few minutes? it coaxed. *You're so lonely! Go on in and see your old friends. What can it hurt?*

Ignoring the cravings, I went home and put on some music. I lit a few candles, turned out the light, and immersed myself in a tub of hot water. Feeling like a vulnerable infant, I longed to go back to my mother's womb where it was safe, warm, and devoid of responsibility.

The following week Joshua unexpectedly showed up at my store looking tired and broke. I made room for him in my apartment as he had no money, no place to live, and his involvement with drugs had him running from the law.

After school let out for the summer Terra's weekend drinking escalated into a daily occurrence. No longer caring about her hair and clothing, she now came to work looking slovenly and hungover. During her breaks she liked to embarrass me by standing in front of the store smoking cigarettes and calling out to her friends who lived in the apartment upstairs. I became distraught with my daughter's bad behavior and after a couple of warnings, I told her she was fired.

Isaac, who was now thirteen, had been kicked out of school for fighting. Like his brother and sister, he was drinking and taking drugs on a regular basis. Recalling the violent exchange with Big Johnny over a drug debt, I became paralyzed with fear when salespeople encouraged me to buy now and pay later.

Drake's irresponsible behaviour continued to fluctuate between drunk and sober, triggering painful childhood memories of my alcoholic father. As a young girl I had been powerless to protect my brothers and sisters from the violence and chaos in our home and now, as an adult, I helplessly watched my children become defiant and their lives out of control.

When Hippie sent the promised plane ticket, I was still afraid to tell Isaac the truth: I wanted him to stay with me and live an honest life. Feeling incompetent and lost, I held my son one last time and then kissed him goodbye. Once his plane disappeared out of sight I got in my car and went back to work.

CHAPTER FIVE

Allurements

Although I had not had the desire to use drugs in over six years, the cravings not only returned, but somehow gained strength during their silent retreat. Naming my store, the Looney Bin, turned out to be a paradox. What was initially meant to be a play on words turned out to be a cosmic joke mirroring my internal state. I felt trapped inside the four walls of my store like a free bird with clipped wings. Unable to cope with the feelings of loneliness and despair, I took a friend's advice and signed myself into the addiction treatment unit at the Yarmouth Regional Hospital.

After filling out the necessary forms, the counsellor on duty showed me to my room. She stepped inside just long enough to inspect the bathroom and then gave her nod of approval.

"You will be sharing this room with another woman. She has not arrived yet, so go ahead and choose a bed." Turning to leave, she pushed up the sleeves of her loose knit sweater saying, "Oh yes, you can take two of the dresser drawers. You'll need them for your clothes."

I sat down on the bed closest to the door. It had been many years since I had shared a dresser like that with my stepsisters, Susan and Liz. Susan the shy, delicate little girl who had let me in that first day at Sue's had become overweight and arthritic by the time she was eleven. As though it were yesterday, I recalled my brother, Don, slipping a rubber lizard on the pillow beside her face the day she came home from the hospital. No parents were home, and I was told to take care of the kids.

"Susan, look out!" the fifteen-year-old boy cried out with alarm. "There's something on your pillow!"

Susan was still quite sick with a jaundiced liver. Before leaving for the bar Sue had wrapped her daughter's leg with a soft bandage. She placed a heating pad under Susan's calf and then elevated her leg with a couple of pillows to drain the pus from the inflamed boil. When Susan saw the toy lizard beside her face, she thought it was real, and bolted from the couch. Seeing the pillows, heating pad, and rubber lizard go flying across the room, Don laughed uproariously.

"You son-of-a-bitch," the yellow-skinned girl sobbed with contempt. "Leave me alone!"

Taking great pleasure in her angry reaction, my brother continued to taunt and tease until Susan limped into the kitchen and grabbed a butcher knife off the counter. My heart constricted with fear.

"Come on, Susan," I begged. "Put the knife down. Don was just teasing you. Boys can be jerks sometimes. Don't pay any attention to him!"

The other kids heard the commotion and came running to see what was going on. Susan, now wild with rage, chased my brother into the garage and hurled the butcher knife with all her might. The flash of the blade's release triggered Don's instinct to move his head before the knife stuck in the garage door beside his face.

I suddenly realized I was holding my breath. The smooth white tiles felt cool on my bare feet as I observed the empty walls and institutional furniture. As the painful memories of my childhood arose in my mind, I felt like there was a frightened bird inside my head, batting its body against its cage, trying to get out.

No, I whispered aloud. *I am tired of running away from my problems. It is safe here and I am determined to find a new way to live.*

The next morning our small group of five was called into the lecture room to meet with the counselor. After speaking to us about how addiction affects the whole family, Deanne put in a video and left the room. For the next hour we watched as a man inflicted with the disease of alcoholism abandoned his responsibilities, spending all his time and money at the bar. Once he was thoroughly intoxicated, he returned home to his distraught wife and troubled children.

The wife on the other hand, focused all her attention on her husband's problems. Neglecting her children, she drank countless cups of coffee, chain-smoked cigarettes, and took pills to cope with her problems. When her husband finally sobered up, he either spoiled the children out of guilt, or beat his young sons during his frequent fits of rage. Terrified by his unpredictable behaviour, the four-year-old daughter hid behind her bedroom door or tried to placate her father by cuddling in his lap.

When the movie came to an end, my roommate, Brenda, got up and turned on the lights. After a few minutes of silence, all five of us began to fidget in our chairs. Doug, the only male in the group, was the first to speak.

"That counselor has a nice ass," he joked. "When she comes in, I'm going to give it a little slap!"

Just then the door opened, and the counselor came in and sat down. Triggered by Doug's ridiculous remark, all five of us began to snicker. Deanne did not move or change expressions but watched as our giggles magnified into hysterical laughter. Finally, one by one, we covered our faces to hide the tears coursing down our cheeks. Without warning, a flood of urine spilled from my bladder. Stiffening with horror I sat up in my chair, struggling to mask the feelings of guilt and shame that were trying to redden my face.

"Today we are going to play a game," the counselor announced pleasantly. "Each of you will receive a piece of paper with a question on it. Read the question and think about your answer. As we go around the circle you will read your question out loud and give your answer to the group." Deanne looked at me and said, "You go first."

I opened my paper and looked at the question. 'What part of your body don't you like?' was written in Deanne's neat handwriting.

I mentally scanned my body from top to bottom.

My nose is okay, I thought, *and I have always liked my green eyes. My hearing is good, and my ears aren't too big or too small. Ever since the accident I can't straighten my left arm but hey, it's strong and doesn't hurt. My feet, legs, breasts, stomach... nope, everything is great... I am attractive, strong, healthy...*

Confused, I stared at the paper.

"Well?" Deanne asked in her straightforward manner.

"The question says, 'What part of your body don't you like?' I don't know what to say. I don't have a problem with any part of my body."

"Then the answer is simple," the counselor smiled. "You just say nothing, or I find nothing wrong with my body."

It was too easy. As soon as the session was over everyone but me got up to leave the room. Giving several excuses why I needed to remain in my chair, I waited for the others to leave and then slipped unseen down the hall to change my wet pants.

The next morning, the counselor spoke to us about the unproductive roles family members assume to cope with the chaos of addiction. To demonstrate the imbalance of co-dependency, she held up a mobile of paper family members dangling from three coat hangers. When she tipped her hand in one direction, the dysfunctional family slid to one side becoming tangled together in their strings.

Deanne explained, "A functional family keeps their balance because no matter what happens, everyone plays their own part. Alcoholism and drug addiction throw the whole family off balance because no one is true to themselves or their own lives. When an addicted parent plays the role of victim, the co-dependent spouse becomes their rescuer. The eldest child generally takes the role of hero, while the middle children either copycat the victim or become the lost child, distant and reserved. The family mascot is the jester who tries to ease the family's hurt by making everyone laugh. Frequently, one of the children becomes a scapegoat, getting into trouble to divert the negative attention onto him or herself. Both the youngest child and eldest daughter have the tendency to become the family caretaker who tries to keep the peace."

After concluding her lecture, Deanne put in a video. Without another word, she turned out the lights and left the room. When the movie was over, she did like she had the day before and gave us a few minutes to process our feelings. One by one the group took on their dysfunctional family roles.

Brenda, a lesbian stonemason, was dressed in dirty sneakers, baggy work jeans, and a sweatshirt two sizes too big. Heaving a sigh of utter disgust, she got up and flicked on the light. When she returned to her chair, she placed her elbows on her knees and clenched her weathered hands together with contempt.

"Oh yeah," she snarled, "that stupid bitch will probably show up late again today."

"Shut up!" cried the woman on my left as she put her hands over her ears.

"Don't talk about Deanne like that. She's just trying to help," I joined in.

"Yeah, right," another woman scoffed. "As if she really cares about anything but her paycheck!"

Once again, Doug's off-color humor broke the tension.

"When she comes in, I'm going to reach out and give her little titties a squeeze," he clowned, opening and closing his hands at chest level.

Just then the door opened, and the counselor came quietly into the room.

"Okay everyone, let's form a circle," she directed.

When Deanne sat down beside Doug, we could not contain ourselves. Doug's ridiculous image flashed through our minds and once again, all five of us burst into laughter. As though she had seen it a hundred times, Deanne quietly watched as our laughter evolved into the same hysteria as the day before. Feeling confused between sympathy for Deanne and the hilarity of Doug's foolish remark, my bladder once again emptied in an emotional river of shame. Shocked, I sat up pale-faced and rigid.

"Good morning," Deanne said calmly. "Anyone want to comment on the movie?"

By the end of the third day I was ready to leave. I had spent the first fourteen years of my life uncontrollably wetting my pants and I refused to revisit the shame and isolation that plagued my youth. That evening I knocked on the counselor's half-open door.

"Come on in!" Deanne called cheerfully.

"I can't do this," I exclaimed, anxiously pacing back and forth in front of her desk. "I have to leave!"

"What's going on?" she asked, with obvious concern.

"I peed my pants every day all the way through the eighth grade," I disclosed. "When it came time to go to high school, I was desperate to find a solution."

"What did you do?"

"Well the problem came whenever I laughed, so my solution was to get serious. When I started taking drugs at the age of seventeen it was as though a heavy burden was lifted from my shoulders. Now that I was high, I was free to laugh and enjoy life, but over the years, my life got worse instead of better. When I stopped using drugs, I intuitively went back to being serious. Now for some reason I have started laughing hysterically with the group during our morning sessions and my problem has returned. Please, just put me back the way I was, and I will go home."

"Do yourself a favor before you leave," Deanne advised. "When you are alone with the group tomorrow stay aware of what is discussed just before the laughter starts. Do you think you can do that?"

"Yeah, sure," I said. "But what will that do?"

"Just watch and see. If you still want to leave tomorrow afternoon, I will personally sign you out."

The next day Deanne lectured us on the harmful effects drugs and alcohol have on the brain. When she finished talking, she put in a video, turned off the lights, and left the room. As soon as the movie was over Brenda got up and turned on the lights. With her usual sneer, she made a negative remark about the counselor and one of the women started to cry. The woman sitting beside her tried to rescue her while Doug responded with an ill-humored joke about something sexual he would do to Deanne when she came back.

The door suddenly opened, and the counselor came in and sat down. The others exploded into laughter, but I was not amused. For the first time I saw the pain behind their remarks. Sitting quietly beside Deanne, I waited for the session to begin. Doug was the first to notice.

"Hey!" he said, wiping the tears from his cheeks. "Kate's getting better. She's not laughing!"

Not only was Sandra Noah the director of the treatment unit, but she was also Drake's aunt. Although he had relapsed many times,

Drake continued his attempts at staying clean by periodically admitting himself into the detox program. As she did with all ex-clients, Mrs. Noah encouraged her nephew to come back and speak with a counsellor anytime he needed support.

When I came out of my group session the next morning Drake was sitting in the day room, talking to one of the counselors. As I approached the table, I overheard him telling her that his girlfriend was downstairs in the hospital having his baby. I was confused.

What does he mean his girlfriend is downstairs? I am his girlfriend!

Slipping on my 'everything is fine' mask I walked up to the table to say hello. Just as Drake got up to give me a hug his aunt stepped out of her office. Leaning back against the wall, she folded her arms across her chest in the same condescending stance she had taken almost two years before. Seeing the hurt look on my face, Mrs. Noah looked suspiciously at her nephew.

"What's going on?" she inquired.

Drake put his arm around my shoulders.

"This is my sponsor!" he said, grinning sarcastically at his aunt.

I didn't need to be a brain surgeon to see that Drake's sexual relationships were the subject of an ongoing joke. Feeling ashamed and humiliated, I squirmed out from his embrace and returned to my room.

The intensive two-week program helped me understand that my drug usage was a symptom of long suppressed hurts. Being in a supportive environment helped me to come out of denial and release some of the pent-up anger and shame I had buried years before. When it came time to leave, Mrs. Noah's advice was the same as the first time we met.

"Remember, alcohol is a drug in liquid form," she warned. "No matter what comes, stay clean from all alcohol and drugs and commit to your

12-Step meetings. The spiritual program will help you and eventually you will pass it on and help many others."

This time I was ready to listen. Although AA was not for me, I committed to another 12 Step fellowship for recovering drug addicts. I studied the fellowship's literature, got a sponsor, and worked the spiritual Steps of the program. Slowly but surely, my feelings of shame and powerlessness began to lift.

It was easy to see that my store was failing. Feeling extremely vulnerable and emotionally distraught, I knew it was time to either close the shop myself or be forced into bankruptcy. I decided to take a chance on the truth and called everyone to whom I owed money. My suppliers were understanding and reassured me that my business failure was not all my fault.

"Don't take it personally," they said. "It's true, you are a beginner to business, so you've probably made a lot of mistakes. But you need to understand, you started at a bad time. Yarmouth's economy has been failing for the past couple of years. With the ferry being redirected to another port it won't be long before many of Yarmouth's long-established shops will also close their doors."

Each sales representative thanked me for my honesty and a total of eight thousand dollars worth of debt was written off. Although my faith in the program was beginning to take hold, liquidating my assets was tedious. I was often overwhelmed by feelings of helplessness and low self-worth. On my way home from work one evening some old familiar thoughts haunted my mind.

Don't worry about your bills! they nagged. *You will never see these people again. Just throw the keys on the counter and take the first flight out of town!*

As though rushing to my rescue, saner, more practical thoughts flooded in to take their place.

Take responsibility for your actions and CALL YOUR SPONSOR!!! they urged.

When she answered the phone my sponsor's stable words were encouraging.

"We do it one day at a time," she guided. "Stick with the process and don't give up five minutes before the miracle happens."

One morning the landlord pulled up in front of my store just as the last of my display cases was being loaded onto a truck. Although it had been over fifteen years since the incident with Big Johnny, my body still tensed with fear knowing I didn't have the landlord's money.

"I don't have the money I owe you for back rent," I admitted, trying hard to control the quiver in my voice.

Mr. Dody only smiled.

"Don't worry about it," he winked. "If you ever win the lottery, just send me a check!"

On the way home I felt relieved but at the same time, empty and alone.

Where would I go? What would I do? How could I tell my father I had failed again?

Every day became a struggle just to get out of bed.

"Stop looking at those old photographs of your family. You're just making yourself miserable," my friends scolded.

The people at the meetings seemed to agree. I repeatedly heard the same advice: "Change all your people, places, and things. Go to meetings. Call your sponsor, and no matter how bad you feel, don't use drugs or alcohol! It is always better to focus on the solution instead of dwelling on your problems."

One weekend a few people from the Halifax fellowship drove to Yarmouth with the intent to carry the message of recovery to our struggling group. They spoke about the steps to freedom and how the tired old lie, 'once an addict always an addict', was no longer true.

The following month our Area held a small weekend convention. We sent flyers to the groups in Halifax and some of the same people came and brought their families. During one of the meetings I got up the courage to ask for help. A friendly woman named Maryanne came over to speak with me after the closing circle.

"Hi, I'm Peter's wife," she said. "Our house is small, but we have a room in our basement if you'd like to stay with us until you get on your feet. Don't be shy! We would love to have you!"

"Thank you," I smiled gratefully. "I would like that very much."

When the convention was over, I went home to pack my things. By the end of the month I was living in Halifax and had a job waitressing at the Clipper Cay Restaurant on the waterfront. It was after midnight one night when I got home. The house was dark except for the dim light above the stove. A note on the kitchen table caught my eye.

It said, "Kate, Terra phoned. She wants you to call no matter what time you get in. I hope you had a good night. Maryanne."

I sensed trouble right away.

"Hi honey." I whispered. "Sorry to call so late, but I just got in from work."

"That's okay Mom," Terra said. "Dad called and wants you to go to the airport at seven-thirty tomorrow morning to get Isaac."

"To get Isaac? Why? What happened?"

"Nothing. Dad just wants him to stay with you for a while."

"Terra, people don't just send their child clear across the country without making plans in advance unless something is wrong. Now tell me the truth! What is it?"

"I don't know Mum," she replied nervously. "That's all he told me."

Pete and Maryanne had two young children and another on the way. All the bedrooms in their small house were full, so I slept in the carpeted section of their basement. Feelings of happiness welled up in my heart knowing Isaac was on his way, but for some reason, dread lurked in the shadows of my mind.

When my son appeared through the sliding glass doors of the airport, I could see the metamorphosis from small town kid to big city teen had come too soon. Although he had never been interested in basketball, Isaac wore a Chicago Red Bull's cap and shirt. The Red Bull insignia seemed to have some significance I did not understand, and his strong jutting chin held too much power for such a young boy.

I sensed my son was happy to see me and I was proud to introduce him to Pete and Maryanne. After showing him around the house, I took him downstairs so he could put his things away. Isaac never said a word, but his disappointed body language spoke volumes about his less than worthy accommodations. Feelings of inadequacy mocked my efforts to explain.

"Son, I just moved to Halifax recently and I'm in the process of finding my own place to rent. I will sleep on that foam mattress on the floor and you can have the couch. I'm really sorry son, but I didn't know you were coming until late last night so I couldn't take time off from work. Would you like to come with me to the store before I have to go to the restaurant?"

"Yeah, okay," he shrugged indifferently.

On the way back to Pete and Maryanne's Isaac seemed agitated. When I pulled up to a red light his gestures toward the people in the car next to me were angry and inappropriate.

"What are you doing?" I demanded, shocked at what I saw.

"Stupid losers, they deserve it!" he retorted.

"Stop it!" I scolded. "Why did your dad send you here so suddenly son? Are you in trouble?"

"I don't know," he shrugged. "Maybe he just needed a break."

A different car pulled up beside me at the next light, and again, Isaac made the same aggressive motions to the people inside.

"Stop that right now!" I insisted. "If you are going to stay with me you cannot treat people that way!"

"I don't need this shit!" he said and jumped out of the car. Slamming the door behind him he yelled, "I'm hitchhiking back to BC!"

I was distraught. Not knowing what else to do, I pulled up beside him.

"Come on Isaac, please, get back in the car," I pleaded.

Zipping up his jacket, my son spit on the sidewalk.

"I'm outta here," he said, and walked up the street.

"Isaac, I have to be at work in fifteen minutes," I called, driving along beside him. "I didn't know you were coming so I couldn't take time off. Now please, get in the car and I'll take you back to Pete and Maryanne's."

What I didn't know was that my fifteen-year-old son was withdrawing from drugs and alcohol. When I walked into the living room, Pete was concerned.

"What's wrong? You look like you just saw a ghost!"

"I don't know what to do," I started to cry. "Isaac is a few blocks up the street. When I pulled up to a traffic light, he jumped out of the car saying he was hitchhiking back to BC. Pete, I have to go to work. I'm already late as it is."

Pete was nonchalant.

"So go to work! Isaac knows where the house is. Don't worry about him. He'll be okay."

Easier said than done! Trusting my friend's words, I changed into my work clothes and dashed out the door. While serving my customers I was haunted by images of Isaac standing at the onramp of the highway. I pictured him with his thumb was out, hitchhiking back to Vancouver in the brisk evening darkness. Once again, the suggestion I heard from people in the meetings popped into my mind.

"Don't worry about the problem, just focus on the solution."

During my break I went to the payphone. Before dialing Pete's number, I paused to pray.

God, I don't know how to be a good mom. I feel so powerless to help my son. Isaac is angry and I sense he is lost and afraid. What can I do to help him?

An idea flashed into my mind. I dialed Pete's number.

"Hi Pete," I said. "Is Isaac there?"

"Yeah sure, he's sitting right here watching TV with me. Here, I'll let you talk to him."

"Hi Mom."

My son sounded different.

"Hi Isaac. Want to go on a date with me?"

"A date?" he asked, obviously confused by my happy demeanor.

"Yes, out to dinner. There's a great Chinese restaurant in Halifax that I'd like to take you to. It's all the way downtown so if you'd like to go, be ready at 8:00. I'll come by to pick you up right after work."

"I don't have any good clothes to wear Mum," he confided.

"You're fine just the way you are son. I'm so happy to see you. Just bring yourself. That's all that matters to me, not your clothes."

"Okay, see you after work!" he said cheerfully, and hung up the phone.

I didn't know what to think. All my worrying had been for nothing. Isaac was sitting there watching TV with Pete. His anger had dissipated and there would be no angry departure back to British Columbia.

When I picked my son up after work he had on a clean t-shirt and jeans. On the way into the restaurant he tucked in his shirt.

"I'm not very well-dressed Mum," he said again.

"Like I told you before honey, you are fine just the way you are."

Although my finances were scant, I told Isaac to order anything he wanted. He began to relax as we chatted and laughed over dinner. On the way home his behavior was normal and all talk of running away had completely disappeared. The following night I invited him to a meeting.

"A meeting?" he asked. "What's that?"

"Well, it's a place where recovering drug addicts get together for support and to find solutions for a new way of life."

"Do I have to say something?"

"Only if you want to," I assured him.

Over the next couple weeks Isaac continued to relax. On the days I had to work he hitchhiked to Bridgewater to see Josh and from there the two brothers drove to Yarmouth to see Terra. Things seemed to be going well until one day, Isaac decided it was time to go back to British Columbia.

Overnight my youngest son's behavior changed back to the belligerent youth I had picked up at the airport just two weeks before. Although I could see that Isaac was in desperate need of help, I was powerless to make him stay and live a healthy life. He wouldn't talk to me about the situation at his father's, but I sensed it was pretty bad. When it came time to leave for the airport, my son was insecure and needy of my affection.

"Mom, do you still love me?"

Wanting him to know my love was unconditional I said, "Of course son, I would love you even if you committed murder."

Two weeks later I was in the shower getting ready to go to work when the phone rang. Grabbing a towel, I ran out to the kitchen to answer it.

"Hello?" I said, drying off while I spoke.

"Kate? Is that you?"

That's odd, I thought. *Why would Hippie be calling me?*

"Oh hi," I said with hesitation.

"Kate, I'm in big trouble."

Hippie's voice was anxious. His breathing was broken, and I was certain he was pulling on his beard.

"What's wrong?" I asked, the previously lurking dread now clenching at my heart.

"Isaac stabbed a boy last night and the boy died this morning," he whispered.

"Hippie, you aren't in trouble, Isaac is!"

I looked at the clock.

"The police came to my apartment this morning and arrested Isaac," he said. "They took him to the Burnaby Youth Detention Centre to await trial."

"I don't know what to say Hip. I have to leave for work in ten minutes or I'll be late."

I felt bad for not having any words of comfort for Hippie. Although I still loved him, I was angry with him for being a bad influence on our son. I was angry with myself for not speaking out sooner. I was angry with us both for the way we raised our kids. I was angry with my parents for how they raised me.

"Okay, talk to you later," he said, and hung up the phone.

The shock was more than I could bear. I couldn't fix it. I couldn't un-ring the bell. Jesse was gone and I couldn't bring him back. It was done.

I felt a protective band shoot around my upper torso, numbing the feelings that longed to wail for my son, the son who was killed, the families involved, and society as a whole.

I looked at the clock. I was now the mother of a murderer and I had five minutes to catch the bus. I grabbed my coat and hurried up the street.

Isaac killed a boy last night.

An eerie chill filled the air as a gust of wind played with an empty chip bag laying in the gutter. I approached the lineup of people waiting for the bus. Painfully aware of the hole in the finger of my blue knit glove, my thumb inadvertently eased its way over to hide the frayed yarn.

It's all my fault. I raised my kids wrong!

Before boarding the bus, I pulled off the shameful gloves and threw them in the nearest trash can.

All summer I had enjoyed waitressing in the fine dining atmosphere of the Clipper Kay Restaurant, which offers a magnificent view of Halifax Harbor. When business turned slow, I worked downstairs at Salty's Bar & Grille, laughing, and chatting with my coworkers as we watched the ships come into the harbor. But this day was different. This day I stood alone and quiet at the back of the restaurant, watching my tables. One of the other waitresses sensed something was wrong. She came over and stood beside me.

"Are you alright?" she asked.

"Yeah sure," I said. "Just a little tired."

A few minutes later the manager passed by on her way to the kitchen. Stopping directly in front of me, she looked deeply into my eyes.

"Everything okay?" she asked.

I was ready to collapse.

Not now, I told myself. *I have to be strong. How can I tell these people that my son killed a boy? I have to keep it together. I'm at work. I can't cry right now. Isaac must be scared. Oh God, please protect my son. Why did he do it? He's so young. Where is he? Oh God, oh God, oh God...*

I looked around at my coworkers. Their eyes were searching my face.

"Yes, everything's fine," I said, struggling to keep my emotions in check.

When I wasn't checking on my tables I was in the kitchen wiping counters and cleaning the fridge. If I held still the hurt welled up in my eyes, threatening to spill down my cheeks. Our last words echoed through my mind.

"Mum, do you still love me?"

"Yes son, I would still love you even if you committed murder."

Even if you committed murder? Oh, God, why did I have to say that? It's all my fault!

I felt like I was going to die from a broken heart. My whole body ached with despair thinking my youngest son was going to jail for the rest of his life. I had seen prison movies and was aware of the atrocities inflicted on young men by the older, more hardened criminals. I didn't know what else to do but call my sponsor, go to meetings, and wait.

When it was time for the trial, I took a leave of absence from work and flew to British Columbia. The long flight gave me plenty of time to think about the victim's family and the heartache they must be experiencing. Although I wanted to extend my sympathy to the parents for their loss, I knew I had to be careful, for anything I said could be misconstrued by the press as an admission of guilt.

While the other passengers nodded peacefully off to sleep, I worried about what I would do if called to the stand to testify during Isaac's trial. I pushed the button on the arm rest and eased back in my seat. Just as I began to relax, I recalled a movie I had seen a few years before. It was based on a true story about a man who had testified against his teenage son for a drug crime he was accused of committing. At the end of the trial his son was convicted and then beaten and killed in prison. The father's remorse was so great that he could not forgive himself for being the one to help the police prove his son's guilt. He said if he could turn back time, he would have been an advocate for his son and let the police solve the case without his input.

Even though Isaac was pleading not guilty, my mother's heart knew the truth. Like the father in the movie, I promised myself that I would not send my own son to prison. I firmly resolved that if I were subpoenaed to testify, I would go to jail for contempt, but I would not do or say anything that might incriminate Isaac. He was my son, and he needed an advocate.

As the plane descended, I rehearsed my lines for the victim's parents over and over in my mind. *I'm really sorry about what happened to your son.* That was it. I could say nothing more.

When I arrived at the courthouse, the grieving mother was easy to spot. Sitting on the edge of a concrete planter, she was surrounded by a volatile group of people wearing white t-shirts emblazoned with Jesse Cadman's picture on the front. I calmly walked up and delivered my sincere sentiment.

"I'm really sorry about what happened to your son," I said softly, looking directly into her eyes.

"Thank you," Mrs. Cadman meekly replied. As I turned to walk away, I heard her call, "Who are you?"

"Isaac's mother," I called back, just loud enough for her to hear.

When her friends and family heard me say 'Isaac's mother' they came running after me.

"Who did you say you are?"

Their fury was palpable.

I picked up my pace. Without looking back, I headed for the safety of the courthouse. I opened the heavy glass doors and quickly went inside. I was relieved to see the clerk standing at the information desk. When I gave him my son's name he pointed at the tiled staircase.

"All court proceedings take place upstairs," he said, motioning upward with his eyes. "You will be in courtroom number three. It's on the second floor at the end of the hall."

When I got to the second floor, five or six people were outside the courtroom waiting for the doors to open. Their scathing remarks were cruel.

"This young punk deserves the electric chair."

"I hope they lock him away forever."

"This is just a preliminary hearing, but don't you worry; this kid will be hung pretty quick!"

Are they talking about my son, Isaac, the boy everyone loved as a child? Stitches, yes, that was the term. He had us all in stitches.

"Adorable!"

"Hilarious!"

"Bright kid!"

"Good musician!"

"Boy, can he draw!"

These were the things people said about Isaac. He was troubled in school, it's true, but then he never had much of a chance with parents who could not provide the kind of home or care he needed to succeed.

Once again, Isaac's words haunted my mind.

"Do you still love me mom?"

Oh God, I think I'm going to be sick.

Just then, someone inside the courtroom unlocked the large, wooden doors. Alone and afraid, I followed the others inside and took my place on the left near the front. Hippie came in soon after and sat down beside me. The seats behind us remained empty except for a few reporters near the back. The victim's family and friends came in and filled the section on the right. I watched in the quiet commotion as the despondent little mother across from me slumped down in the vacancy of her loss.

Just then the side door opened, and Isaac was brought in wearing handcuffs and shackles. As soon as the court officer got him settled in the small cubicle designed for the accused, the lawyer handed Isaac a pen and paper to help him stay focused during the trial. From the audience's point of view, my son appeared cold and nonchalant, like he felt no remorse at all for what he had done.

Although my son pleaded guilty when he was first arrested, his attorney insisted his words be stricken from the records.

"That statement cannot be used in court," the lawyer informed the sheriff. "This boy is a minor. He was supposed to have either his parents or his lawyer present when you interrogated him."

Although it went against his own conscience, sixteen-year-old Isaac listened to his lawyer's advice and obeyed his father, who was desperately trying to keep his son out of prison. On the first day of his trial, the Vancouver attorney instructed Isaac to keep his eyes down throughout the hearing.

"If we are going to beat these charges you cannot look up at the judge, jury or the gallery. And absolutely do not *ever* make eye contact with either Dona or Chuck Cadman," he warned.

The next day Hippie stopped by Josh's apartment to drive me to court. As we neared the government buildings he parked around the corner from the courthouse.

"Why don't we park closer?" I asked.

"You'll see," was all he would say.

And I did see. Aggressive reporters waited on every corner like greedy vultures stalking their prey. When they saw Hippie's red Volkswagen van pull up to the curb, they flocked around us pointing their cameras in our faces, asking questions we knew not to answer. Neither of us spoke, we just walked straight ahead with an even gaze and steady pace.

When I got home from court that evening, Josh wanted to know if I wanted to watch the news.

"They've been reporting on Isaac's trial, showing videos of you and dad on every channel," he said.

"No thanks son. I don't want to listen to the reporters sensationalizing our tragedy."

If Hippie couldn't pick me up for court, I had to take the bus. Since the other riders had seen my face flashing across their television screens, they were repulsed by the thought of sitting next to the mother of a murderer. If I sat down beside them, they got up and moved. To avoid their scorn, I kept my focus on the scenery outside the bus windows. I could feel the people staring at me with anger and hatred. They clearly thought I was evil, and were afraid that somehow, my darkness would get on them. I, however, knew I was not a monster, and neither was my son.

One day Hippie showed up with one of his friends. Inappropriately dressed in tight jeans and a revealing t-shirt, the young woman paced back and forth during recess, loudly cursing the unfair ways of the judicial system. Hippie's shoulder-length hair was greasy and unkempt, and his mannerisms identified him with the drug life. Wanting to keep to myself, I went to the cafeteria to buy a cup of tea. On the way back I noticed a group of police officers huddled together with several reporters. Their eyes turned away when they saw me, and their voices dropped to whispers as I passed.

"Click, click, click," my high heels echoed in the tiled corridor.

I crossed the hallway and stood alone with my back against the window. The warmth of the sun helped me to relax as my mind drifted back to the first morning I practiced yoga with Kareen Zebroff, the woman on television. The sun illuminated Isaac who lay peacefully beside me on the bed. His smooth baby skin was still soft from the womb and his breath held the scent of my own sweet milk.

Sounds of people gathering in the hallway jerked my consciousness back into the present. Feeling ostracized by the community I stood alone, a veritable pillar of strength. I suddenly got a glimpse of myself from the other peoples' point of view. Rigid and unapproachable, I had unknowingly locked myself away in an imaginary fortress of steel.

My anguished body started to convulse with grief. Through my tears I saw two fifteen-year-old girls hovering nearby. I could tell they wanted to comfort me, but they were afraid of my unpredictable reaction. I calmly held out my hands.

"It's okay," I said softly. "I'm Isaac's mother and I just feel really sad right now."

The dark-haired girl stepped in close to give me a hug.

"My name is Melissa. I was Isaac's girlfriend before all this happened."

The blonde girl stepped up next followed by her mother.

"I knew him too," she said. "I'm Natasha, and this is my mom. We were wondering if you would like to come with us to the cafeteria for lunch."

I appreciated their support and accepted the invitation. Although they didn't come every day, it felt good to have friends who knew and cared about Isaac.

By the end of the week all the testimonies were in. The judge called a recess so the jury could begin their deliberations and then left the courtroom. As soon as the officer took Isaac away, Hippie went for a walk while Dona's family and friends went to the cafeteria, looking for coffee and a bite to eat. When I looked up, I realized Dona and I were alone with our pain on opposite sides of the now silent hallway. Not to say we didn't have people nearby; we did. We could hear the quiet chatter of reporters and police officers further up the hall, their voices echoing in a void we could not touch.

My mind searched helplessly for some understanding, some reason why life had taken our sons so young.

They were only sixteen!

I stepped into the middle of the corridor and held out my arms. To my surprise, Dona came forward to meet my embrace.

"We're in this together," I whispered.

The fragile woman hugged me back and then quickly pulled away.

Glancing up the hall she said, "I have to go back to my side of the corridor. My family is going to come back soon, and they won't understand."

I knew it had to be bad news when the jury returned with their verdict in less than two hours. Isaac was brought in after everyone was settled in their seats.

"All rise," the bailiff's voice was monotone.

When the judge came in and took his seat an expectant hush flooded the room. Everyone else followed his lead except Isaac who was asked to remain standing. The judge shuffled through his papers and then turned to the jury.

"How do you find the defendant?"

"Guilty your honor, of second-degree murder," announced one of the jurors.

The judge's sentence was stiff.

"Life with eligibility for parole after ten years," he commanded. He hit the striking block with his gavel and said, "Court adjourned."

When the officer came over to escort Isaac out of the courtroom Chuck Cadman unexpectedly jumped up and pounded his fist on the banister in front of him.

"May you burn in hell!" he cursed, his pain exploding in a fit of rage.

As my son walked past me my spirit plunged downward, seeking comfort in the gloomy abyss of darkness and despair. Just then, an indomitable surge of energy filled my body and mind with light. Fighting off the demons of dread, a silent wail arose from deep within.

NO! I cried, and a determined force pulled my spirit upward. *If I lose the will to live, my son will feel responsible for the loss of two lives instead of one. Not only will I live, but I will live and be happy!*

That night Josh tried to make me feel comfortable in his small apartment.

"You can have my bed Mum," he said, carrying his sleeping bag out to the living room couch.

As soon as I closed my eyes brutal prison scenes of rape and violence flashed through my mind. Relentless sobs racked my body with grief until I fell into a tortured sleep. Toward morning, the victim's mother appeared in my dream like a prophetic vision. Leaning over my bed she compassionately held out her arms to give me a hug.

"I'm really sorry about what happened to your son," she consoled. When she leaned down to embrace me, she whispered, "We're in this together."

"Thank you," I said, reaching up to accept her hug.

When I awoke my arms were in the air and the dead boy's mother was gone.

After the trial, I visited Isaac a couple times in the youth detention center and then returned to Nova Scotia. Sensing my grief, my friends Pete and Maryanne, invited me to move back in with them. Their kind offer didn't take much convincing. I quickly cleaned out my small apartment and moved back into their basement.

Nova Scotia summers tend to be quite humid. One particularly hot afternoon, Pete and I took their 8-year-old daughter to the beach. While she played with the other kids near the shore, I swam out to the floating wharf and took a few dives. The fresh air, soothing water, and warmth of the sun were much appreciated after the long ordeal in court.

When we got back to the house, Maryanne was sitting on the sofa chatting with an Italian man with short silver hair. The mature-looking man nonchalantly leaned back and stretched his arm across the back of the couch. The top two buttons of his silk shirt had been left undone, revealing a tanned chest adorned with a golden cross hanging on a thick gold chain.

At the beach I had slipped a black cotton dress over my bathing suit. My wavy, auburn hair was still wet, and the white shell beads around my neck made an alluring contrast against my glowing tan skin. When Maryanne introduced us, the man grinned without reserve.

"Hello Kate!" he said, seductively caressing his expensive leather boot. "I remember you from the regional conference last year."

I recalled the day very well. Leaning back in his chair, Mario had flirted with me while I poured water for all the members on the committee.

"You would make someone a good wife," he arrogantly predicted, loud enough for everyone to hear.

Mario's casual remark triggered the good memories I had with Hippie during our fifteen years of marriage. Without looking up, I poured the rest of the water and quietly left the room.

Mario Poletti worked as a counselor at a recovery house in Montreal. Clean of all drugs and alcohol for the past six years, his service in the 12-step fellowship to which I belonged, had evolved to the world level.

Could this be the silver-haired man Edna saw in my cards? I wondered.

Mario appeared to have a lot of money, which to me meant he could take care of a woman properly. Since he spoke with great passion about his love for God, I invited him out to the back porch to talk. When it was time for Pete to drive him to the airport, the romantic Italian kissed me on each cheek and promised to call. I was downstairs that evening when I heard the phone ring.

"Kate!" Pete called. "It's for you. It's Mario!"

The next day the florist delivered a dozen red roses. The following week, a gift-wrapped box of Italian chocolates arrived in the mail. Over the following month Mario's long-distance phone calls became more and more frequent.

When he came to visit, Mario took me to one of Halifax's finest Italian restaurants. Skillfully twirling his spaghetti, he bragged about his past involvement with organized crime. While savoring a rich dessert of tiramisu, Mario boasted of the large shipments of guns he had helped send to other countries. His manicured nails glistened in the lamplight as he sipped espresso, boasting clever innuendos about how people were tracked when they tried to escape their fraudulent drug deals. Although he assured me it was all in the past, I became frightened one day by an unexpected phone call.

I had flown to BC for Isaac's preliminary trial with no idea where I would be staying or with whom. All I knew was that a friend of a friend had arranged for me to be picked up at the airport when I arrived from Nova Scotia. When I came through the arrival gate, a woman holding a sign with my name on it was waiting for me in the crowded Vancouver Airport. We made the usual small talk during the drive to her house and as soon as we walked in the door the phone began to ring.

"Hello?" she answered. "Yes, she's here. Just one moment." Seeing the puzzled look on my face she said, "It's for you."

As she handed me the phone I was surprised. I couldn't imagine who would be calling me at her house since I hadn't given anyone her phone number.

"Babe, I found you!" Mario laughed, as though he was playing a game of hide and seek with a little child.

Chills waved over my body. I was already so vulnerable over my son's upcoming trial that I easily became paranoid and afraid. Mario had only been in recovery for six years. His glorified tales of crime, nightclubs, and beautiful women made me wonder what an espresso-drinking man with manicured nails, expensive silk shirts, and seven-hundred-dollar alligator boots wanted with a vegetarian woman who drinks chamomile tea wearing cotton dresses and Birkenstocks.

I promised I would stay in touch but as I hung up the phone, I missed Hippie's homemade gifts and longed for the simple way of life we enjoyed on our land. Kerosene lamps, tending our garden, chopping wood, raising kids; these things meant more to me than expensive clothes and fancy restaurants. Wanting to understand what a healthy relationship looked like, I sought help from a few happily married women once I returned to work in Nova Scotia.

"Mario seems to be a good man, but I don't love him the way I loved my husband. Do I trust my heart or stick with reasoning?" I asked, but their answers varied.

Not knowing what else to do, I decided to try the truth.

"I'm sorry Mario, but this relationship isn't working," I admitted the next time he called.

"You are still in love with your ex-husband!" he accused defensively. "Most divorced women are quick to let go of their ex-husband's last name, but you kept his. And besides, you still have his name tattooed on your arm!"

For once my response was calm.

"All my life I have hidden the truth about who I am and what I want. That is how I got divorced in the first place. You are absolutely right. Night and day, I think of my ex-husband and children. My youngest son is alone in prison with no spiritual support. It's time for me to start listening to my heart. I am moving to BC."

"Does that mean we're through?" Mario asked.

"Yes," I admitted. "I'm not in love with you Mario, and we both need to get on with our lives."

"I'm going with you. Please, Kate," he begged, "if you would just give our relationship a chance you would see we belong together!"

Not wanting to hurt his feelings, I gave in to Mario's desperate plea but as soon as we moved into our apartment in BC, I knew I had made a serious mistake. For the first time in fifty years, Mario was away from the comfort zone of his family and friends in Montreal. His insecurities were suffocating and his need for control intimidating. Before going to bed one night I told him I needed some time alone.

"Tomorrow morning I'll be going into the spare bedroom to fast and meditate for three days," I said. "I need to get clear on what I want for my life."

I had just finished my morning meditation on the second day when Mario started pounding on the locked door.

"Kate! Open this door right now! I need to talk to you! Kate! Open this door!" he demanded, violently jiggling the handle.

Sensing his fear, I kept my voice calm but firm.

"I need to be alone, Mario. We will talk when I come out."

Enraged by my refusal to do as he commanded, Mario banged on the door a few more times and then went downstairs and left the house. I looked around at the newly carpeted bedroom. It was empty except for my sleeping bag, journal, pen, and two books, *Silence Speaks* and *Autobiography of a Yogi*. During the flight from Halifax to BC I read the book, *The Cross and the Switchblade* by David Wilkerson. Like Gideon from the Bible, the small-town minister sought direction by putting a fleece before the Lord. Wanting to do the right thing for myself, my family, and Mario, I got down on my knees to pray.

Lord, I need a sign. If you want me back with Hippie, please get him clean and in recovery in the next three days.

It was late that night when Mario came home. I heard him in the kitchen getting something to eat before going to bed. About four o'clock in the morning I awoke to the sound of my own voice calling, "HIPPIE!" Startled by my heartfelt summons, my hand flew up to cover my mouth. Afraid that Mario might have heard me I sat up and listened until I was sure he was still asleep.

I was cooking supper that evening when Mario came in from work. Glad to see I was out of the locked bedroom, he came into the kitchen and cornered me against the counter.

"Babe!" he cried, kissing my face.

His male bravado was really getting on my nerves. I struggled to back away, but Mario blocked me by pressing his hard, bloated belly against my body.

"C'mon babe," he taunted. "One little kiss won't hurt anything now will it?"

Now clear that the relationship was over, I turned my face away in disgust. At the supper table my conversation was guarded. "Please pass the potatoes" and "Would you like more salad?" was the best I could do. We did the dishes in silence and then Mario went upstairs to read. Knowing my appearance in the bedroom would arouse him sexually, I stayed downstairs to write in my journal. When I heard his bedside lamp click off, I waited until I thought he was asleep, and then hid my journal in the downstairs closet.

I was relieved to see Mario's back as I climbed beneath the covers. Lying stiffly on my side of the bed, I controlled my breathing so as not to trigger his unwanted affections. Just as I was beginning to relax, he got out of bed and crept stealthily downstairs. Acutely sensitive to his every move I sat up in bed to listen. When I heard the slow squeak of the closet door my mind raced with fear.

Mario is looking for my journal!

Although I trusted this man to be sincere on his spiritual path, his insecurities had awakened his old defects of character. With a quick toss of the covers, I flew down the carpeted stairs before he had a chance to touch my book. Knowing better than to provoke a jealous man with angry accusations, I slowed my pace near the bottom of the stairs and casually walked past him, yawning on my way into the kitchen.

"I need a drink of water," I said, without raising my eyes.

Looking sheepish, Mario closed the closet door and went back upstairs. I sat down at the kitchen table and shuffled a deck of cards. After several games of solitaire, I took my journal out of the closet and went back up to bed. Once my writing was safely beneath the mattress, I once again controlled my breathing and drifted cautiously into sleep.

The next morning, I phoned Hippie as soon as Mario left for work. After three rings the answering machine clicked on.

"Hippie if you're there, please pick up the phone. I really need to talk to you."

"Hello?" he sounded puzzled.

"Can we meet?" I asked. "We really need to talk."

"Give me a couple days," he said, and wrote down my address.

The sun's warmth felt good on my face as I stood in front of the apartment building waiting for Hippie to arrive. The dreary spring rains had finally let up after two months of continuous downpour. Trees were sending out new shoots and the tightly formed buds framing the lawn were just beginning to bloom. I felt at ease seeing the red Toyota van pull up to the curb. Hippie handed me a rose through the open window and then snapped my picture.

"I would have come right away but I needed a couple days to get clean," he explained.

The fleece I placed before God three days before flashed through my mind.

Lord, I need a sign. If you want me back with Hippie, please get him clean and in recovery in the next three days.

As Hippie made his way up the mountain highway, I watched the jade waters of the Fraser River ease their way around the rocks far below. As soon as he found a spot to pull over, he turned off the van.

"Hip', the divorce wasn't entirely your fault," I confessed, when we got out to enjoy the view. "I wanted so much to have a good home for our children that I lost sight of our family as a whole. Then, when the kids started getting into trouble, I tried so hard to be a good example that I became self-righteous and drove everyone away. I'm really sorry. Please forgive me. I don't know how to do everything right, but I do know I love you the same as I've always loved you."

Hippie was surprised.

"I love you too," he admitted. "All this time I thought everything was my fault. I never seemed to be able to measure up to your high standards, so I felt like a failure no matter what I did. When you left, I thought I was going to die from the loneliness. I couldn't stand seeing you with other men. That's why I went to the West Coast."

When I explained what was going on with Mario, Hippie took me back to the apartment to pack my suitcase. He arranged for me to stay with one of his friends and then drove me over to meet her and her infant son. He picked me up every night to go to recovery meetings and when he was clean from all drugs and alcohol for six months, we decided it was time to move in together.

Hippie's carpet cleaning business began to pick up and one night after our 12-Step meeting, a man offered me a job at an emergency center for troubled teens.

"I think you would be good at the job," he encouraged, handing me a card. "Here's the number. Call for an interview. The supervisor's name is Faye Dunphy. It's a great place to work and you couldn't find a better boss."

Faye had worked with troubled youth many years before coming to Ballam House. A short, stout woman with piercing black eyes, she had a special love for damaged children such as these.

"Most of them have been raised in an atmosphere of physical, mental, and emotional abuse," she instructed her staff. "Study their backgrounds so when they come home filthy, drunk, and stoned you will understand it's all they knew from their childhood environment. That is the familiar for them.

"We must treat each of them as individuals and not see them as bad kids. Their successes are not like normal, more nurtured children, and placing unrealistic expectations on them is the worst thing we can do. At the same time, we cannot write them off as stupid or incapable of growth.

"Part of your job will be to attend workshops where you will learn to protect yourselves as well as the kids. You will also be taught to work together as a team. The leaders will demonstrate how to safely restrain the teens if they are out of control, but it is imperative that you learn how to break down their hysteria before it escalates into violence. Sometimes experiencing compassion will be the only success needed to surmount the problems of the day."

Two house parents, one male and one female, were on duty fourteen hours a day. To give consistency to the kids' lives, our shifts were four days on and four days off. The night watchman did all the cleaning and checked on the kids every hour until the morning crew took over at eight o'clock. During the day Faye helped us problem solve with the kids. Some of our duties were to take them on special outings, arrange their health care appointments, and accompany them to court. When I arrived for my shift one afternoon Faye was in the office speaking with a co-worker.

"Connie is coming back to Ballam. She and the social worker will arrive at about three o'clock," she informed, as we gathered together for our shift change.

I detected a slight waver in her voice.

"Who is Connie?" I asked, tossing my jacket over the back of the chair.

"You'll see," Faye promised. "Connie is one of our more difficult kids, but we love her just the same."

When the social worker dropped Connie off, the young girl waved goodbye and then went directly into the office to talk to Faye. She seemed like a decent enough kid, sweet, well-behaved, and courteous. When she went to her room to put her things away, I questioned Faye about her nervous reaction earlier.

"I don't get it. When you said Connie was coming back to Ballam you looked like there was a monster on the way. This girl seems like such a sweet kid. I don't understand why she's even in care."

"It's called the honeymoon phase," Faye explained. "At first the kids are on their best behavior and then suddenly, all hell breaks loose. Remember, we are the end of the line for most kids who come to this emergency facility. Their own parents either don't want them or can't handle them, and they have been in and out of foster homes for years. Since most of them are thirteen, fourteen, and fifteen years of age, the police don't even want anything to do with them until they are sixteen. They are devious, self-absorbed, and totally lacking in empathy or any sense of other.

"Connie has been in and out of Ballam House six times over the past year," continued Faye. "Although she just turned fourteen, she has been drinking, taking drugs, and having promiscuous sex since she was eleven or twelve years old. This girl has been our greatest challenge as well as our greatest opportunity for compassion."

By the next morning, I realized just how much Faye knew her business. Sensing my vulnerability, Connie targeted me right away. She sarcastically refused the kindness I offered, and cruelly made fun of me when I emotionally held back. When she was finally accepted into a new foster home, I was relieved to see her go.

The atmosphere at the group home quickly returned to a sense of normalcy now that Connie was gone. There were still the everyday ups and downs, but generally speaking, we had a pretty good group of kids. One morning Faye called us into the office. Her dark eyes were filled with concern.

"Connie has been drinking and staying away from her new home for two and three days at a time. When she does show up, her language is vile, and her attitude is obnoxious and rude. Her foster parents are distraught. They called social services this morning saying they want her out of their house NOW. Since we have an empty bed, we have to take her."

"I need to go for a walk," I said, trying to hide my loathing for the intolerable brat.

"Perfect," Faye consoled. "Take care of yourself at all times. That is the success of a great house parent. Know your limitations. We can't be there for others if we are not balanced and okay within ourselves."

Tears streamed down my face as I walked the streets of the quiet residential neighborhood.

I hate her, I admitted to myself with deep remorse. *How can I possibly hate a kid?*

Images of my stepsister Liz suddenly flashed through my mind.

Connie reminds me of Liz when she was a kid! I thought. *All those times Mom and Dad left me alone to care for her I was just a child myself. With no training or family support I was expected to cope with a disturbed little girl who had been emotionally and physically abused most of her young life.*

Suddenly filled with compassion, I stopped at the corner and bowed my head to pray.

Please God, show me the way. I want to love, not hate. Please help me to understand and be kind to this girl.

"Connie is a pearl of great price," whispered the all-knowing Voice from deep within.

For some reason I looked up at the signpost I was leaning against. As though in agreement with my inner Voice, the prophetic words inscribed in bold black letters read PEARL AVENUE.

I suddenly knew what to do. I ran all the way back to Ballam House and filled a pail with warm, soapy water. It was our duty to clean the rooms for new arrivals, but this time I scrubbed every corner with concentrated love and attention. After vacuuming the carpet, I searched the linen closet for a matching set of sheets and the best quality towels that I could find. Instead of our usual way of placing them on the dresser, I made up the bed and then went out to the garden to pick a bouquet of flowers.

When everything was ready, I closed the door and stood in the middle of the room. Holding Connie's face firmly in my mind, I mentally invited her to come as one of my greatest teachers. About ten minutes later, the social worker pulled into the driveway. With no show of emotion, Connie got out of the car and went into the office to see Faye. Unlike ever before, she remained well-behaved throughout her stay. The following week her social worker called, saying she had found new foster parents for Connie. Six months later, Connie stopped by with her mother.

"Here," she said, proudly handing Faye a tin of homemade Christmas cookies. "I made these myself."

Seeing our hesitant faces, she started to laugh.

"Don't worry, they're not poisoned! I just want to thank you all for helping me through such a hard time in my life."

Hippie and I had been back together for a little over a year when I started noticing some of his old friends coming around. They never came upstairs into the house but stayed in the basement speaking in whispers while Hippie worked on his Harley. Whenever I came downstairs to say hello all conversation stopped, and they would give reasons why they suddenly had to get going.

Every weekend that I didn't have to work, Hippie and I drove into the mountains to see Isaac. During our visits I noticed silent gestures passing between father and son. Whenever I left to go to the bathroom, they put their heads together to whisper; upon my return, their speech was inundated with codes I didn't understand. If I asked any questions the uncomfortable cutting of their eyes told me I was on the opposite side of the fence and not privy to their secrets.

Although Hippie often spoke about going into treatment, the right time never seemed to come. He continued to go to meetings but remained on the perimeter as though it were all a game. Still unable to speak openly with my partner I kept my suspicions inside, hoping things would somehow resolve themselves with no input from me.

At home I continued to do the energization techniques and study the lessons from Paramahansa Yogananda. One day I received a notice in the mail from the *Self-Realization Fellowship* in Los Angeles. The Mother Center was announcing its yearly convocation and all members were invited. Since Yogananda's book had helped me so much over the years I prayed for guidance on how to proceed.

Dear Lord, all these years I hoped you would send me a living guru to guide me and be an example in my everyday life. I am beginning to accept it is not meant to be. Like Jesus, Paramahansa Yogananda is alive in spirit even though he has left his body. If it is Thy will, I am happy to take initiation at the Mother Center in Los Angeles.

I dialed the phone number listed in the invitation. After asking several questions about my spiritual practice, the receptionist assured me that I was ready to receive initiation. She gave me the nearby hotel prices for the duration of my stay along with the cost of the retreat.

"Can I call you right back? I need to consider my financial situation before deciding where I will stay."

"Of course. Just give us a call whenever you are ready," she replied.

I went to the kitchen to make a cup of tea.

Going to Los Angeles will be expensive, I thought as I poured the boiling water into my cup.

I returned to the table and settled back in my chair. The warm afternoon sun felt good as it filtered through the geese crocheted along the bottom edge of our white lace curtains. Sipping the fragrant chamomile tea calmed my busy thoughts as I flipped through the *Common Ground Magazine*. A large black and white photograph suddenly caught my eye. It was the silent monk from Silence Speaks; the book Elizabeth brought to the cabin in Nova Scotia so many years before. According to the article, he was teaching at a yoga retreat that weekend on an island not far from my home. Excited by my good fortune, I dialed the number given in the ad.

251

"Will Baba Hari Dass really be there, or will it be his students teaching at the retreat?" I asked the receptionist.

"Oh yes, it will be him. He comes every summer," she assured me.

Excited with the prospects of meeting such a One, I booked my reservation and went to get ready. When Hippie came home, he saw me packing.

"Where are you going?" he asked, looking confused.

"I know this is short notice, but I just found out there is a four-day yoga retreat this weekend on Salt Spring Island with Baba Hari Dass. You may remember him; he's the silent monk who wrote *Silence Speaks*. I've been studying his teachings for many years. The receptionist at the Center arranged a ride for me with two other people. They should be here in about half an hour."

After boarding the ferry, I stood outside on the deck watching for whales. A serene-looking man approached me from behind.

"Where are you headed?" he asked.

"I'm on my way to a yoga retreat on Salt Spring Island to meet my guru," I responded easily.

"I've been there many times," he said. "Ask for an appointment as soon as you arrive."

"You mean I can speak with him personally?" I asked.

"Yes, just ask for Anuradha. She will be the one with the long blonde hair who is buzzing all around taking care of details. Oh, and while you're in the meeting with Babaji ask for a name and a mantra."

A loud voice suddenly boomed over the loudspeaker, interrupting our conversation.

"The ferry is now approaching the dock. All passengers are asked to please return to their vehicles."

"A name?" I asked, but when I turned around, the man was gone.

Well that was strange. Ask for a name? I wonder what he meant by that.

The lobby at the retreat center was crowded with people waiting to register for the retreat. Newcomers stood quietly in line, while old friends hugged and talked in groups. Staff wearing aprons deftly weaved their way through the crowd, sweeping, mopping, and restocking the tea bar. As the man on the ferry predicted, a woman with long blonde hair suddenly rushed in through the open double doors. I watched as she flitted from room to room welcoming new arrivals and directing staff. She was just about to dash back out the door when I stepped out of line.

"Excuse me," I said shyly. "I'd like to make an appointment to see Baba Hari Dass."

"Sure," she said, taking a small notebook out of her pocket. "What's your name?"

After quickly scribbling on one of the pages she said, "Your appointment is tomorrow morning during yoga class. I will come in to get you so be ready. And by the way, we call him Babaji," she smiled, before running back out the door.

That evening many of the retreat participants gathered on the floor of the main room for a devotional service. Feeling insecure and disconnected, I sat near a post in the middle of the room. A woman dressed in white got up and knelt in front of an altar decorated with fresh flowers and pictures of saints. She made some motions with her hands and then waved a small brass lamp with five burning wicks while the audience sang and clapped their hands. As soon as the ceremony was finished, the woman went around the room offering sweets. Pleasantly lulled by the music, I did like the others and waited with upheld hands. I suddenly remembered my guru and sat up with a jerk.

Babaji! I gasped. *I forgot to bring Babaji a gift!*

In Paramahansa Yogananda's book *Autobiography of a Yogi,* he educated his readers on the importance of bringing the guru a gift.

I must have a gift for Babaji! I inwardly demanded.

Just then a small orange blossom plopped into my lap. I looked up to see the lady in white smiling at me. The colorful flower had fallen from her plate when she leaned forward to put a spoonful of candies into my open palm. As soon as she moved to the next person, I hurried up to my room to put my simple offering in water.

That night the August air was sweltering in the cramped quarters of my small room. The registrar had assigned me to a dorm that was shared with three other women. They noisily discussed their kids, pets, houses, and gardens while I rested quietly on my bed mentally chanting, *Babaji! Babaji! Babaji!*

After the last lamp clicked off, I waited for the women's breathing to deepen before taking my sleeping bag outside where the night air was fresh and cool. Lying on the grassy mound beside what looked like a large circus tent, I fell asleep gazing at the stars shimmering in a clear black sky. Early the next morning, I awoke to the gentle sound of someone playing a guitar.

"Ha-ree Krishna, Govinda, har-ay, har-ay," sang a balding man with wispy, shoulder-length hair as he walked about the land to awaken the retreat participants for morning meditation. Not wanting to miss anything, I quickly rolled up my sleeping bag and ran inside to take a shower. By the time I got to the meditation hall it was already filling with people. I grabbed a cushion and took my place on the floor at the back of the room. After a few minutes, an Indian man dressed in a white robe came in and sat cross-legged on a low seat at the front of the room. He wrote something on a small whiteboard which the man to his right read aloud.

I thought my heart was going to burst. This was him! The guru I had prayed for so many years before in the backwoods of Nova Scotia. When it was time to instruct us on the yogic methods of breath control, the man sitting beside Babaji suggested we close our eyes for the duration of the meditation class. I did as he asked, but every now and again I peeked through my slightly open lids, trying to catch a glimpse of my newly found Master. Like the porcelain sage of my childhood, Babaji's silver hair embellished the shoulders of his white robe, and he spoke without saying a word.

After the class ended, the guru stood up, pressed his hands together in prayer position, and left the room. The retreat participants noisily dispersed to various classes, taking their pillows and mats with them. I was just unrolling my yoga mat at the back of the room when Anuradha slipped through the crowd and quietly tapped me on the shoulder.

"It's time for your appointment," she said.

"Do I have time to run upstairs?" I asked. "I have a gift for Babaji."

The blonde woman looked at her watch.

"Yes, but hurry!"

When I entered the room, the silent monk smiled as though he had known me for a thousand years.

"Here Babaji, it's a flower for you," I said, shyly placing the nasturtium bloom on a corner of his seat.

Without even a blink, he took the small blossom and flicked it into the large potted bush beside him. The magnitude of his Presence was so peaceful that all the anguish and confusion in my heart lifted, and I began to cry. He waited a moment and then wrote, "What do you do?"

"I work with street kids," I said, wiping my face with my sleeve.

The faces of the young men I had seen in prison while visiting Isaac suddenly flashed through my mind.

"Babaji, all our children are in prison!" I exclaimed.

He pointed to the inner fold of his elbow as if to ask if I had used intravenous drugs.

"Yes," I nodded, wondering how he knew.

"There are no drugs in your aura," he wrote.

"No, I have been clean a long time," I admitted, my tears beginning to dry.

"Keep your focus on the Divine and you need never fall back again," he advised.

"Okay, but that won't be easy!" I laughed nervously.

He nodded his head and made a slight clicking sound with his tongue as if to agree with me.

"Oh, yes," I said, "I almost forgot. May I have a Sanskrit name and a mantra?"

"Write your name and birth date on a piece of paper and give it to Anuradha," he wrote.

Just then, Anuradha opened the door.

"Time's up," she said, pointing to her watch.

Touching my head respectfully to the floor, I thanked Babaji and left the room.

During teatime that afternoon Babaji held up a folded note and motioned for me to come up and get it. I was excited. I was getting my new name. Feeling accepted and loved, I quickly made my way through the friendly crowd of people who were sitting on the grass eating watermelon and drinking chai. Babaji handed me the note and I went off by myself to read what it said.

"Your name is Supriya: It means one who is loved by all. It's a name for a goddess."

My Sanskrit mantra was written below along with my guru's direction to keep it to myself.

On the last day of the retreat I was standing all alone on the front porch of the main house when Babaji unexpectedly walked by. For some peculiar reason he too was all alone and walking quite fast.

"Goodbye Babaji!" I called like a forlorn little child.

Hearing my innocent voice so full of yearning, Babaji suddenly stopped and turned to look at me. The words *'come to Mount Madonna,'* flashed through my mind and then he continued walking up the road.

Mount Madonna? I thought. *What is Mount Madonna?*

I went back inside the lobby.

"What is Mount Madonna?" I asked the lady at the information table.

"Oh, it's our sister center in California," she said, pointing to a stack of brochures on the table near the wall. "Please take one. All the information you need is right there."

When I got back home, I was once again bothered by the distinct feeling that something was not right. Hippie's carpet cleaning business had picked up over the past several months, but it could not possibly provide the amount of money he was spending on restaurants, concerts, and expensive chrome for his motorcycle. Although he was the Area Service Representative for our 12-Step group, Hippie remained distant from the members of the fellowship. He went to meetings and spoke at the local detox unit, but I never saw him do any written work. When we went to the prison for special events with Isaac his aura became dull and contracted.

Before leaving for the retreat I told myself that Hippie was new in recovery and to give him more time. After a couple months of doing the daily spiritual practices from Babaji, I no longer doubted what I saw. I decided to call my daughter in Nova Scotia.

"Hi Terra," I said. "I have to ask you something. Where is your dad getting all the money?"

"I don't know Mum," she said, and began to cry.

I was surprised by her reaction.

"Terra, what's going on?" I asked, now concerned for the welfare of our whole family.

"Mom, Dad has been sending one of my friends marijuana through the mail," she admitted. "I felt bad all those times you said you were glad there were no more family secrets. I'm sorry Mom. Really sorry."

I felt numb.

"I have to go Terra," I said.

"Please Mum," she said. "Don't be mad at me."

"Terra, your dad has to do what he has to do, but so do I. I'm not mad at anyone honey. I'm just really tired of all the lies and have some things I need to think about."

After hanging up the phone, I sat down on the couch. I didn't know what to do next. *What* I would say to Hippie was not the question, but *how* I would say it. Preserving Terra's anonymity was not going to be easy.

Terra!

My mind was in shock.

My daughter was the one who always spoke out against such things. Terra, the noble one. Terra, the one I could trust. And Hippie is our Group Service Representative! Every Thursday night he speaks at the detox. How can he do this? Do the men he sponsors know he is selling marijuana? And are they buying it from him?

My mind reeled with suspicions and condescending moral judgements.

On the way to the meeting that night Hippie was sensitive to my silence.

"What's wrong?" he asked, keeping his eyes focused on the road ahead.

"I'll tell you later," I replied, wanting to clear my mind before broaching the difficult subject.

As soon as the people at the meeting were settled, the chairperson called on Hippie to share. Listening to him speak about the miracles of recovery I recalled my daughter's recent disclosure.

Just like he has done his whole life, I thought. *Even in recovery he's bluffing his way through. Why can't he just get honest and be who he truly is?*

Still spiritually immature, I was unable to understand and tolerate Hippie's shortcomings. The survival skills he had learned as a boy and then honed for many years of his adult life could not be overcome in a few months. On the way home I stayed quiet until he pulled into our driveway.

"Hippie, where is all the money was coming from?" I asked.

He turned off the engine and leaned forward on the steering wheel.

"Cleaning carpets, why?"

"Are you selling pot?" I asked directly.

"No!" he snapped defensively.

His eyes darted about like a scared rabbit ready to dash.

"Hippie please, tell me the truth. Are you selling pot?"

"No!" he repeated a second time. "Who told you that?"

"Terra," I admitted, knowing the truth had to come out.

"She's lying!" he protested.

"No Hippie. Terra started to cry when she told me. I know my daughter; she is telling the truth."

"She's lying," he repeated, and went inside the house.

The next day I wrote to Babaji asking him to be my teacher. I told him I would like to come to Mount Madonna Center to study with him for one year. A week later his reply was in the mailbox.

"Dear Supriya," he wrote. "If you have taken refuge in God then yes, I will be your teacher. You can write to me if you have any questions about your spiritual practice. Contact the Mount Madonna staff for information about coming to stay at the Center."

I phoned right away and then made arrangements to go. When Hippie came home that evening, I told him I was going to California to study with Babaji.

"I will be gone for one year," I said. "If you want to get your life together that's up to you, but this is something I need to do for myself."

The following week Hippie angrily threw my luggage into the van and drove me to the airport. When my plane landed in San Jose my brother, Don, was waiting to drive me up into the mountains.

"Are you sure you're going to be okay Sis?" he sounded worried as we set up my tent. "I mean, you're up here all alone in the mountains. You don't know who or what could be prowling around in these woods at night."

All I could think of was Babaji.

"I'll be fine," I promised. "Thanks a lot Don, really. Hey, look! There are a few other tents right over there. I won't be alone. If anything happens, I'll call out for help."

"Okay Sis," he said. "But I feel kind of strange leaving you here alone like this. Are you sure you are going to be okay?"

I gave him a hug.

"Yes, Brother," I reassured him. "Everything is going to be fine. You'll see."

Right from the beginning I had it in my mind that I would be staying at Mount Madonna Center for a year. Although it was obvious that I was fit for ashram life, the staff kept reminding me that I had to finish my three-month probation period and then apply for an extension. It became the ongoing joke that when anyone asked how long I was staying at Mount Madonna I responded, "For one year!"

Toward the end of my three-month program, I was unexpectedly invited to a private meeting in the downstairs room of the Community Building. I had no idea I was about to be offered the job as supervisor of Mount Madonna's 500-person capacity Conference Center.

"No thanks," I quickly replied. "I'm just here to live in my tent and study with Babaji."

"We have been watching you and think you would be great at this job," said Sunanda, the spokesperson for the middle management staff.

"Thanks, but I don't have any experience with this kind of work. Besides, I want to keep my time open for studying with Babaji," I said.

A few days later Sunanda called me back for another meeting.

"We would really like you to reconsider the job as supervisor of the CC (Conference Center)," she urged. "Your organizational skills are excellent, your ideals match those of the Center's, and you have a good way with the staff. As long as your responsibilities are taken care of you can make up your own schedule.

"We encourage everyone who lives here on the land to attend Babaji's classes and participate in the Center retreats. If you accept the position you will receive a stipend and your monthly fee will be waved. Your food, lodging, retreat attendance, and classes will all be free. You will also have one of the nicest rooms on the land. And just think, you can move out of your tent and have your own shower right in your room!"

"I'll have to think about it. It's a big responsibility and I have never done anything like this before. And what about my observance of silence every Monday? I don't break my austerity no matter what comes."

"We have watched you communicate on your chalkboard on Mondays and you do very well. It's generally pretty slow here for programs that day so you can make Monday one of your days off. We believe in you and hope you will agree to take the position. We work as a team here so if you need any help just let us know. Think it over and give us your decision by the end of next week."

Other than my lack of experience, the job at the CC sounded perfect for me. My three-month program was almost over, and I didn't have the money to pay for an extended stay at Mount Madonna. Besides, it was now the end of November, which meant it was dark when I climbed the mountain to get to my tent after dinner and taking early morning showers in an outdoor stall was a little chilly.

I accepted the position and quickly became an integral member of the community. I learned all the yogic practices and flourished in the spiritual atmosphere of ancient rituals and Vedic mantras. By the end of my first year I not only ran the Conference Center but organized and ran the staff for every program space on the entire land.

At the beginning of my stay I called Hippie from the lobby payphone a couple of times, but our conversations always left me crying when I hung up. Even though I gave him my phone number and address he never tried to call or write to me even once. I finally realized that if I were to find peace, I had to let go of the past and keep my focus on where I was. Although I was lonely at first, I slowly adapted to the new people and ways of ashram life.

Three days a week one of Babaji's devotees picked him up and drove him up the mountain, about an hour from his home in Bonny Doon. On those days he guided us in meditation and taught classes on the Bhagavad-Gita and Patanjali's Yoga Sutras. Thanksgiving, Christmas, and Easter were all celebrated with traditional feasts and devotional worship.

Not only did our 70-year-old teacher participate in the Center events, but he spent three months of every year at the orphanage he and his devotees built in India. At night he answered our letters and wrote scriptural commentaries which were edited and published by his students. During the day he taught classes and worked with the rock crew, building temples, caves, and rock walls. And even with all of that, Babaji still had time for walks with us in the morning and tea in the afternoon.

My first year at the ashram was spent watching my teacher's every move. I had heard about false gurus and morally debasing cults and wanted to make sure that Babaji's actions matched his words. Every Sunday many devotees went to the Pacific Cultural Center (PCC) in Santa Cruz to sing, play devotional music, study scripture, and meditate with Babaji. Since one of my duties was to run errands for the Conference Center, I drove the work truck into Santa Cruz every Sunday to pick up what I needed after the spiritual gathering ended.

The day finally came when I was ready to trust Babaji as my spiritual guide. Feeling safe to love him without hesitation, I bought a dozen roses and then proceeded to the PCC. When I arrived, the main room was already crowded with people singing and playing the harmonium, guitar, and tabla[6]. Feeling extremely self-conscious with my bouquet of flowers, I went to the kitchen to get a vase. Once the flowers were arranged to my satisfaction, I ignored the curious stares from onlookers and walked straight up the center aisle to where Babaji was sitting. Mustering up all my courage, I looked him in the eye and then set the vase of roses on the small tile near his seat.

After taking my usual place on the floor near my teacher, I noticed that I could no longer gaze adoringly at Babaji as I usually did. Wanting to overcome my avoidance, I forced myself to look at him. Seeing his thinning gray hair, aging skin, and bloated belly triggered my childhood abandonment issues, causing tears to well up and spill down my cheeks.

Babaji is old and will die soon, leaving me alone and unprotected the way my mother did when I was two, I worried.

To stop the onrush of tears, I closed my eyes and a flash of energy whooshed out from the center of my forehead. The sounds of people singing and playing music completely disappeared and I found myself in what appeared to be a railyard in another country. As though awake in a dream I walked without legs, saw without eyes, heard without ears, smelled without a nose, and tasted without a tongue.

A cacophony of honking vehicles filled with soldiers suddenly pulled up to a crowd of frantic people inside what looked like a large pen for wild animals. The men were being herded off to the left of the barbed wire enclosure and the women were grouped together with their children on the right. The dusty air vibrated from the drone of waiting trains as the barrage of low-ranking soldiers ruthlessly grabbed wailing infants away from their mothers. Frightened toddlers clung to their mothers' legs, and hysterical women screamed as their babies were ripped out of their arms

---

[6]   Tabla: a set of twin hand drums from India.

by the uniformed men. If any of the men moved to protect their wives and children, they were brutally beaten or killed.

As the chaos ensued, I noticed a couple of the soldiers casting reluctant glances at their superior officer who was standing off to one side. Watching with icy indifference, his steely gaze met their hesitant looks with a slight nod, and he made a stiff, cutting motion with his hand. His silent response was clear. His men were to take the children and get the women onto the waiting trains as fast as possible. My chest began to heave.

THAT OFFICER WAS ME!

"I'm so sorry! I'm so sorry! I'm so sorry! I cried over and over from the depths of my soul.

As quickly as the vortex of energy expanded outward, it suddenly withdrew. No longer in the devastating turmoil of Nazi Germany, I was now sitting back in the room full of devotional people singing and clapping to the spiritual music. Unrestrained tears flooded down my face as my guru's thoughts merged telepathically into my own.

"It's okay, you can go to the orphanage to be with the children whether I am there or not," Babaji said compassionately.

"Okay, but I'm really, really sorry,""" I said, transmitting my thoughts back to him in the same manner.

"Now you understand why in this life you had to experience the loneliness a baby feels when separated from its mother and the excruciating pain a mother feels when her children are taken away," he explained.

Buried memories emerged of my frightening and lonely childhood, deprived of my mother's presence. I remembered how painful it was when the uniformed officers grabbed baby Joshua out of my arms and how my little daughter, Terra, had desperately clung to my legs when any stranger tried to pick her up. I recalled going numb from grief when my children were taken away each time I was arrested; how powerless and repulsed I felt seeing my husband in a cage after his face had been shoved in a toilet of urine and feces; and how I thought I would die when my three-year-old son was sent away for testing after the accident in Donnie's van.

For so many years I had hated Liz for impudently grinning at me while her brother handed her my baby and then falsely arrested me. After glimpsing my karmic debt, I finally understood that it had been the divine Mother all along, smiling at me with deep compassion while my karma worked itself out.

For as long as I could remember I had nurtured my blame and hurt as though they were treasures to be protected. Now that the veil of ignorance was lifted, I was able to see a current of memories lying beneath the surface of every person's consciousness. With deep understanding, I realized that like hidden underground springs, those latent impressions from past lives would draw these people back again and again to experiences beyond their control. Compassion flooded my being as I realized that we must take responsibility for our actions if we are to advance spiritually. When Babaji got up to leave I bowed deeply before him, glad that I had made the decision to love him with all my heart.

About three months later, Muneesh, a young yogi who lived at Mount Madonna, passed me in the lobby while I was doing my morning chores.

"After supper tonight a few of us are going to see Ammachi," he said with an inviting smile. "She's called the hugging saint from India. You're welcome to join us if you'd like but be prepared to stay until at least four in the morning when Amma leaves. I hope you'll come. The music is awesome, and I think you will like it a lot."

"Sure," I said. "Where will we meet?"

"Be in line to get your supper when the kitchen opens at five o'clock. Kishori will want to get an early start, so we'll eat on the way. Her van will be parked out in front of the community building. She doesn't like to wait, so be on time."

A little after five, Kishori drove her van down the winding mountain road. After an hour of patiently switching from lane to lane through rush-hour traffic, she took the Crow Canyon Road Exit just beyond Pleasanton. The sun had gone down half an hour earlier and it was getting hard to see on the rural road.

"Keep your eyes focused on the right," Kishori told us. "The sign to Ammachi's ashram is small and easy to miss."

"Is that it?" I called a few minutes later.

Without any show of excitement Kishori said, "That's it."

It was completely dark when we turned onto the unpaved road. Attempting to dodge the potholes, Kishori swerved this way and that until she came to the head of a long driveway. Four men with walkie-talkies stood off to one side as Kishori slowed to a stop. When she rolled down her window it was easy to see this wasn't her first time to visit the hugging saint.

"OM Namah Shivaya[7]," she said, with a disinterested smile.

"OM Namah Shivaya," the men responded in unison.

One walked up to the van and peered inside the window.

"How many?" he asked.

"Four," Kishori grinned, knowing more than two people in her van meant she could park up near the main building.

After several short bursts of static, a woman's voice spouted parking directions over the hand-held apparatus. Kishori uttered a word of thanks and then followed the long line of vehicles to our designated spot. As

---

[7] OM Namah Shivaya: I bow to Lord Shiva. According to the Hindu Religion, Shiva is the destroyer of darkness or spiritual ignorance.

we got out of the van, we could hear a male voice broadcasting over loudspeakers in deep, even tones.

"OM, AMRITANANDAMAYI NAMAH! OM, AMRITANAN-DAMAYI NAMAH! OM, AMRITANANDAMAYI NAMAH!"

The four of us walked single file through the trees until the trail opened into an expansive courtyard. Long strings of white Christmas lights had been draped across the front of a large wooden building, giving a carnival effect to the festivities. Off to our left was a pond surrounded by trees and thick underbrush. Seemingly oblivious to the commotion above, a couple swans glided contentedly on the dark evening water.

Kishori pointed to a large, well-lit structure off to our right.

"Let's go wait for Ammachi inside the food tent," she suggested, and then easily led the way over a short, planked bridge.

An old, stooped Indian woman tended the cash register just inside the door. Beside her was a well-used placard on which the evening's menu had been painted in simple red letters. As we passed through the food line, gentle-natured Indians spooned generous portions of dhal, curried rice, and chapattis onto paper plates and passed them out with a smile. The din of voices suddenly went quiet.

"Amma is coming! Amma is coming!" hushed whispers passed from one person to the next.

The droning voice chanting over the loudspeakers rose louder and louder until it was joined by the whole crowd.

"OM AMRITANANDAMAYI[8] NAMAH! OM, AMRITANAN-DAMAYI NAMAH! OM AMRITANANDAMAYI NAMAH!"

"What's going on?" I whispered to Kishori.

---

[8]   Amritananda Mayi: another name for Ammachi. Namah means I bow to.

"Amma's coming," she said. "Come on, let's go out front to greet her."

Influenced by the devotional fervour of the crowd I began to chant with all the rest.

"OM AMRITANANDAMAYI NAMAH! OM, AMRITANAN-DAMAYI NAMAH! OM AMRITANANDAMAYI NAMAH!"

Just as our voices reached a crescendo a white van pulled into the courtyard. A man got out and helped a short, robust Indian woman dressed in a white sari to step down from the back seat. Her charismatic smile radiated love to the people and her eyes glittered with the brilliance of a hundred suns.

Pressing her palms together in front of her chest, Amma gaily saluted the crowd and then entered the well-lit building. Inside the door, throngs of people crowded the aisles trying to get a glimpse of the Indian saint. Amma suddenly stopped and pointed at a young girl who knelt huddled with her family.

"Birthday!" she announced in broken English.

The sixteen-year-old girl began to cry. Amma bent down and patted her cheek and then proceeded to a homemade throne adorned with flowers at the front of a large stage.

"We'd better get our number," Kishori's voice was barely audible over the loud Indian music.

"Our number?" I shouted back.

"Yeah," she motioned, pointing to the long line of people waiting at the back of the room. "It's the only way the ashram devotees can deal with so many people wanting to see Amma."

Several rows of chairs were arranged theater style on either side of a roped off aisle. Whether in groups or by themselves, hundreds of people

269

slowly advanced up the center aisle to receive Amma's darshan[9]. When our numbers were called, Kishori and I took our places on the crowded carpet.

Five Indian musicians sat cross-legged on the stage behind Ammachi. Their music created a devotional atmosphere for self-reflection and prayer as the people inched their way up to the holy woman who was laughing and chatting with her devotees. As we moved close to the front, I took Isaac's baby picture out of my pocket.

Please Amma, I prayed. *Won't you please, help my son?*

Just then one of Amma's devotees handed me a tissue.

"Wipe any perfume and sweat from your face, and be careful not to kneel on Amma's feet," she instructed from the sidelines.

"You okay?" Kishori asked, as we scooted a little closer.

"I guess so," I replied, nervously. "I've just never been in the arms of a saint before!"

As soon as the woman in front of me was released from Amma's embrace, the two devotees who had been passing out tissues grabbed my arms and ushered me forward. Two others took hold of my body and deftly positioned me in front of Ammachi. Being careful not to kneel on her feet, I let them press my torso into her lap.

Amma took me in her arms while continuing to laugh and converse in some unknown language with the devotees standing behind her. When I looked up at her face, the saint's ascetic smile and shining eyes were unlike anything I had ever seen. I handed her Isaac's baby picture and Amma dotted his forehead with sandalwood paste and handed it back. Thinking she was finished, I started to get up, but Ammachi pulled me back and held me tightly in her arms.

---

[9] Darshan: spiritual audience.

"Daughter, daughter, daughter, daughter, daughter," she chanted into my right ear with rapid succession.

The fragrant aroma of sandalwood exuded from her soft body as her words echoed deep inside, to a place long forgotten. Placing her hands on my shoulders, the holy Mother once again gazed deeply into my eyes.

"Okay?" she asked with a laugh.

Before releasing me into the hands of her devotees, Amma placed a few rose petals and two chocolate kisses in my hand. Swooning with spiritual intoxication, I made my way to the edge of the stage and sat down. As soon as I was stable enough to walk, I made my way back to my seat on the floor beside Kishori.

From her arrival at seven-thirty in the evening until her departure at four o'clock the next morning, Amma did not get up to eat, drink, or go to the bathroom. After the last person was released from her arms, the still radiant woman stood up and bowed. Walking down the now empty center aisle, she cheerfully waved goodbye to the sleepy crowd, and then climbed into the waiting van which quickly disappeared down the road.

There is a permanent black mark on Amma's cheek from continually pressing it against people's faces over the years. Her devotees told me that the saintly woman travels all over the world and nearly every day of her life she hugs thousands of spiritual aspirants from different cultures and religions.

In the courtyard behind the new resident building of the Conference Center, Babaji had directed the rock crew to build an authentic looking cave. It was embellished with colorful flower gardens and a waterfall that flowed into two fully stocked koi fishponds. While making beds with my staff one afternoon, I happened to glance out the window just in time to see Babaji and several devotees observing the fish. Without stopping to put on my shoes, I ran downstairs to join the group.

As I approached, Babaji gazed into the water for a moment and then wrote something on the small whiteboard he carried with him. Sudhir read his words out loud.

"I see a baby in the pond."

My interest drew me closer. Babaji leaned forward and pointed as I strained to follow his finger.

"Where Babaji? I don't see a baby," I said.

"He's right there swimming near the top of the water," he wrote. "His name is Pinhead; he is smart and funny."

From that day forward it became my routine to run out every Tuesday afternoon to be with Babaji at the fishpond. One day Sudhir Dass showed me how to clean the pond filter and asked if I would like to feed the koi. Although I already had my hands full with the CC duties, I loved the fish and appreciated the special new connection with Babaji.

"I would love to take care of the fish," I replied happily before heading back to work.

From then on whenever I came into the main room for supper Babaji would set his fork down to write something on his chalkboard.

"How many fish are in the pond?" he'd ask, or "Did you see Pinhead today?"

Delighted with all the attention, I tried to anticipate what Babaji would ask next. One morning while counting the fish, I noticed a patch of scale rot on one of the adult koi. When I called the pet store, the owner suggested isolating the fish to protect the others from getting sick. While I drove into Santa Cruz to purchase the medication, Sudhir put a large plastic tub in the CC basement and filled it with water. As soon as I got back, I scooped the sick fish out of the pond and placed it in the tub with the prescribed tablets.

After a couple of days, I started feeling sad for the isolated koi, so I transferred it to my room. Throughout the day I would drop in to visit my patient knowing that if the fish felt safe and supported, it would heal faster than if it was left alone in the darkened basement.

One Tuesday evening I had to work late preparing the rooms for incoming guests at the CC. On my way to the Community Building for supper I realized I had forgotten to feed the sick koi. It was already five-thirty and I knew Babaji would be leaving at precisely six o'clock. Torn by my strong desire to be with my guru, I tried to ignore my inner prodding to go back and feed the fish.

The koi will be fine until later! I argued, but it was no use, I had to go back.

From the very beginning Babaji taught us about dharma,[10] explaining the importance of doing our duty no matter what desires try to pull us away. I suddenly remembered how it felt to be a child with no one home to care for me and how I in turn had neglected my own children when they were small.

I ran back to my room and opened the door. The large, orange and black koi was flopping around on my carpet which was now spattered with blood. Without hesitation I tenderly scooped him up and placed him back in the tub of water. I sat and talked with him for a few minutes and then gave him some food. After placing a rock on the partially closed lid, I ran to the Community Building to see Babaji.

When I entered the room full of people, Babaji was just finishing his evening meal. With twinkling eyes, he flashed me one of his all-knowing grins and then wrote something on his whiteboard. He handed it to the person next to him to read aloud.

"You are the Mother of the fish," he said, and a soothing light flooded my being with peace.

---

[10] Dharma: a person's innate duty which is always based in righteousness and virtue.

That night I had a dream. Aware that I was the observer, I saw a battlefield on which many soldiers had been blown to pieces. Deafening bombs blasted nearby as nurses smeared with blood, rocked soldiers who were screaming from the pain of their severed limbs. All of a sudden, the screams and blasts stopped. The nurses, soldiers, and even the dead bodies that were scattered in bloody heaps, got to their feet. Looking directly into my eyes they linked arms and then all together, they smiled at me and took a bow.

Watching from my lucid state, I remembered wanting to understand the song, "Row, Row, Row Your Boat" that my father taught my brothers and me on the way back from Nebraska. Just before I woke up I thought, *this is what Babaji teaches in Sutra class... life is but a dream!*

The next day I asked Sudhir to help me move the sick koi to the fountain area so it could be near the other fish. The rushing fountain water naturally aerated the upper pond which emptied into another pond directly below it. After placing the blue plastic tub on the ledge separating the two pools, I partially covered it with a lid anchored in place by a large rock.

As usual, Babaji came the following morning to teach the Bhagavad Gita to the students gathered in the Community Building. After breakfast he changed his clothes and went to work on the rock crew. As soon as I finished my morning chores at the CC, I went to check on the sick koi. I was shocked to see it floating on the surface of the water, gasping for air. I quickly ran to where Babaji was sitting in the dirt pounding old cement off a small pile of rocks.

"Babaji, the sick koi fish is dying!" I sobbed.

Sudhir overheard me and called from the group of men working nearby.

"Let it go Supriya. It's just the cycle of birth and death."

"I can accept that everything dies, but the fish is suffering!" I called back.

Babaji stopped his work and looked up at me. As though reading my mind, he took out his small whiteboard and wrote, "Unless you kill it."

That was exactly my dilemma. From early childhood I had been taught that you "put an animal down" if it is suffering. I pictured myself taking the fish out of the tank and hitting it over the head to end its life. For some reason it didn't seem right.

"That's what I'm wondering Babaji. Am I supposed to kill the fish?"

"Let it die naturally," he wrote.

I dejectedly went to my room to get my parasol and then went out to stand near the sick koi. I was certain the visitors gathered in the courtyard thought I was crazy, but I was determined to stay and shade the poor fish until it died. Over and over I chanted the sacred words of the Sanskrit healing mantra until finally, I looked down to see what was taking the fish so long to die. Its little mouth was right up to the water's edge, gasping for air.

Air! Fish need air pumped into their tank to breath!

I ran back to the rock crew looking for Sudhir.

"Come quick!" I called. "The fish needs air. What can we do?"

Babaji looked up at me like a proud father. Sudhir climbed down from the work project and went with me to the CC basement to get an air filter. As soon as the bubbles formed in the water the fish started to swim in the confines of its makeshift hospital room. The medication cleared up the scale rot and the following week the koi was placed back in the fishpond with the other koi. Once the temple ponds were built the koi fish were moved to their new abode. Every time I went back to visit over the next twenty years, the fish that survived my learning curve as the "Mother of the fish" was still contentedly swimming with its peers.

Patanjali's Yoga Sutras are a collection of aphorisms that reveal the essence of yoga philosophy. It is said that without a guru, these Sutras are extremely difficult to understand. During Tuesday morning Sutra Class, it was Babaji's way to dispassionately glance about the room while one of his senior disciples read his commentary. After the reading, Babaji would patiently respond in writing to any questions asked by his students. One day a strong urge came over me to have Babaji look directly into my eyes.

Please, Babaji, I prayed. *Give me a glimpse from your divine eyes! That is all I need, just one quick glance. It doesn't have to be long, just a simple look in my direction. That will be enough.*

After class Babaji laughed and joked with the others while eating his breakfast, but my heartfelt prayer seemed to go unheard. The following Saturday a woman from the Pacific Cultural Center stood up after morning meditation to ask for volunteers.

"We have decided to build a fountain in the courtyard at the PCC," Pratibha announced. "If anyone wants to come and give us a hand, Babaji and the rock crew will be starting work this morning right after brunch."

I quickly finished my breakfast and then ran to my room to change my clothes. When I arrived at the PCC our elderly guru was already at work. Dressed in work boots, gloves, and dhoti,[11] Babaji hauled rocks and shovelled dirt in the scorching sun with the rest of the crew. After a couple hours of hard work, he came over near where I was digging and sat on the edge of the pond liner to rest in the shade. Keeping one eye on Babaji and one eye on my work, I continued to dig until suddenly, my guru toppled over backwards!

Dropping my shovel, I quickly rushed over and fell to my knees. Sudhir, Babaji's long time devotee and personal bodyguard, quickly jumped inside the circular container. Carefully picking up our guru, he cradled Babaji in his lap while someone else called an ambulance. Heartfelt sobs wrenched pitifully from my throat as I clung to the liner's edge.

---

[11]   dhoti: an ankle length cloth many East Indian men wear tied around their waist

Please Babaji, I prayed, *not yet. I just got here to study with you. Please don't die. I really need you. Please, stay a while longer. I need your guidance. Please stay alive, please, please, please!*

Just then Babaji's head rolled over to one side and he looked directly into my eyes for about seven seconds. His piercing gaze reached deep inside my soul and then his eyes closed, and his head rolled back into Sudhir's lap. Simultaneously shocked and calmed by his gaze, my heavy sobs began to diminish. By the time the paramedics arrived Babaji was sitting up on his own. One of the men took his blood pressure and asked a few questions, which of course, Babaji did not answer.

"Don't take it personally!" Sadanand quipped with a grin. "We've been asking him questions for years and he doesn't talk to us either!"

Babaji sat in the shade to rest while the rock crew returned to work. As I began to dig, I realized my guru had heard and answered the sincere prayer I made in Sutra class.

During my stay at Mount Madonna Center I not only kept my focus on Babaji, but his interactions with those around him. It was through these close observations that I noticed many of his long-time students wore a single bead on a white cotton string around their necks. While looking through some of the old black and white photographs of Babaji I noticed the same beaded string around his neck, so I did a bit of research. During my next appointment I asked him for one of my own.

"I'm ready to take nun vows," I said.

Babaji smiled mysteriously and wrote, "Nun or flying nun?"

The following week he called me up front and passed me an envelope. Inside was a note accompanied by a bead strung on six strands of thick cotton thread.

"Wear this witness bead now and I will tell you the rules as we go along."

Besides my job as supervisor of the CC, I also worked in the gift store a couple of days a week. My spare time was dedicated to studying Babaji's writings, memorizing Sanskrit prayers, practicing meditation, and learning the ancient rituals. Never wanting to leave his side, I worked on the rock crew with Babaji and went to his kutir[12] for music classes and teatime.

One afternoon my friend, Yamuna, asked me to cover her shift at the store. Although I never missed teatimes with Babaji, I agreed to help my friend because she wasn't feeling well. After the last customer left, I went out to the front porch where I could see Babaji's kutir right up the hill. My inner longing to be with my guru was so great that I silently cried out with great distress, "Babaji! Babaji!" Just seconds later the elderly master came out of his kutir and ran fast down the steep dirt path toward the gift store. I was shocked.

Did he hear my call? Did he think I was in trouble?

I instantly changed my thoughts to let him know I was sorry and that I was ok. Without looking up he stopped outside the store near where I was standing and then got in the passenger side of the truck to wait for Sudhir to drive him back to work on the rock crew. As they drove away, I vowed never to call out to Babaji again unless I was truly in distress.

Every other Sunday I went to see my father in Mountain View. We would have brunch together at his apartment and then go for long walks in the park, talking easily about whatever was on our minds. Now that the two of us were off alcohol and drugs we could see each other in a different light. His friends told me that he often spoke about me with admiration and pride and I accepted him as the gentleman and scholar that he truly was. Even in his nineties, my father traveled by himself, took care of his own finances, and kept his living space tidy and free from clutter.

One Saturday after work Babaji came into the Community Building at precisely five o'clock. After changing out of his work clothes he came into

---

12 Babaji's kutir was a small cottage built for his use during weekend retreats and teatime with his devotees.

the main room and took his seat. Prepared for the crowd of devotees that generally surrounded him, I held my note tightly in my hand. Oddly, no one came. Babaji was all alone. Amar Dass, a white-haired devotee with big blue eyes, stepped up behind me.

"Well that's odd. I've never seen this before," he said.

"Me either and I'm going to seize the moment!" I said.

I bravely went up and knelt on the floor beside Babaji. Ignoring the note, I spoke directly to my guru.

"Babaji, I'm writing a book," I said, inwardly seeking his approval lest problems of money, property, or prestige divert me from my spiritual path.

Babaji held out his hands as if to ask the number of pages I had written.

"Yes, exactly that much!" I said, amazed at his accuracy regarding my pile of hand-written pages.

"Why do you want to write it?" he asked.

"Because I think my story may help others."

"WRITE IT!" he wrote in large capital letters.

"Okay," I said.

I started to get up but Babaji continued to write so I lowered myself back to my knees.

"Five chapters," he wrote.

That is exactly where I was stuck, breaking my life into chapters.

"Okay," I told him.

Once again, I began to rise but Babaji kept writing.

"Chapter one: *Growing in The Dark*; Chapter two: *Unreality Seems Real*; Chapter three: *Going Through Sufferings*; Chapter four: *Turning Point*; Chapter Five: *Allurements*."

When he picked up a cloth to erase his board, I put up my hand.

"Wait Babaji! Please, don't erase your board! I want to copy it exactly the way you wrote it."

Babaji dispassionately tossed me the pen and tablet that were sitting on the small table beside his chair. When I was finished writing, I folded my hands in front of my chest.

"Thank you Babaji," I said, deeply grateful for his blessing.

People were beginning to enter the room, so I gave Babaji back his pen and tablet and stood up to leave. With a disinterested nod of his head, my guru turned back to the pile of letters heaped on the small table before him.

A few years after Babaji's arrival in the West his sponsor, Ma Renu[13], helped him find and buy land for an orphanage in India. For three months out of every year several devotees went with Babaji to develop the land, expand the orphanage, and visit the kids. On the day of their departure those of us who couldn't go travelled to the airport to sit with Babaji before waving our goodbyes. Ever the mischievous one, our guru liked to tease us. With a jovial sparkle in his eye, Babaji would point at us and write, "Leftovers!"

It was now three years since I had left Hippie to study at Mount Madonna Center with Babaji. I had developed many lasting friendships and loved my job as the supervisor of the Conference Center. During that time Isaac had been viciously attacked in prison by five other inmates. Fearing his revenge or deadly repercussions from his attackers, the officials at the penitentiary had him involuntarily transferred to Quebec. When he called me at the ashram one evening, I told him my good news.

---

[13] Ma Renu: previously Ruth Horsting, art professor at the University of California at Davis.

"I'm so excited!" I told him. "I have just about saved up enough money to go to India with Babaji."

"Wow, that's great!" my son replied cheerfully.

When I hung up the phone my heart didn't feel so good.

What am I doing? I thought. *My son is alone in a maximum-security penitentiary where he never gets a visitor and can't even speak the language. How can I go to India to be with well-loved children who receive many visitors every year?*

That night I had a dream. I was sitting with Isaac in a room filled with small square tables. Out of the corner of my eye, I saw Babaji slip by on the far side of the room, almost undetected. During meditation the next morning, my inner Voice whispered, "It's time to go to Quebec and help your son." Recalling the previous night's dream, I knew exactly what I had to do.

The next day was Saturday which meant Babaji would be coming for our early morning meditation class and then remain to work on the rock crew until five o'clock. Many students from on and off the land stayed after class to eat brunch with Babaji in the main room of the Community Building. Now that my courage was gaining strength, I felt more comfortable speaking with my teacher, even with others around. As soon as Babaji finished eating I went up and knelt beside him.

"I wanted to tell you first," I said evenly. "I'm going to Quebec to stay near my son who is in prison."

"It is your duty," he wrote and then as usual, he glanced dispassionately about the room.

When the people at Mount Madonna Center heard I was going to Quebec they became worried for my welfare.

"Where will you stay and what will you do for work?" they asked.

"You might fall spiritually if you're away from Babaji and the satsang[14]," another warned.

"You can't help people once they've gone to prison," someone else reasoned. "I used to work with inmates and it's a thankless job."

What they didn't know was that I had already spoken with Babaji.

"There is only one thing I know for sure," I answered. "I love my son and he is alone in a vicious environment. In the Bhagavad Gita Krishna tells us that if we just do our duty without expectation of the results then everything will work out for the best. God will provide everything I need. He always has and He always will."

A few days later, I was sitting on the carpet near Babaji eating my supper when Babaji suddenly put his fork down and motioned to a man I hadn't seen before. The man came right up to the front of the room to see what he wanted. Babaji wrote something on his whiteboard and then pointed at me. After reading the message the man came over to introduce himself.

"Hi, my name is Maheshwar," he said with a friendly smile. "Babaji said you need a place to stay in Montreal."

"Yes, my son is in prison in Quebec and I'm going to support him during this difficult time in his life."

Maheshwar flashed another smile saying, "You can stay with me as long as you need. I have a three-bedroom apartment in Montreal that I share with my son, Jonathan. I'm sure he won't mind if you join us."

"Thanks so much. I appreciate your kind offer and I would love to stay at your place!"

I looked at Babaji to thank him, but he had gone back to eating his food and didn't seem to notice.

---

[14] Satsang: the association of truth seekers

Like all real mothers, I was always able to feel my children but for some reason over the next few weeks, Isaac disappeared from my field of awareness.

He is either extremely depressed, on drugs or...dead, I worried.

I called the prison that evening and left a message for my son to call his mother. The next day the telephone rang. It was Isaac.

"I am coming to Quebec to be near you," I said.

"No, don't come!" he said. "It's too dangerous. I want you to stay at the ashram with Babaji. You are safe there and I don't have to worry about you getting hurt."

"I love you Isaac, and no matter what, I'm coming to stay with you and help you through this."

"Mom, it may take years for me to get out of prison."

"Isaac, if you had a son how long would you give him to walk?" I asked.

The defensiveness in his voice was beginning to weaken.

"As long as it takes," he admitted.

"Well that's exactly how I feel about you. I'm sorry for the way I acted as a young woman. It is a mother's duty to assist her children when they are sick, poor, or in trouble. I will stay by your side for as long as it takes and together, we will get through this."

My flight was on a Sunday, so I stopped in at the Pacific Cultural Center in Santa Cruz to say goodbye to Babaji on the way to the airport. As usual, he was sitting among a crowd of devotees who were clapping and singing devotional music. Determined to live the truth now blazing in my heart, I walked up the center aisle and lay face down on the carpet before him as a sign of complete surrender to all that is good and right. When I got up, I humbly touched his feet and then turned and walked out of the building. Radha, a long-time devotee who had been sitting next to Babaji got up and hurried outside after me.

"Are you leaving right now, Supriya?" she called.

"Yes, we're on our way to the airport," I said.

The beautiful woman came down the steps and took me in her arms. I felt waves of peace emanating from her body and I knew that through her, I was receiving Babaji's blessing.

On the way to the airport my friend Diana was quiet, giving me time to reflect on the long journey ahead. As she maneuvered her way through afternoon traffic I relaxed back in my seat and closed my eyes. Vibrant, smooth energy suddenly flushed upward from the base of my spine, saturating my being with indescribable joy. The secret place behind my eyes that was obscured so long ago suddenly opened, and I could once again see that beyond all activity of life there was another world; a silent garden, where people moved slowly and kindness was the way.

At the airport, Diana waved a tearful goodbye as I headed through the boarding gates. On the plane, I tucked my bag in the overhead bin and then took my seat. After fastening my seatbelt, I closed my eyes while the rest of the passengers settled in.

Where will I live and how can I support myself if I can't even speak French? I began to worry.

My hand reached up to touch the witness bead hanging around my neck. I suddenly recalled the words of Edna, the psychic woman in Nova Scotia, who had read my tarot cards so many years before.

"You're gonna meet an older man who will be very good for you," she said. "He has silver hair and he's gonna help you a lot. He has hair on his face and he's a good man. I like this silver-haired man. Yes, he's a VERY good man and he's gonna help you a lot!"

As the engines revved for take-off, I recalled the courageous little girl who had faced her childhood fears in the dark house on Gary Avenue. I thought about the movie *The Nun's Story* that Mr. Stevenson had taken me to see, and my ensuing vow to help people find peace even though everything around them was hopeless and cruel. And finally, I smiled remembering Babaji's witty response, "Nun or flying nun?" when I asked him for a witness bead.[15]

It's time, I thought. *My son is alone in prison and he needs my love.*

My mind suddenly flashed back to the porcelain sage of my childhood that sat on Kaye's coffee table.

"Don't be afraid or worry about a thing," he had whispered without moving his lips.

Now as the plane lifted into flight his memory was reassuring.

---

[15] A witness bead is a single (often hand carved) wooden bead threaded on 6 strands of twisted white cotton string worn around the neck by the devotee as a witness to their spiritual practice.

Printed in the United States
By Bookmasters